FAST
CAPITALISM

BEN AGGER

FAST CAPITALISM

A Critical Theory of
Significance

University of Illinois Press
Urbana and Chicago

© 1989 by the Board of Trustees of the University of Illinois
Manufactured in the United States of America
C 5 4 3 2 1

This book is printed on acid-free paper.

Library of Congress Cataloging-in-Publication Data

Agger, Ben.
    Fast Capitalism / Ben Agger.
    p. cm.
    Bibliography: p.
    Includes index.
    ISBN 0-252-01578-9
    1. Books and reading—Sociological aspects. 2. Authorship—
Sociological aspects. 3. Capitalism and literature. 4. Critical
theory. I. Title.
Z1003.A37 1989   88-14432
    306′.488—dc19   CIP

For Buddy,
again

"This book is obsolete."

—Max Horkheimer

Contents

Acknowledgments

Paul Diesing read this manuscript—fast. As ever, he provided sharp, sympathetic criticisms, guiding me in my revisions. Beth Anne Shelton read the manuscript and offered her typical blend of generous encouragement and no-nonsense advice. She provokes me to refine my version of Marxism/feminism. The work of Russell Jacoby continues to enlighten me. His *The Last Intellectuals: American Culture in the Age of Academe* (Basic 1987) figures centrally in this book. Lisa Nowak Jerry again did a fine job editing the book for style. My editor at Illinois, Lawrence Malley, makes all of this possible. His faith in my work is sustaining at a time when, as I say in the book, the literary culture of academia further declines.

Fast Capitalism is a book about the decline of books. Instead of merely acknowledging the irony, I make sense of it. We must learn from the fact that it is difficult to gain distance from the world in criticizing it. That insight forms the basis of my empirical theory of "fast" capitalism. In this stage of capitalism the membrane between text and world is increasingly fragile. The world swallows traditional texts and disperses them into money, science, edifice, and figure. As such, they compel "readings" merely repeating, reliving, their encoded imperatives to accept, adjust, acquiesce. Even Marxism and feminism have not successfully resisted their absorption as texts into the exterior world. They have become slogans doing little original work on their own; they substitute for thought. I restore them by using their basic understanding of the hierarchy of valued and valueless activity to understand the erosion of book culture, and thus of critique, in fast capitalism.

Introduction:
Writing a Book When Books Do Not Exist

THE THESIS SEEMS outrageous. This book surely exists. It is between covers; it was purchased or borrowed; it has a title. Nevertheless, I want to advance the notion that books do not exist at a time when the boundary between text and world is fading fast—thus, my term fast capitalism. The irony of writing about books when I claim books do not exist is only apparent. I am talking about tendencies just as Marx talked about tendencies when he predicted an imminent class revolution, the "expropriation of the expropriators." That he was neither proletarian nor capitalist does not make his argument any less compelling nor, necessarily, does the fact that the revolution *did not occur* in the way he foretold. Similarly, in what follows I discuss the tendency for the signifying nature of writing to degrade where the exterior worlds of money, science, edifice, and figure become "texts," thus compelling adjustment and precluding the possibility of new versions standing at one remove from the world they address. I want books to exist not only because I value intellectual culture but also because what I call book or "text" in standing apart from the world it confronts preserves the possibility of critique's utopian imagination, desperately needed today.

My argument begins with Marxism and passes through a variety of recent traditions of interpretation and cultural critique from the

Frankfurt School to feminism and deconstruction.[1] However, this is not a book about those books as much as a book about books in general. I understand books both literally as what they are and metaphorically as examples of critique's ability to stand apart in order to think the world differently. Marxism, critical theory, feminism, and deconstruction all risk losing their ability to conceive and thus act their difference from the world. Instead they increasingly become mere slogans, canons, parties, committees, and courses identical with whoever mouths them or claims them for themselves. Although my own approach is closer to that of Adorno and Marcuse than to literary theory and orthodox Marxism,[2] I am not interested in compiling authority strings of citations in support of a fragile argument. The argument will be fragile anyway. No amount of Adorno references will strengthen it except to show how he may have thought the same problem differently—thus giving credibility to my notion of a problem if not my resolution of it.

Let me describe how I came to the problem of the disappearance of textuality as a way of beginning. This is less autobiography than a coming to terms with my sources as they inspired me to think about the deficiencies of traditional approaches to emancipation, particularly Marxism and, more recently, feminism. I do not think I am any less Marxist or feminist, as I will argue in Chapters 6 and 7. However, no one knows what these names mean or ought to mean in a world where slogans are dispersed into the external environment and then compel certain readings of them, indeed certain lives, without pause for interpretation or mediation—thought. In the late 1980s it is not useful to reformulate Marxism and feminism *de novo;* that fails to address the more general problem of the thoughtlessness requiring discussion in the first place. Nor is it adequate to take a poll, for I am sure that 9 out of 10 self-appointed Marxists and feminists will convict me of apostasy, maybe even treason. So what? The majority is rarely right these days. At least, there is no reason why it should be.

At one level, then, I propose some empirical variations in critical theory helping address the present circumstance. The nature and force of ideology have changed significantly since Marx, even perhaps since *Dialectic of Enlightenment* (Horkheimer and Adorno 1972). Fast capitalism, as I call it, is characterized by the quickening erosion of writing's—mind's—ability to formulate the world in terms that do not borrow so heavily from it that text can only imitate or iterate. Text's eroding powers of signification enhance the capacity of the exterior environment, now a "text" of sorts, to compel certain intended readings and lives—think of Marx's famous account of money. The eclipse of text suppresses the possibilities of critique, thus of imagination. These are essentially empirical processes, and I will talk about them even acknowledging that there is much work to do in actually reading money, science, edifice, and figure as dispersed texts of the kind I am addressing. That is for others to do, at greater length. Here I want to provide a hermeneutic framework within which that critique can carry on. The critique of theory makes theory possible.

At a second level, then, I want to consider the changing nature of the public sphere directly as a political problem. Much has been written about the decline of public "man" (Sennett 1978), the culture of narcissism (Lasch 1979), and the eclipse of reason (Horkheimer 1974b). In advanced capitalism the public sphere is increasingly colonized (Habermas 1984, 1987) by administrative imperatives of control. In turn, we lose the forum for debating public issues, notably including the demise of public space and the rhetorics with which to engage in constitutive discussion and critique. I want to approach this problem by considering not only the administrative apparatuses privatizing us in the interest of control but also the way in which textuality, a possible medium of critical resistance and dialectical imagination, fails to stand apart. As public space is administered, we lose the capacity to write the world in estranging ourselves from it.[3] Books become things provoking their thoughtlessly ready readings as things become books.

Finally, this will suggest a notion of reading at once authorizing textless books like money, science, edifice, and figure and then reformulating them in better terms.[4] Critique fights for power by insisting on the textuality of versions appearing not to be texts at all. Then it argues with those versions freezing the present into an irreversible social nature. Critique joins community with other versions that accept the corrigibility of discourse as a way of prefiguring a future in which versions flourish. As such, critique opposes the discipline imposed on mind in the bureaucratic university.

These are all ways to understand this book's problem. Writing today is easily reduced to a simple recipe or slogan that need not be read, considered, engaged. The bureaucratization of mind promotes a categorizing mindlessness when it comes to interpretation. To use names and concepts—Adorno, fast capitalism—virtually guarantees a certain reception. Language cannot stand outside the preestablished nest of meanings attaching to its signifiers. But if significations degrade into the things they are thought to connote, writing loses its ability to say anything different from what the words ordinarily are heard to suggest. Adorno as a code word robs the ability of Adorno to speak for himself—sometimes surprisingly so. Furthermore, when

I use the word Adorno it destines a certain reception by preventing me from having "Adorno" do analytical work not ordinarily covered under the slogan Adorno.

I am not talking about the generic tendency of language to be misunderstood. Rather the degradation of signification—the ability of words to do thoughtful work—is both the risk I run and my empirical topic. Adorno now means the shelf full of books called critical theory at the local intellectuals' bookstore or perhaps a certain citation or bibliographical reference in the secondary writing. Adorno's books, indeed Adorno himself, have become things in fast capitalism, losing the capacity to stand apart from the world and then think it otherwise. When refusing the Nobel prize, Sartre[5] expressed this well where he resisted his own "institutionalization." Today the degradation of signification is more than that; it is sheer objectification of text into an exterior world at once compelling passive "readings"—so-called everyday life—and vitiating the possibility of critique from the outside.

I want to understand this tendency of text to become thing and then thing to become self-reproducing text as an intensification of the process of the alienation of labor first addressed by Marx. Fast capitalism is still capitalism, although literal Marx is unhelpful where he theorized ideology as traditional text standing apart from the world it addressed and intended to fatalize. The problem is that books no longer convey the codes of adjustment and acquiescence formerly called ideology by Marxists. The codes are dispersed into the world itself; money, science, edifice, and figure increasingly encode significance. These "texts" constitute a *positivist world* in which reading passively iterates and thus reproduces the things given to it as ordinary parts of social nature. Old-fashioned books are left with virtually no work to do except to entertain trivially or to convey formulaic knowledge—calculus, engineering, positivist social science.

Capitalism today quickens the pace at which significance diminishes away from text and moves toward things themselves. As the original Frankfurt School knew, this is the nature of a society characterized by administration or what Habermas later calls the colonization of the lifeworld. Capitalism subsists economically by objectifying and commodifying all human experience, subjecting it to the rule of equivalent exchange. Marx did nothing more than read money as a telling medium of this objectification, as I have tried to do in my reading of mainstream social science positivism (1989). There is nothing new about fast capitalism other than the rate at which it happens; the mind is short-circuited to the world without passing through the discursive media of speech and text.

The challenge is twofold. First, I must make some empirical and theoretical sense of what I have called the degradation of signification once I establish the way textuality as an example of generic reproduction is dominated by the public/profit imperatives of production. Then I will address Marxists and feminists about their own eclipse in fast capitalism; no one escapes these tendencies absolutely. Second, I must somehow rescue my own argument from its reduction into recipes, citations, dismissals, or blind approval by talking about it in a way that this reflexivity becomes part of the argument itself, a mode of ideal speech I sketched in my *Socio(onto)logy* (1989). It is one thing to suspect that one's own prose will degenerate into its slogans themselves, and it is another to make that suspicion a rich source of insight. By anticipating it I can try to prevent it, especially where I write and rewrite the argument in light of what it becomes: add a chapter, subtract some prose, write this introduction at the end, then rewrite the whole in light of it.

The original Frankfurt thinkers, especially Adorno and Horkheimer, tried to prevent the methodologization of their own critique through a penetrating indirection. Some have called it simply obfuscation. But take a sentence, usually short, from Adorno's *Negative Dialectics* (1973a) and insist that it does not "make sense." For example, "No theory today escapes the marketplace. Each one is offered as a possibility among competing opinions; all are put up for choice; all are swallowed."[6] Sounds simple and it is. But *he included his own* as a way of putting a dialectical spin on these words. Every line of Adorno resonates the totality he tried to illuminate without leaving open his particular formulations to methodologization, simplification, stupefication.[7] The falling rate of intelligence continues to fall. Thus, we must be clear without letting clarity be ruled by the administrative principles of epistemological rationalization congealing into what I have called positivism. Capitalist clarity disciplines and thus in its own way obfuscates. Writing that merely iterates is least clear of all where the world complexly conceals itself in order to be reproduced thoughtlessly.

I work on different levels. I present an argument about the fate of textuality in fast capitalism directly as a mode of ideology-critique, and I stay attuned to the tendencies of my own version to be disciplined, reduced. For me the tendency of significance to erode in fast capitalism is no more absolute than the tendency for the rate of profit to fall was for Marx. All sorts of things can intervene to prevent it: smart readers, my inability to hear my prose as others will, the state of political resistance today; these might work against the tendencies I describe and want to avoid. This is how one can write about the demise of writing. There is no fate, only the obdurate empirical present and the way it pulls the future to it relentlessly. Indeed, one *must* write in a time when writing is dispersed into an exterior world not bearing the mark of its textuality as a susceptibility to historical transformation.

The most political thing about writing is that it could be written differently, offering a metaphor for the possibility of all social change and directly participating in it where it takes the form of critique.[8] I not only authorize hidden texts but also argue with them about their version of social nature. In positivist culture imagination is limited to the texture and text of the present. In this sense, the nature of ideology remains the same.[9] It wants to open the door of limited personal betterment—money, entertainment, salvation—while closing the door of fundamental social change. It wants the world to repeat itself by inserting signifiers into it, recommending various states of affairs to which behavior would conform. Formerly these signifiers were books themselves—the Bible, economic theory. Today, although those texts obviously still exist, most of these subtly hortatory and proscriptive texts have become things themselves, as such unreadable in a critically evaluative way provoking the enactment of the versions they suggest: valorization and acquisition of money,[10] repetition of the hidden sociopolitical agenda of positivist social science,[11] compartmentalization into the hierarchized structures of edifice,[12] and reduction of qualitative judgment to sheer number.[13] Money, science, edifice, and figure become texts even though they do not read like them and thus are the more effective for all that.

In fast capitalism, books that become things compel a certain world, indeed one that looks just like itself. Textuality imagines the world differently, what Foucault called "thinking otherwise." The eclipse of text into thing moronizes "reading"—all our unthinking adjustments to the given in so-called everyday life—and at once dries up the transformative medium of critique, collapsing what Marcuse (1964) called the first and second dimensions of human experience. That is what I mean by the positivist world. Critique must read the world as a text, the empirical contribution of this book, and then insist on its own right to be a book—to stand apart and think otherwise. In the meantime it must attempt to prevent its own reduction to terms of given discourse in order to say what it wants to say and be heard as such.

I presuppose Marx's critique of the alienation of labor and his sketchy vision of a better world. I agree with many feminists that Marxism frequently misses the sphere of reproduction as an arena of value. I follow the original Frankfurt theorists where they tried to address culture and sexuality as thoroughly material forces in their own right. Habermas and certain literary theorists suggest a textual approach to problems of ideology. And Foucault suggests an understanding of social control, of *discipline*, enriching my understanding of positivist culture. What is original about this book, it seems to me, is the way I understand the material nature of textuality as a crucial factor in the entrenchment of domination and thus model a critique both reauthorizing the world's undisclosed texts and suggesting a better world in terms of its own democratic norm of dialogue.

In this regard, Habermas (1984, 1987) offers the most systematic rethinking of the original Marxian approach to the conceptualization of ideology. Although his communication theory in crucial respects regresses behind the sweeping utopianism of the original Frankfurt School and even Marx, Habermas at least raises the issue of a possible renewal of historical materialism in compelling terms.[14] By learning the various disciplines, Habermas explodes their narrow territoriality and undoes their discipline of imagination. In his intellectual reach, Habermas has made critical theory virtually impossible to ignore by serious social thinkers. My dissatisfaction with his new version occasions this work; I must take him seriously.

Yet Habermas is generally ignored under sway of the fast-capitalist degradation of significance. Either he is refused disciplinary status, or he is reduced to a slogan—a "Habermasian" perspective, a "Habermasian" application. Perhaps he has been read.[15] But it is unlikely that his readings—Kant, Hegel, Marx, Freud, and so on—have been duplicated in the strenuous labor required to understand his understanding of them. It is cheap to read Habermas and claim him; it is much more difficult to make sense of him and then reformulate him in an original way. Perhaps this is only to observe that theory has its own hierarchy and canon, more so today than ever where names become stars and cease to require reading and reformulation. This is more than an argument for reading in original sources inasmuch as so-called secondary sources can be constitutive in their own right. It is no more than a warning about the self-objectifying tendencies of text in fast capitalism; even Habermas becomes "Habermas" and so ceases to matter in the way he intended. He likely remains unread.

This would not happen if critique formed community and community swelled into a universal social order, the topic of my last chapter. *At stake is power,* particularly the power to dictate the fate of reading and writing, of critique and imagination. This is not an epistemological but a political issue. The positivist world ensnares all textual versions as ontological reproductions of itself precisely because it is the dominant world, reflecting and provoking the given economic and political order. It could be different. But until we understand the forces of administration, commodification, and reification as political forces we fail to understand the dismal fate of our own versions. Disciplines discipline in part by usurping the economic power to hire and fire and by controlling publication and distribution outlets. Critique often loses sight of its own unmysteriously material nature in a putatively postmodern world in which politics is denigrated as groundless perspective, even hubris.

Deconstruction has failed to become a political force because it views the world entirely as a text with no outside, thus losing the ability to theorize what is happening—to make distinctions, abstract, recommend. The fetish of the postmodern is intended by capitalist modernity as the ultimate end of ideology.[16] Where a universal reason is denied on grounds of its Prometheanness, as Derrida and Foucault do, they refuse history and thus the possibility of political transformations. In a seemingly centerless world centerlessness is not adequate resistance—especially in that world. But an apodictic social philosophy need not repeat the arbitrary elitism of the Greeks as an alternative to the valuelessness of postmodernism. There are options, notably Marxism. Post-Marxism is invented by anti-Marxists to disqualify not only Marx's literal formulation of economic and ideological critique but his millennial philosophy of history driving to create a universal reason.[17] Post-Marxism is fashionable because it derives truth from fashion, precluding the hard work necessary to "think otherwise." It is easy to dismiss Marxism where the world is littered with versions, practices, and nation-states mouthing Marxist words but thereby vitiating them.

There is another reason why Marxism is anathema to postmodernists. *He is heavy,* abstruse, structuring—textual. This is the same reason why few read Habermas or Adorno. Weighed against the expected payoff, the amount of mental labor required is too great. Marx lived in a slow capitalism, when books could not only stand apart from the world but also comprehend its totality and thus begin to remake it. Things have speeded up in the meantime; attention span has shrunk. This is not to constrain the possibilities of language using pop psychology but to address a crucial symptomatic of millennial oppression.

10

People do not read, cannot read; their reading is done for them by texts lacking both covers and critical distance from their topics. The faculty complaint about student illiteracy is only a telling tip of the iceberg. Book culture dissolves where books are things and things books. Postmodernism only apes these tendencies by endorsing them profoundly.[18]

Thus, I am writing against the postmodernist acquiescence to the miserable present. History is neither cyclical, random nor linear. Rather the past, simply by having happened, creates structures within which determinate possibilities are arrayed before us. Postmodernist thought, indeed virtually all thought today, misses history where it wants to live in the instantaneity of the eternal present, a typical sign of a dumb civilization. In this way philosophical and political questions are decided episodically with reference to whatever standards prevail—today no apparent standards at all. This is fine because to think evaluatively would require the difficult work of estranging oneself from the moment sufficiently to appraise it from the outside, even realizing that one is never completely outside but always partly inside.

Standardlessness appeals where the argument for standards is usually conservative—particular standards inflated into a universal. The present popularity of Allan Bloom's (1987) *The Closing of the American Mind* in its Platonism repels liberals and radicals alike who refuse his unexplicated absolutism. Why study great books and not all books? Why the liberal arts? Conservatives' unexplicated standards of reason suppress the search for other, arguable, more humane standards in a postmodern age. When the prevailing absolutes are bad, it is tempting to indulge the orgy of decentering signifiers, each as worthless (or worthwhile) as any other. We must resist this tendency no matter how empirically compelling it is, especially where the world already imposes its own absolutes on us.

Postmodernism, as I understand it, is an inadequate response to the decentering of traditional discourses about the good. In this work I discuss this decentering process as a loss of book culture.[19] There are other ways to understand it. I do not dismiss what I exclude from my argument, especially where focus prevents me from attaining encyclopedic breadth. The answer is not all here, only a questioning about why it is so hard to present the totality textually when books are things and things books. Where bookishness marks the stagnant, reactionary intellectual culture allowing all this to happen, it can have a directly political role in writing that stands apart and thus rethinks. This is not the typical argument for intellectual autonomy; that is only apology.

Rather by gaining distance one can both criticize and reformulate the world in a way defying the world's suctionlike pull on minds and bodies.

To write a book with a certain relation to its topic and audience, intending its undecidability as a norm of all community, is a political act today.[20] Fast capitalism reduces books to copy and thus provokes what copy represents ahistorically. Critique can break the hold of positivist culture where it models itself as a norm of gentle, democratic practice. Intending community, critique hopes to overcome its isolation. That is its difference from bourgeois intellectuality prizing disengagement as moral purity. Today mind gains distance so as not to be coopted and thus to see clearly and imagine forcefully. Although inadequate politics in itself, this revaluation of intellectual culture offers some resistance to the bureaucratization of mind in what Jacoby (1987) calls the age of academe.

Resistance already exists. In this book I theorize the world opposing it in order to broaden and deepen it. On the way, I must be alert to the tendency of my version to degrade itself into a slogan for someone else. Words only work where they mark their difference from the world they hope to capture in its particular concreteness; they stimulate thought to question the adequacy of concepts to cover the things they address, thus provoking rethinking. Marxism and feminism have run out of ways to prevent their own degeneration into slogans; their methods are excuses not to think at all. The world swallows them by disciplining them, robbing thought of its political moment. Marxism and feminism are not simply shelves of books but lives devoted to naming and thus opposing injustice.[21]

We tend to forget this because "we" are already isolated in the bureaucratic university. I raise the question to which Marxism and feminism are answers: How is it that we lose freedom to the world engulfing all political options? I name this fast capitalism, yet I want to start discussions and not create another edifice of unassailable definitions and abstractions. Perhaps it is a conceit to call this political work. But look at the options: career academia with its persistent attention to the local scenes of department and discipline or the apologetic "life of the mind" celebrating its disengagement as a mark of moral virtue. Either way, thought sacrifices itself. In this book, following a host of others unbound to canon and yet uncomfortable with political isolation,[22] I suggest an alternative political role for intellectual work. Of course, there are other political versions; not mentioning them does not mean they are neither real nor important. But this is my version;

it is how I define my own relationship to the large structural issues of domination and freedom.

By suggesting this version of political work I anticipate a community of like-minded people doing similar and different work. It is irrelevant that the probabilities of creating such a community are slim. Indeed, *why* they are slim is a crucial empirical topic. Here is my answer.

CHAPTER 1

Fast Capitalism?

I NECESSARILY WORK within the dialectic of language. While avoiding definitions and discursive argument in order to ensure that they do not become slogans—the very problem of a "fast" capitalism—I must establish a framework within which the argument can proceed. Adorno was confronted with much the same problem of presentation in numerous works, notably his (1973a) *Negative Dialectics*. Indeed, a reviewer of this book noticed that the argument is "Adornoesque," recommending earlier attention to my argument's structure, even going as far as to offer "definitions." He urged that I relate the term fast capitalism to other usages of late or advanced capitalism in defining its specificity. I do that in various places throughout the book, allowing my distinctive sense of fast capitalism to emerge in counterpoint to and convergence with the arguments of others, notably people in the Frankfurt School like Marcuse and Adorno. I do not overdraw a conceptual apparatus at the beginning precisely because I do not want terms like fast capitalism to become mindless slogans substituting for thought and analysis. Nevertheless—the reviewer's point —they are my terms, and I am stuck with them. It is better to proceed with at least a glance at what I mean by fast capitalism before I undertake an argument dialectically presupposing its definition but realizing that its sense must emerge in the context of usage.

My editor seconds the reviewer's suggestion that I provide a road map of my subsequent argument in order to talk to "unconvinced" readers. Anyone who preaches communicative democracy, as I do, must acknowledge its importance. Private language is not language;

by indulging in it, one only hastens the demise of book culture, the problem I suggested in my introduction. Yet to pretend that fast capitalism can be defined outside its rhetorical context—that is, in terms of its analytic work—is artificial. Worse, it courts the tendency of the term itself to become a cliche used willy-nilly when I otherwise cannot deal with the empirical world in its fine-grained subtlety. Fast capitalism as a dead definition can be marshaled whenever I cannot think my way out of the problems I feel are important; I must avoid this at all costs. If I cannot avoid it, my analysis of the decline of book culture and thus of modern capitalism will tend to exhaust itself in the semantic controversies it stirs among readers more concerned with the argument's pedigree than with real empirical substance.

The only way to provide a road map for the uninitiated reader (and, after all, every reader is uninitiated) without allowing definitions and a conceptual apparatus to do my thinking for me, enslaving the subsequent argument, is to be reflexive about my writing. Concretely, this means that I must think back on what I have said already about fast capitalism and then recoup that in a summary way to proceed with the balance of the argument. In effect, the manuscript reviewer asks me to consider readers inquisitive about the genealogy of the concept. The adjective "fast" is unusual and might be heard to trade on a number of different usages. Let me suggest these as a way of moving ahead with my argument, yet without pretending that what I write here is not also argument. I want to return to my short introduction and prise out of it the four ways in which I used the term fast capitalism to house the remaining argument in which I will necessarily refine and deepen these notions. This sort of self-reflection constitutes an alternative to straightforward definitions. By now thinking about my quick introduction to fast capitalism, I slow down my argument and give the reader time to breathe before proceeding.

The Boundary between Text and World

In the book's sixth sentence I suggested that "books do not exist at a time when the boundary between text and world is fading fast—thus, my term fast capitalism." I say this regulatively; that is, by exaggerating my strong claim that "books do not exist" I write a book opposing the further decline of book culture and thus of critical intelligence. Books threaten not to exist because we are no longer sure what constitutes a book's independence from the world it addresses. Thus, I say that the boundary between book and world is fading quickly. I try to support this empirical claim in my subsequent analyses of the four modal "texts" of money, science, edifice, and figure. I am talking about tendencies, not inert realities. Prose tends not to resist its absorption into the various codes and slogans degrading its significance; instead, it is swallowed into the world as a secret text compelling everyday lives of comfortable conformity. In any case, my first sense of fast capitalism concerns the very boundary separating book and world, a boundary that we have taken for granted virtually from the beginning of written civilization. But I do not take this boundary for granted, and I explore the implications of this for social analysis.

Imitative Writing

My second mention of fast capitalism in the introduction discusses "mind's [in]ability to formulate the world in terms that do not borrow so heavily from it that text can only imitate." When losing independence from the world, writing swallowed by it loses its toehold in possible social criticism. This is very much the thesis of the Frankfurt School (e.g., Marcuse's (1964) *One-Dimensional Man*) where it suggests that reason has been "eclipsed" (Horkheimer 1974b) in advanced capitalism. The more prose is degraded into slogans, cliches, and codes, particularly on the model of advertising, the less writing can construct imaginatively the possibility of a very different world. Thus, a central feature of my analysis of fast capitalism concerns the tendency of writing merely to reflect and thus reproduce the given order of things, a theme initiated from within Marxism first by Lukacs and then extended by the Frankfurt School in its analyses of false consciousness, reification, and domination.

I go beyond Lukacs and the Frankfurt School in locating the eclipse of reason directly in the literary oppression of utopian thinking. We cannot propose radical social change today in large measure because we are insufficiently distant from the world to be able to speak about it in terms that are not immediately turned upside down, even used apologetically. Thus, "freedom" is obtainable at 7-Eleven grocery stores, not in egalitarian social relationships. Even if we understand the deformation of language, as the Frankfurt critics did, we cannot effectively write about it because "books do not exist," my earlier claim. Prose becomes simple reflection of the frozen world, not a lively challenge to it issuing from its self-conscious distance. This has enormous implications for the possibility of social criticism and thus political mobilization, largely neglected by the Frankfurt School. At some deep level, Adorno, Horkheimer, and Marcuse believed in the power of reason to pierce the ideological haze of mystification and doubletalk. By writing esoteric books they could kindle the possibility of critique and utopian imagination. Although I share their hope, my empirical analysis of present capitalism suggests to me that critics face grave problems where text itself is increasingly sucked into the legitimation and reproduction processes. The banality that Adorno contradicted his own thesis of "total administration" or Marcuse "one-dimensionality" by writing about it contains truth. However insuperable the problems of reception they confronted in postwar America, the original Frankfurt theorists assumed that books could still refuse and thus negate the dominant world order. I too continue to write and hope. Yet it seems to me that a new era of capitalism exists in which one can no longer assume that critique's textual vehicle—reasoned prose— will not be immediately swallowed, even turned against itself. Witness the domestication of critical theory itself into yet another academic specialty.

The original Frankfurt theorists accepted Marx's model of the critique of ideology and felt that they could make a political difference if only they could secure themselves an educated audience. Once they secured this audience, they could complexly unravel the layers of deceit covering the exploitative and self-contradictory logic of capital. Although I too engage in much this sort of analysis here, I think more than an audience problem exists. It is not simply that people do not read or write public books exposing the world for what it is but that *the autonomy of bookness itself* is at issue in fast capitalism. We can write and then publish works of critical theory, but they are not public books in the sense that they stand apart from, and thus oppose, the dominant world. We lack not simply readers but a public forum in which textuality can play a political role, both energizing and organizing the passion to change the world.

Relationship to Marx I: Dispersed Ideology

My difference from the original Frankfurt School is friendly; Adorno and Marcuse could well have written about the demise of book culture had they paused to consider the decline of the public sphere in literary terms. At some level they still believed that language could penetrate oppression. Although not absolutely wrong (there are no historical absolutes here), they are even less right today than they were in the 1930s and 1940s. Yet my analysis of fast capitalism not only extends original Frankfurt themes but also Marx's original analysis of the logic of capital. In my third use of the term fast capitalism I say that we can understand the eclipse of book culture "as an intensification of the process of the alienation of labor first addressed by Marx." Thus, I am not changing the terms of Marxist discourse so much as bringing them up-to-date. Where the original Frankfurt School was slightly hopeful about the possibility of a "negative dialectic" (Adorno 1973a) and "negative thinking" (Marcuse 1960a), Marx was even more optimistic that straightforward social criticism in the form of ideology-critique could stimulate revolutionary opposition and organization. I fully accept Marx's labor theory of value and his implied critique of the alienation of labor, but I would revise his theory of ideology (and thus his concept of ideology-critique) where, as I say, "books no longer convey the codes of adjustment and acquiescence formerly called ideology by Marxists . . . [but] are dispersed into the world itself [as] money, science, edifice, and figure."

Capitalism today is both the same as and different from Marx's and Frankfurt's capitalism. It is the same in that it rests on the exploitation of labor power (now crucially including sexuality and housework, missed by sexist Marxists); it is different in that what Marx called ideology does not simply stand over against the world in book form (e.g., the Bible, bourgeois economic theory) but is also dispersed into the world as the unreadably deauthorized versions comprising "everyday life" for almost everyone. Although ideology in the old sense still exists, it is supplemented by new forms of ideology, including what I call dispersed texts constituting a positivist culture. Ideological directives are no longer issued only from the pages of principled (if false) prose; they are encoded into the numerous layers and levels of a public world in which money, science, edifice, and figure in effect become the new "books," compelling adjustment to what they reflect as ontologically unalterable (ever the nature of ideology).

Where Marx recognized only one type of ideology—untrue books —there is now a second type characterized by the language games of a disempowered everyday life in which reading has been degraded into mindless rehearsal of social life's various subtexts—buy, work, privatize, count, capitulate. Ideology today has sunk deeper than Marx imagined. It takes both textual and metatextual forms; thus it cannot be opposed simply from the outside through what Marx understood as ideology-critique, particularly economic analysis. Where ideological texts have been dispersed into rhetorics seeming not to have been authored at all—money, positivist science, buildings, number—they cannot be disputed merely in books offering different accounts of reality.

The dispersed texts of fast capitalism "compel a certain world, indeed one that looks just like itself." Where for Marx ideology taught values from the outside, today people learn conformity from the inside, without having to read in the old-fashioned sense. One learns a sense of metaphysical and thus political possibility simply from surrounding signs and structures. Not only do books make the wrong claims (e.g., religion promising an afterlife as compensation for earthly suffering); much social learning does not take place in the traditional ways. Instead of learning a world and then reproducing it, people are inculcated with conformist values in a lifeworld that appears to have no outside and thus no exit. Books do not mediate reality for people in fast capitalism; if they exist at all they exist merely to divert and entertain. Reality mediates itself where texts are dispersed into things themselves, a claim I unfold in the course of this book.

Relationship to Marx II:
Pace—from Quantity to Quality

The basic difference between slow and fast capitalism is simply that today "the pace at which significance diminishes from text and moves toward things themselves . . . quickens." The question of where quantity becomes quality, slow capitalism becoming fast capitalism, is empirical and not theoretical. Fast capitalism more quickly shields ideological claims from critical counteranalysis; ideology resides not between covers but in the interstices of an everyday life incredibly difficult to resist. Whether this makes fast capitalism qualitatively different from slow capitalism is purely rhetorical. It both does, and does not. In any case, it is more difficult to oppose the quick world of the 1980s than it was to recognize and then act upon the miserable world of the 1880s, when Marx voiced his extremely persuasive model of ideology-critique as well as socialist organization. In saying this, I do not romanticize the past; that is cheap, and it is beside the point. Rather, I apply a version of the model of ideological domination inherited from Marx and later the Frankfurt School to a later stage of capitalism without assuming that the boundary between book—thus, critique—and world can resist the pace at which significance erodes today.

Fast capitalism speeds up the rate at which people live out the historical possibilities presented to them. They do this by "reading" a public world in which deauthorized texts have been dispersed into the built and figural environment. The books still sold at the bookstore are archaic remainders, not the salient texts of the time; thus, things have become worse if we are talking about people's abilities to resist and then reconstruct. I locate the rising rate of public deception in the demise of a textual world in which thought could at least hope to make sense of and then oppose the dominant world order. In a certain way, the past was better. Although few people had the luxury of occupying a genuinely public space in which they could participate as critical citizens, at least in some sphere of existence reason subsisted. Marx could be Marx and Adorno Adorno. Today the odds against such invigorating examples of public intellectuality are long indeed. If thought lives anywhere, it is housed in the university, disciplined to the narrow codes of department, field, specialty.

Saying this risks being heard as romantic; yet realists know that one cannot turn back the clock. I differ from most Marxists and feminists and virtually all liberals in that I believe things are, in fact, getting worse. Specifically, the longer domination endures the harder it is to uproot, even to recognize and then write about it. Although slow capitalism ground down almost everyone, at least it was amenable to Marx's world-making dissent in *Capital*. Today it is almost impossible to imagine a book or oeuvre having the sweeping impact of Marx's Marxism. I want to learn from that, not simply lament the academization and absorption of critique. I will return to these senses of my term fast capitalism in deepening it. I labor not to refine a theory, for that too quickly becomes a consuming exercise in pedantry; nor do I want to proliferate slogans that think for us instead of the other way around. Instead, I want to confront a world in which literary activities like this one (or like Marx's or Adorno's) are scarely imaginable. It is tempting to insist that critique conclude with positive nostrums, but I must resist that temptation in the interest of intellectual and thus political rigor. It is enough, or at least the most that can be hoped for, that we understand our difficulties, hesitatingly joining community with others who share our sense of the world.

Fast capitalism obviously trades on Marx. It also borrows from the Frankfurt School's thesis of the eclipse of reason. I bend the Frankfurt School's version of critical theory in a literary direction so as to explain how not only reason is at stake today but, more directly, the public world of ideas in which reason plays itself out. Capitalism reproduces itself frenetically by consuming the book world, both replacing profit quickly and degrading reason. By laboring in the British Museum Marx threatened the whole capitalist world. Today such labor only adds to one's curriculum vitae; at most it earns one reputation. Although this may sound incredible to people on the left convinced that critical theory was too gloomy and thus overly resignatory, I propose an even more pessimistic version of our capitalism. But pessimism does not constitute epistemological failure. Intellectuals need not be cheerleaders.

The Domination of Reproduction

TRADITIONAL MARXISM HAS failed to bequeath a suit-
able intellectual and political legacy with which to make sense of the
world that has survived Marx's apocalyptic expectations of its demise.
Of course, this begs debate about the nature of the word *traditional*
just as it threatens to undercut a rich heritage within which this writing itself is conceived, albeit in shameless revisionism. Likewise, more
recent versions of feminist theory and poststructuralism parochially
canonize themselves in the same oppressive way as Marxism. Nonetheless these are the best available emancipatory traditions in western
society, and my own work spirals out from within them. Yet in themselves they are insufficient to conceptualize fast capitalism, a world in
which it is increasingly difficult for thought and voice to resist their
dispersal into the built, textural, and figural environments engulfing
mind's attempts to remain apart—and thus *to criticize*. In fast capitalism the mark of intellection fades into naturelike inertness. The world
zips by too quickly for us to resist the signifiers it imposes on us as
a second nature. In fast capitalism texts do not stand apart; they are
written to be lived immediately.[1]

This book is about critical theories as well as the world they address.
When discussing common versions of Marxism and feminism I intend
a more empirically and politically adequate version of critical theory.
My main thesis is that the process of signification has become virtually
automatic, dispersing meanings it would provoke as behavior directly
into the inert environment, notably through the media of money, science, edifice, and figure. "Texts," another word for Marx's ideology but

23

trading on various theories of interpretation since Marx, no longer appear to be authored acts standing apart from the reality they address but are part of nature themselves; thus, their significances are to be received uncritically and then enacted.[2] By appraising and opposing mainstream sociology (1989) I read disciplinary versions of positivism as an example of textual dispersal, making way for this more general study of degraded signification.

Money, science, edifice, and figure are the main texts of fast capitalism, defying their ready reading and thus reformulation. They comprise a positivist culture in which writing loses its distance from reality and thereby reproduces it. These accounts of the real in provoking behavior ironically prove them. In this book I consider how a positivist culture swallows textuality but then expels it into the exterior world. As a text itself these dispersed versions exercise a power over "readers" who live them as unalterable versions of the unalterable.

Criticism to criticize must read texts where writing appears absent. It must excavate authoriality from naturelike text-objects dispersed into the built, textual, and figural environments in order to engage these subterranean versions in dialogue and thus provoke their reformulation. Ideology today is deeper than Marx found it simply in textual mystifications, whether religion or *The Wealth of Nations*. Ideology now belongs to the reality it formerly described as eternal, and thus it is difficult to read it as a literary version at all.[3] In fast capitalism texts dispersed into the exterior environment compel lives unselfconsciously, only reproducing what the "texts" reflect in ontological amber. Readers no longer mediate the words that tell one version of the world or another.

My project is to offer a critical theory of signification within which to understand a host of discourses including money, science, edifice, and figure as these have taken hold materially and thus politically. I do not have to apologize for my seeming diversion into cultural critique; the base/superstructure distinction of orthodox Marxism is as wrong today as ever. I address reproduction's subordination to the valorized realm of productive work as a way of understanding the eclipse of textuality. Unfortunately, this subordination is only reinforced by a Marxian economism and a cultural feminism continuing to dominate thought. Thus, I develop a critical theory of fast capitalism through a version of Marxism and feminism alert to their own derivation from dominant western dualism and its fateful hierarchy of value.[4] Marxism and feminism do not invent the western order of value, denigrating valueless activity, but only contribute to its momentum.

Marxism and feminism have become mere words, slogans provoking obedience or apostasy. As such they have largely ceased to do valuable analytical and political work. This is only partly their fault. Primarily they have been engulfed by the same forces reducing everything else to terms of given discourse. Marxism is the books we own, where feminism is merely a personal and cultural style differentiating some women from other women. Of course, that is an oversimplification. There is much labyrinthine intellectual labor behind the two traditions; there is also vibrant political practice. Yet I am talking about tendencies of thought, even oppositional thought, to degrade into routines suppressing their essences in mere appearance. Readers think they know what they mean when they say "Marxist" this or "feminist" that, even if arguing for one iteration over another. Critique has become mindless.

One might ascribe this simply to the institutionalization and especially academization of Marxism and feminism, as a sociologist might. But there is more to it than that. Like all mind today, critique has lost itself in the topics and objects it addresses. Thus, Marxism and feminism are unexplicated; they are what people who claim them for themselves "do," whether in the university or in extraacademic politics. They have lost their theoretical power but are merely applications—a Marxist study of AIDS, a feminist position on surrogate motherhood.

This is bad for two reasons. First, critique is coopted where it forgets to think; Marxism and feminism are whatever people claim for them, even the powers. Indeed, much of American social science has selectively adopted the conceptual apparatus of these forms of critique precisely to turn words like class and gender in patently conservative directions. The current Weber renaissance narrows his distance from Marxism to vitiate Marxism, not the other way around. Attention to liberal-feminist concerns of pay equity only fuels the western order of value degrading nonwaged, largely household, labor. Second, by forgetting to think, critique becomes ritualistic and fails to introduce new empirical work. Marxists in naming themselves no longer think their Marxism; they ignore the differences as well as sameness between capitalism then and now. Feminists duplicate a common cultural style but thereby fail to break out of personal politics to the "other" politics, that of massive economic and cultural structures.

I understand these tendencies as tendencies, not absolutes. Conservatives trace the falling rate of Marxist intelligence directly to Marx, thereby precluding a living Marxism. I also understand these tendencies as outcomes of a certain drift in fast capitalism away from book culture and toward lifeworlds in which books compel unthinking adjustment, what passes for "reading" today. The left is not invulnerable

25

to this tendency of degrading its concepts into slogans; it happens to everyone else. But the left should foresee its own tendency to degrade precisely because Marxism is above all a view of totality. Yet totality is sacrificed in a postmodernist spirit where a universal structuring reason is dismissed as the sin of pride; instead, people cherish their own particularism in a desperate urge to avoid being Archimedean, absolutist, male. Unfortunately, they fail; a decentering heterogeneity is cultivated by the stewards of totality so that we are kept isolated, stupid, disorganized.

I will discuss the dispersal of Marxism and feminism into author-less "texts" compelling unthinking readings. In this sense they are like anything else in fast capitalism. The basic problem is loss of the defiant force of writing where the allegedly more valuable sphere of production continues to subordinate the realm of ideas. Thus, Marxism and feminism are not powerful forms of authorial mediation and constitution but the folkways associated with *being* Marxist or feminist —ownership of certain books, clothes, a certain cultural orientation, a lingo. Book culture preserving the autonomy of thought is vanquished where books are dispersed into an exterior world as deauthored accounts of our implacable fate. Marxists have always understood this as economism—a civilizational tendency anchored in an overarching dualism only concealing a deeper hierarchy.

Ironically, the disempowering of textuality secretly empowers writing to provoke system-serving behavior on the part of muted readers who approach texts as naturelike objects reflecting unalterable being. I do not urge textuality to become productive in its own right; it already is. Rather, I understand the domination of reproduction, including textuality, as an occasion for a reading strategy liberating us from the thrall of seemingly transcendental versions bearing the imprint of no authorial artifice. I call this critique, trading on Kant's interrogation of what is possible as well as Marx's sense of sharp opposition. Ideology-critique in Marx's original terms does the work here of opening authored practices dispersed deceptively into money, science, edifice, and figure to the eye of critical scrutiny and thus to reformulation by readers who defy their ontologizing by *living differently*. Therefore, my approach to interpretation as a mode of political critique avoids disengagement.

In fast capitalism thought is dispersed into the built, textual, and figural world so that reading forgets that signs were originally authored and thus can be reformulated. Signs inherently criticize where they acknowledge their difference from the reality they represent. As an inert, obdurate text, word reflects a supposed social nature as it

is engulfed in nature itself. Thus, I will discuss the way the degradation of signification in fast capitalism poses us the task of excavating
text-objects virtually blurring with nature and thus fatefully relived
as accounts of unalterable necessity. I propose a radicalized hermeneutics,[5] a way of reading these dispersed and degraded texts that in
its own version of authorial excavation, of resignification, prefigures
a communicative world; Habermas began this project (1984, 1987) in
his version of critical theory.

Theoretical synthesis fails to address the complicity of theory itself
in the world it makes its object, falsely aping the natural sciences and
reducing nature to a manipulable domain of protean human mastery.
Instead, I want science to be a directly transformative practice welling
up in oppressed human beings who by understanding their situation
as remediable immediately begin to relive it; the gap between theory
and practice shrinks to the time it takes to read and write the world
that writing calls forth as its correction and completion. A literary
version of science, in understanding itself understanding, opens itself
to dialogue with people who have other versions of the world—and
thus together we create a better political community.[6] I will try to
demonstrate the notion that reading is immediately a valuable form
of political practice today, an issue I rejoin in Ch. 5.

This is not to say that theory is politically sufficient but to interrogate the meaning of sufficiency in avoiding made-to-order assumptions about the nature of the political. In Ch. 6 I address the politics of
textuality in these terms. At the outset it is enough to distance my version of critical theory from traditional Marxism simply by suggesting
that the transformative scenario exhorted by Marx is virtually unreal
today in a world order more complexly interrelated than the relatively
simple capitalism Marx confronted in the mid-19th century. Marxism
is not a shelf full of books but an ongoing engagement with those
books in a literary community, where reading and writing join people
in a permanent dialectic of ignorance and enlightenment. I want to
probe the possibilities of a version of critical theory informed by developments in literary theory as a way of exploring the possibilities of
new literary versions and thus of a new world.[7]

Marxism and feminism have been born of a world preventing critique from hitting its target. A notion of the *domination of reproduction*
suggests a way of thinking about the deceptive role of textuality in
fast capitalism. Marx was a product of his time just as one cannot ignore Freud's context in Viennese morality and sexual politics. I do not
attempt a sociology of knowledge clarifying Marx by reductively re-
moving the traces of time, place, and passion from his work, precisely

27

the effort of the many Marxologists who still seek definitive versions; instead, I address the bourgeois concepts of reason and liberation insufficiently rendered self-conscious by Marx and his epigones in allowing them to avoid the irony that the world they propose is all too similar to the one they attack as inadequate.[8] Criticism borrows so heavily from its orienting texts and practices that it frequently internalizes their fatal contradictions and thus only reproduces the world it makes its topic. The subsequent history of that critical movement, then, is taken up with the frantic attempt to purge criticism of its opponent's flaws, occasioning works such as this. This is not to reject critique as endlessly iterative of its bad object but to attend to the embeddedness of critique in a central text in a way that would make critique self-conscious of its unconscious borrowings from what it professes to oppose.

This project becomes urgent when critique shades over into construction, whether Marx's infrequent utopianizing or feminism's quite self-conscious discussions of androgyny, family, sexuality.[9] Critique risks infection by its topic; today the entire administered world is virtually impossible to put into enough words. This is not to make the common argument that Marxism was folly from the beginning because the world is inherently intractable. Just the opposite: critique that sticks so close to its object loses its difference, offering itself as the artificial negativity (Piccone 1978; Thompson 1981) a totalizing liberal society seems to require. It is important to turn critique toward its new object by resisting the centrifugal forces otherwise transvaluing it into a plural interest group scrapping to get its voice heard or, worse, only another academic specialty with its own journals, conferences, and superstars.

Marxism as the dominant emancipatory philosophy of our time has to be rethought continually as empirical theory for it to avoid becoming the shark's remora, its negation rendered complacent.[10] This invigoration proceeds not scientistically by turning Marxist microscopes toward an inert material world, thus risking the fetishism of Marxist measurement so abundant as to be prosaic today. It distances critique from the suctionlike world swallowing nearly everything. Not a call simply for abstraction, critique breaks thought's dependence on the convenient concepts it has made virtually second nature. Few Marxist discussions these days fail to invoke the cliches of contradiction, capital, surplus value, theory of the state, determination in the last instance, social formation. Marxism risks losing its mind as its homilies cease to think for it.

It is tempting to criticize Marxism's academization as if that were the problem. But academization is hardly the most pernicious sequence in the disciplining of Marxism. Is the nonacademic somehow a more propitious venue for Marxist disputation—a Marxist rock video, hamburger chain, political party? The critique of academization is merely a moment of an anti-intellectualism only hastening the integration of thought and its object, especially ironic where Marxism depends so much on its critical distance from the world it opposes.[11]

In this book I want to expand the distance between a version of critical theory and its object to develop a better mode of opposition and hence construction. In no sense does this shift the burden "from" politics "to" theory, as if theory were not already fully political; it acknowledges their inherence in each other as a central topic of a nearly totally administered society. Whether we call its object ideology, hegemony, or reification, theory as a text participates in the objects it makes it topic, its writing a textual practice as much practice as text. Capitalism, even more broadly domination, thrives where it can be reproduced through the reflexes of a scripted "everyday life" prompting its ritualized reproduction. As such, "texts" are nucleic units of an everyday life only entrenching its domination by the imperatives of capital, patriarchy, and racism. Yet in fast capitalism money, science, edifice, and figure are not easily read as authorial versions precisely because they do not want to be read that way but only duplicated slavishly in their ontological foreshortening. Text is neither derivative nor inferior to the other material practices thought to subordinate it; today it produces its own seeming subordination to frozen being. The crucial challenge for the left is to conceive of a qualitatively different order in images that not only make sense to people inured to classic Marxism but also energize them defiantly to relive their routinized lives in ways attaining a significant difference from the present order. Indeed, the word "significant" can only be argued through systems of significance increasingly at peril where texts are things and things texts, the topic of Ch. 3.

I move along the plane of the textual not because I restrict emancipatory projects to the literary but because it is impossible to conceive a different social order outside conception itself, beyond the pages and images presenting themselves as the possibilities of their own enactment. This avoids idealism, the bugbear of 19th-century materialists, where it challenges textuality to enact itself in the myriad million ways that readers and writers narratively turn text into a genuinely social relationship—Wittgenstein's (1953) well-named language games. While acknowledging that all the world is not a text, all writing is worldly in the sense that it proffers a version of the world it would provoke

29

out of the reading practices making writing only a version. This book is about the thin boundary between text and world, a construction obscuring writing's worldliness and blocking its transformative potential. Similarly, all idealism has been subordinated to the material, its electric imagination shortcircuited.[12]

Let me cast this in a way more comprehensible to empiricists: texts *matter* because they are matter, entering the world as its simultaneous transformation. These last words have changed the world just as have the inventions of the microchip and missiles. Fiction as much as science, textuality joins lives and recommends various states of affairs and courses of action and thus produces the world it seems only epistemologically to reproduce—reproduction in the double sense of copy and perpetuation.[13] *King Lear* depicts a perfidious world just as Graham Greene inhabits and would ironically relive a world in which innocence is absent; although not manifestos, fiction enters the world as the invitation to readings that *would enact themselves in the various rituals of obedience or disobedience to text's version.* If we read science (and here especially Marxism and feminism) as a mode of narrative, we can excavate the authorial intentionality methodology cleanses out of writing in order to reproduce its topic in reality, science reflecting and thus reproducing a frozen social horizon.

As I will explore in Ch. 6, that texts matter because they are matter does not deeconomize traditional left perspectives on such things as unemployment, rape, and genocide but understands the muting of their victims as a literary problem. Rape becomes a text when the victim screams for help, identifies her attacker, and then writes (about) rape in joining community with other women. Rape is the most extreme form of monologic patriarchy, transvaluing sexuality into power. This is not simply to let rape victims write, although that would be a beginning, but to understand gender relations as significative-signifying entanglements in which men both usurp women's dialogue chances and impose on them the phallogocentric discourse of male mastery of nature and concept; so-called feminist methodology is an ineffective response, biologizing abstraction as male essence.[14]

The most pressing strategic problem is not to convey esoteric truths to a dulled public but to empower them to the same conclusions through their own education and self-education. Marxism has failed dramatically where it has imposed truth. As Korsch (1970) said in the 1920s, this only ends in a dictatorship *over* the proletariat; Lenin's truth "from without" prevents the Russian working class and peasantry from learning to live and write their own freedom. The search for a female imaginary eschews male standards of scientific iterability and promises, indeed requires, a nonphallogocentric textual/sexual practice. Feminism more than classic Marxism has understood the textuality of domination both in stereotypical language and in reproduction's domination by male productivism and its scientism.

Feminism needs Marxism where it fails to differentiate the concept of world-historical patriarchy sufficiently to gain political purchase in a totalizing stage of world capitalism and state socialism. The notion of patriarchy requires its historicization from outside itself, its differentiation into classes and races as well as sex classes. For its part, Marxism needs feminism where it has lacked a sufficient focus not only on sexual politics but also on the whole politics of reproduction, including both biology/sexuality on the one hand and culture/textuality on the other. My contribution here is to rethink Marxism and feminism in a way that moves toward a *critical theory of significance* as well as an ethic through which critique becomes a binding norm moving us from the personal into the political and back again.

The discussion of the relationship between Marxism and feminism has been hampered by the very phallogocentrism the French feminists decry.[15] Marxism needs feminism as feminism needs Marxism yet not because each is only half the truth; independently each only reproduces the epochal separation *and thus hierarchy* of production/reproduction, object/subject, nature/world, heaven/hell, man/woman, white/colored. The sundering of feminism and Marxism undoes defiance where defiance is carefully compartmentalized. They are not untrue apart; rather they cannot even exist apart as competing constructions of the axiologies of domination without shattering against each other long before they take on the preponderant world frequently crushing opposition. The hierarchization of dominations only dominates.

The movement politics of male domination has so preoccupied feminists that they approach the male left with a good deal of trepidation about territoriality.[16] But Marxism and feminism are versions of the same textual practice, a larger critical theory addressing the range of dominations of center over margin from capital/labor and man/woman to society/nature and concept/thing; *all emanate from the central diremption and thus hierarchy of object and subject both as a mode of knowledge and concrete social practice.*[17] This construction of domination pivoting around the axial antagonism of subject/object, a Promethean subject mastering the seemingly unresisting object world but thereby provoking its subsequent revolt, risks unnecessary ontological prioritization read to evince a hierarchy of dominations with some being lower than others in importance. Domination, however, resists this

31

hierarchization by its very nature as a practice that feeds off itself re-productively; one domination leads to another, and is frequently contained in another, inasmuch as *domination drives relentlessly to totalize itself,* overdetermining its constituent levels such that thought can grasp its structured complexity only with great difficulty. Indeed the notion of the hierarchization of domination itself dominates inasmuch as it implies the possibility of dominations' analytic separation and thus isolation. The world pits Marxism, feminism, and antiracism against each other to prevent their crystallization in a unified critique as practice. The social order relentlessly isolates dominations from one another to prevent their totalization of the lousy world as a topic in its own right. The reality "domination" does not exist discretely out there, in the concretely factual object world, but is as much a product of the mind that thinks it as it is a mind that produces a world. The fundamental nonidentity of subject/object or concept/world itself makes possible a nonidealist dialectic of gentle writer/rewriter, person/person, man/woman, white/black, society/nature.

A positivist version of science pretends presuppositionlessly to describe the object world without addressing its own contribution to that world; its desire to produce a world in its image becomes the topic of self-reflection and thus textual transformation. Domination is both external and internal, both done to us and by us. The prioritization and hierarchization of dominations marginalize those dominations remote from the writer, exemplified in the frequent notion of a Third World somehow distinct from and subordinate to First and Second ones as well as in the Marxist derogation of the woman's question and the feminist essentialism of an undifferentiated patriarchy.

If domination is construction as much as a context in which construction takes place, then it is useless to attempt a reductionism grounding it in a singular principle of expressive logic, whether capitalism, sexism, or racism; *that reduction only contributes to its object by privileging one domination over another,* mirroring the world as it "is"—that is, as we have made it. Domination in Adorno's (1973a) terms is non-identical to itself because it evades the mirror in which we would lucidly capture it and thus subject it to dissection.[18] The mirror dominates our efforts to relive the world by silencing the great majority of the world's billions. Thus, the construction "domination" either provides a way through and out of it or simply privileges one group of dominated at the expense of others—ever the rule in a hierarchized world in which the next best thing to being at the top is to be on top, over at least one other even more oppressed group or version.

Domination splits apart the margins pitted against each other so as not to challenge the dominating center. The more Marxists and feminists contend the less they bear on the center decentering them. The center holds by constructing margins in its own image, that is in terms of center/margin hierarchies further marginalizing the margins. The margins are split into good and bad versions, the one safe and incrementalist, the other wild and threateningly incorrigible; *both* constructions preclude authentic versions like western Marxism and socialist feminism.

The left cannot oppose the hierarchy of center and margin without resisting its own hierarchization. This is not simply a moral pluralism where everyone's suffering is "appreciated" but an awareness of the indissolubility of dominations overdetermining and overlapping each other precisely because *the victims are never different.*[19] It has become popular under sway of Derridean deconstruction to reject single-cause models of domination for decentered ones, acknowledging a plurality of dominations. Although valuable as a counterpoint to reductive notions of totality, this proto-Nietzschean marginalism so typical of postmodernist thought tends toward its own absolutism, here an absolutism of the relative, the fragmented, the marginal.[20] In this book I present some of the central themes of emancipatory theory not to totalize the various regional dominations (that Derrideans rightly point out are strictly irreducible one to the other) but to orchestrate them discursively into a concerted whole.

Deconstruction evades the political where it becomes method, tempting in an age when it is difficult to think let alone write the totality of a billion dominations. To save deconstruction from the myth of its own method it is necessary to interweave its textual-critical approach to the aporias of dualism with a more substantive *sociosexual approach to the relation between production and reproduction,* that is, Marxism and feminism.[21] Deconstruction is not lacking in substance; yet its Nietzschean impulse to transvalue all centering values, crucially necessary in a decentering world today, tends to get the better of its political possibilities as critique. Nietzsche did not aim to change the world but to interrogate the notion that "change" has occurred. Critique goes further; it harbors the positive in its negation of the world, unafraid to stand for substantive values like justice, freedom, reason—indeed, acutely aware that we must recoup the competence to signify *and then signify anew.* For his part, Derrida declares himself a Marxist. Yet this is external to his own philosophical ("grammatological") program in the sense that he needs to say it at all. If transformativeness is not there from the beginning, so deeply embedded in method it becomes inseparable from it, then no amount of self-clarification will rescue the text from its fateful spiral into methodism, the tendency of virtually all isolated thought today.[22]

This is not preciousness disguised as strategic expediency, the charge too frequently leveled against Adorno (1973b) where he tried to extrapolate a mode of political resistance out of some of the most unusual voices of modernism like Schoenberg's composition and Beckett's literature. He was correct to think that critique can only subsist at the furthest removes from the totalizing center; otherwise it is sucked into the dominant logic of administration patterned on the model of the Promethean subject mastering a recalcitrant object. That Adorno did not have a political program is simply wrong; his writing reeked of the political, if not a kind recognizable by either orthodox Marxism or liberal scientism.[23]

Distance from the dominating object is not simply abstraction or evasion; the system not only accommodates but also encourages the shifting, depthless expressions of the postmodern as a safety valve for deeper resentments and unsated desires. Texts proclaiming foundationlessness as a reprieve from the foundationalism entrenching the wrong foundation (capitalism, sexism, etc.) only marginalize themselves innocuously, absorbed into the babble of the ephemeral as so much noise. Distance differs from this self-trivializing abstraction in that it works through its isolation in order to understand both *why* it is so remote from the center of the world and *how* it can remake that center in terms of a logic of emancipation defying the either/ors of dualist society. Distance in this sense buys time and encourages real reflection, both scarce in an age of instantaneity, inflation, innovativeness. If this is not political "enough," so much the worse for politics. Or better, although writing is not an adequate political practice we must interrogate the meaning of adequacy as a part of the transformative process. Otherwise the books that inspire us become our tombstones.

We are so deeply ensconced in the problematic of duality concealing hierarchy that we conceive our liberation too frequently in terms only reproducing the vain Prometheanness of subjectivity. Politics is not a heroic gesture but a web of relations of writers, readers, and nature. Correct politics in left cant is politics that buys into the dominant power order by using its own currencies of exchange value, hierarchy, division of labor, and the like. Although this tells us something, namely how the system is ultimately aporetic in its tendencies to undo itself (too much x for some, too little y for others, precipitating their revolt), it does not work free from the embedded ontologies valorizing exchange value, hierarchy and the division of labor—administrative power *for its own sake*. This foreshortens imagination into what amounts to a duplication of the given or its inversion into an ever-the-same version of itself (e.g., state socialism for capitalism; motherright for patriarchy).

I have chosen the domination of reproduction, particularly of textuality, as my initial topic in order to refract Marxism, feminism, and deconstruction toward some useful authorial work in a quick world defying distance from itself, ever the requirement of liberation. Every reading is a new version, regardless of the author's credentials: my Marx is me, as is my feminism. This does not reintroduce the Derridean decentering too frequently only skirting the dominant center in an orgy of ontological pluralism; instead, it underlines the literariness of reading and thus empowers readers heretofore muted before the authoritative texts of canonical literature, whether the Grand Theorists of a certain tradition, embalmed for posterity, or the everyday mainstream of a research discipline.

Writing joins community with both tradition and other writers, thus making way for much more than Hegelian "synthesis," a notion connoting simple arithmetic or centering. Hegel himself intended synthesis as a process of *Aufhebung,* negating-preserving-transcending the object or topic under address. Rendered in English frequently as sublation, this process of negation-preservation-transcendence dereifies writing's canonized topics by reading in a creatively dialogical engagement with other writers, empowering them toward their own versions. Of course, the dominant dualisms dismiss this notion of literary democracy as hubris, doing violence to great books and minds that have only to be interpreted and thus iterated. Unfortunately, because Marxism came from one pen the tendency of canonization within Marxism has been virtually irresistible, later matched by the hagiography of the various European representatives of one or another version of Marxological explication. This is largely why Marxism so urgently needs a discourse-theoretic grounding to overcome its own hierarchization of (Marx's) writing and (our) criticism, denying vital sources of theoretical and political redirection decried as revisionism.

The logic of administered society in reducing negation to an inversion of the positive so saturates it with both deep and surface scars of its own neutralization that critique becomes almost entirely parasitical. The dialectic of process and product is thus understandably a central problematic for a Marxism and feminism intent on preventing the short-term authoritarianisms allegedly necessary to vanquish counterrevolutionary vestiges of the old regime. Although necessary to avoid precisely this outcome, too much emphasis on process fails to achieve that critical distance from its topic protecting it against the fallout of the old world's implosion once it can no longer live within its own aporetic parameters of "progress" and the like. Yet too little emphasis on process risks the Gulag. This is an invitation to rethink the polarity between closeness and distance by underlining the hidden closeness of distance, its relevance in a world demolishing the concrete under its world-historical logic of abstracting administration.[24] As ever, survival is the most "practical" thing to do, especially in order to fight another day and in ways that give real substance to the notion of fight, of negation.

The embeddedness of liberation theories in one rhetoric of pragmatism or another conditions a reading of critical theory and especially Adorno as perversely disengaged, occupants of Lukacs's "Grand Hotel Abyss." But this fails, indeed refuses, to interrogate the notion of engagement and implies that the most political thing to do, "strategy," is engage with the existent in its own terms; thus, it either reproduces itself or an inverted, ever-the-same manifestation. But the phrase "its own terms" is subject to construction. When deconstructing capitalist economic theory Marx did not accept the world's terms of discourse but imposed on it a new construction transfiguring not only its concepts of itself but also, through the emerging institutionalization of Marxian "practice," the world itself.

Distance approaches proximity to the most relevant political tasks to the extent to which those tasks are deeply encoded in the textual practices today entwining and delimiting our imaginations—hence Adorno's (1973a) dictum that we must break out of the objective contexts of delusion only "from within," that is in terms of our rhetorical stances to other writers, the world, and nature. Less heterodox Marxists would rephrase this as the timeworn program of ideology-critique toward the rehabilitation of class consciousness. I differ from this classical Marxism in the way it separates both temporally and ontologically this process of ideological demystification and more "real" political practices to which ideology as superstructure is subordinated. As Habermas (1971) argued in *Knowledge and Human Interests*, Marxian mechanism obscures the distinction between instrumental and communicative/reflective rationalities, affording Marxism no basis on which to provoke active knowledge-constitution and thus community building outside the predestinations of a naturelike history.

Although Habermas takes his Marxism in a somewhat different direction from me, it is common ground between us that the old conception of ideology defeats thought's active interrogation of its own autonomy as the most basic possibility of radical social change.[25] If it is required that one subordinate intellection to economic practice in order to be a real Marxist, so much the worse for Marxism. Better to say that Marxism is a version of critical theory than the other way around.[26] Acquiescence to official constructions of subject/object as a version of center/margin, notably science/nonscience, will always defeat the left because it accepts the dominant discourse valorizing the notion of *identity as hegemony;* subject is defined by the object it masters, manipulates, defeats. Hegemonic identity explored deeply by Sartre (1976) and de Beauvoir (1953) achieves itself at the expense of the Other, nonscience, nature or other people denigrated for their less-than-humanness.[27] The logic of duality is fascist, conquering the object world as a validation of the arrogant subject's Faustian selfhood. This is not to settle for retreat as a sufficient political result but to address engagement as the secret subtext of conquest it really is, the replenishment of subject with spoils wrested unselfconsciously from the object world constructed as a mute horizon of not-I-ness and not-it-ness.

Some feminists intriguingly trace this Promethean arrogance of conquest back to the originary subordination of maleness to femaleness in early hunting and gathering societies. To come to terms with the seeming magic that women survive monthly bleeding and reproduce themselves it is theorized that men developed productivism as their own version of reproduction, making of nature a kind of self-validating infant and then extending that power drive into a virtually world-historical impulse for control, ending with nuclear weaponry. Even if only an allegorical device akin to Freud's notion of the primal horde, this notion of the originary primacy of (female) reproductiveness over (male) production devised precisely as compensation for seeming male inferiority (of course a biologistic misreading in its own right)[28] provides a historical-materialist foundation for the notion of the domination of reproduction.

Without such allegorizing, the subject/object problematic could be explained with reference to a deep structure of mind and society, the route taken by Lévi-Strauss (1963, 1966) among others. But (Diamond 1974) structuralism lacks history, even if only the mythic history of this account of originary female primacy. This reconstruction of Faustian self-externalization in nature as an artifact of men's debilitating sense of their biological inferiority allows us at the very least to develop alternative, non-dualist/sexist/capitalist modes of concourse with ourselves, texts, other people, and nature energized by this prehistoric construction of the fateful primacy of reproduction—of *textuality*—over (male) production. To put this another way, the feminist left lacks images of liberation appropriate to the overdetermined, overadministered world today, both energizing resistance and stimulating prefiguration of new forms of life. We need such images that sufficiently break with the dominant dualities deconstructing into what Adorno called the preponderance of the object—the epochal domination of nature, other people, and desire by the driven ego of reproductively deprived men, capitalists, state socialists, and racists.

Although clearly old Marxism fails to address the present in concepts stimulating imagination, clinging to outdated words from the *Manifesto* and *Capital*, most feminisms fail to provide suitable images of liberation; instead, in Hegel's terms they badly negate the patriarchal present with imprecations against male culture counterposed to a "female imaginary" as an alternative. The metaphysic of women's knowledge fails to be real negation because it plays into the pluralism of a totalizing system scattering and thus disempowering dissent in the various "interest groups" privileging their particular domination with respect to other dominations. It is no solution to play feminism off against Marxism as if either could be "corrected" with the other; instead, they must be rethought *together* and thus reformulated.

Critical theory wants to reprivilege reproduction by examining the way in which its devaluation only reproduces dominant hierarchies. Critique itself politicizes texts dispersed into nature, thus only provoking the lives they portray as ontologically inevitable. Marx read money in this way.[29] Reading politicizes by authorizing versions like money appearing not to be products of human artifice at all but simply dumb pieces of nature. Radical hermeneutics, as I will call it in Ch. 5, makes social nature speak openly about the social agendas it encodes much the way Marx made money disclose its desire to fall disproportionately into the pockets of capitalists. Reading in politicizing is a form of politics itself, albeit a heterodox one by most standards.

In particular reading insists on the material relevance of textuality. The derogation of the realm of intellection only reflects and then reproduces other hierarchies of the useful and useless, the valuable and valueless. Money hierarchizes itself over the nonmonetarized precisely to perpetuate its own dominance as a legitimate standard of value. In fast capitalism value is increasingly encoded in things that thus dictate whole theories of being; writing already contains an interpretive rule for its own reading. I want to write reading as a form of writing, arguing for the strength of critique against its apparent subordination to money's and science's rules of value. In this sense critique insists on the textuality of the real as well as on its own constitutive role in authorizing and then reformulating invisible texts. Critique strongly reclaims the power apparently denied writing by showing that texts make the world go round—money, science, edifice, figure, all forms of what I have called *discipline* (1989). And the most powerful texts in fast capitalism are those concealing their authoriality precisely to provoke lives that then validate their original accounts. Money is valued the more it conceals its narrative identity with value—the less it reads as the text it is.

By rethinking the role of ideology in fast capitalism Marxism opens itself to a feminist version of text's subordination to a rule of productive value. We must resignify the exterior environment as the authored accomplishment it is. As things, books do not read anymore as corrigible products of analytic intelligence but simply obtrude into the exterior environment as codes of adjustment, adaptation, acquiescence. Labor is capital's rule over labor power that then disperses itself as truth in the textual form of money. Science in provoking the world it freezes on the page thus confirms its own account. Edifice structures public life by seeming rationally conceived as a form of nature. Figure robs number of thought in monetarizing philosophical standards of meaning and value. Yet the goal of liberation is not only to empower money, science, edifice, and figure into the hands and minds of the people but to change the way we signify value. We must create a world in which writing is not inferior to labor; indeed, it is a part of labor as generic human praxis.

The irony of programmatism is that it must already write in the voice it recommends.[30] Thus, my analytic reconstruction of fast capitalism intends a different world prefigured in the way I talk. By raging against a western order of value tautologically subordinating the valueless to the valued I passionately model a new order in which nonalienated activity like writing solicits its gentle reception and correction in human community. Hate and love blend in critique that neither loses itself in its object, thus losing its identity or even its mind, nor so distances itself that it ignores history's deadly direction to date. In authorizing the exterior world I make it read like fiction—a world made up of literary possibilities. Yet in understanding myself understanding and then writing about the world, I remake it on the model of what Habermas calls ideal speech. Good talk vanquishes bad by admitting, even celebrating, its literary corrigibility, soliciting correction as the norm of utopia. Duality's secret hierarchy of public and private can only be undone by writing about it in a way that sheds the constraints of dualism as much as possible. This does not privilege form over content but sees them in each other.[31]

Too little thought has been given to revolution's process; as a result, critique suppresses its utopianizing desire in favor of its science. Both

39

belong. Yet critique, failing to attend to its own prefigurative implications for the world it would create, only reproduces an order of being subordinating critique to construction, private to public, subject to object. While I do not immediately give rise to a new world in a single version, neither will the world spring full-blown from world crisis. Analysis does not guarantee a good outcome; it only helps understand the aporias of the present. Critique must add poetry to its science in order to exemplify an alternative mode of social being. Where critique rejects the rule of productive value in the way it hierarchizes itself over reproduction it offers utopia the norm of dialogical reciprocity, mutual respect, literary self-understanding. The good society emerges in the talk and work it takes to vanquish its enemy; the two are inseparable.

Who is to blame Marxism for its scientism when the capitalist totality veils itself in so many layers of illusion? Yet critique that loses its poetry fails to put a dialectical spin on negation, thus, as Habermas suggested, failing to secure a ground for its social criticism. If poetry is the wrong metaphor for a version at once opposing and prefiguring, then think of critique as dialectical. If dialectic rings the wrong bell, imagine science as fiction. In any case, one's relation to one's topic and audience contructs as much as deconstructs, and thus one must attend to the auspices under which one attempts to copy the world. Objective knowledge is possible, yet only by thinking the relation between knowledge and the object world in a literary way. Text produces as well as reproduces. Forgetting this only entrenches a positivist culture in which signs do little overt work but thereby do a lot; they provoke the world they attempt presuppositionlessly to conceal in their ontologizing account of it. The domination of reproduction reproduces itself where textuality concedes to the world from which it is born as its teleological completion.

At the very least, critique learns something empirically important by understanding the process of textual dispersal in fast capitalism where books become things and things books. It realizes that the world is not seamless and that money, science, edifice, and figure must do crucial political work. They make social history into social nature thus forestalling reformulations unbidden to a positivist model of the relation between truth and the world. The fact of money as a congealed text can be read as both the social order it conceals in which labor power is ripped off and the contingency of a market economy in which the labor contract embedded in the money form needs to be occluded not as text but as invariant nature. Critique learns the untruth of a seemingly sufficient world and thus gains a modest measure of political optimism. Although this is not a lot, where can we find more in the way of political sustenance? The labor movement? The Soviet Union? The National Organization of Women? Eldridge Cleaver? Critique in confronting the narrative nature of domination at least addresses the possibility of resistance. What "use" it makes of this is another question and one that cannot be answered theoretically. The world already contains a billion different rages of which this is only a local version. Conditioned by university, theory, and social movement, it is no less truthful than the rage of Central American peasants or Soviet political prisoners.

As ever, resistance must think itself and thus gain distance from the world swallowing it: *critique*. Thought should not be ashamed at its effort to comprehend itself comprehending; therein lie all sorts of empirical clues about how opposition tends to be defused. And thought faithful to its utopian imagination at least models a better address to things, a more humane discourse through which to inhabit the social world. We must resist the tendency to reduce thought to operational terms, refusing to strategize imagination; otherwise, we lend credence to the dominant notion that ideas are only as good as the work they do—popularity gained, money earned, hypotheses tested. This version of critical theory puts distance between itself and things in order to read things in fast capitalism as the enmeshing codes they have become. In the process, I suggest a different order of value. I cannot be sure how "much" this version contributes to that order; indeed, that is the wrong way to view critique's analytic and poetic possibility.

Instead, thought in differentiating itself from things gains a clarity of vision without giving up the passion of polemic. Critique models the norm of democratic speech in order to remake the world oppressing dialogue and enslaving imagination. That I do not know the extent of my contribution does not make it less vital. Intellectual and political conformity always finds comfort in the seeming futility of defiance. But they imagine that. No one can reckon the probability that someone will write another *Manifesto*, or even what form it will take at a different point in world history. To say that is what I want to do risks hilarity among true believers as well as cynics. So what? They temporize anyway.

CHAPTER 3

Books and Things:
Texts in a Material World

WRITING IS A material practice in the way it objectifies thought into a public world. A positivist version of writing disperses itself into naturelike text-objects defying their reading as narrative instances of construction and thus, possibly, critique.[1] In this regard writings dispersed into the built, textual, and figural environments are all the more compelling in the way they provoke reading that, in effect, is practice itself. In fast capitalism writing concealed in text-objects defies reading as authored acts thus provoking the worlds they intend to portray as inescapably invariant. Examples of this abound. Bourgeois political economy made thematic by Marx portrayed a naturelike economic universe embodying an implacable rationality. More recently, within disciplinary sociology Parsons and Bales's (1955) well-known defense of patriarchal family is "proven" empirically by the familied behavior it provokes. This is not to say that anything and everything can be "read" as text but only that textual practice is a powerful material force, especially in the way it conceals its own authoriality. Positivism as a theory of knowledge is a paradigmatic form of this self-concealing version of prose, blurring its own distinction from the reality to which it is an address. Writing ideologizes by occluding its difference from its topic, the essence of a presuppositionlessly representational model of knowledge. Writing in fast capitalism is detextualized precisely to hide its own attempt to overcome its difference from the world it would ontologize as an invariant history, inducing either the love of fate (Nietzsche) or simply resignation, even resentment (Scheler).

These are *tendencies,* not absolutes. Books still exist as does the possibility of critical mediation. I run the risk of ontologizing what are merely tendencies by naming them. But the opposite risk is worse—to assume that thought enjoys a distance sufficient from the centrifugal force of things that it can pick and choose the topic and timing of its interventions. It cannot, especially where the public status of Marxism and feminism seems to have been settled behind the heavy momentum of their literatures and cultural styles. By desperately resisting its tendency to degrade into slogans and folkways thought fights for its political life. One cannot assume its success, especially where the preponderance of evidence indicates its failure. Capitalism and sexism subsist, and thought has been largely academicized. Critical theory must make its own isolation an empirical topic in learning from its failures.

What is "fast" about this version of writing in capitalism is that it zips by the eye and mind so readily that we do not read it as an act of meditation or mediation at all. As text congeals into nature, like nature it appears to be an unalterable piece of eternity, irrefutable in its obdurateness. In particular, text's nature is to reflect or represent the given order of things, and so in becoming a thing it provokes the nature of what it portrays narrativelessly. Positivist science, concealing its own literariness, is a strong literary version provoking what it wants to prove in the beginning, a twist of Merton's notion of self-fulfilling prophecy turned back against the social text itself. Fast capitalism capitalizes on the inherent temporality of the text/topic relationship further to deauthorize versions otherwise appearing not to have been written at all but simply copied from a timeless cosmos—thus only reproducing it.

This is not to suggest simply that we slow down the process of the degradation of signification, texts' dispersal into naturelike objects defying their reading and hence reformulation.[2] The rate at which signification degrades only represents the more fundamental problem of the deauthorization of the built, textual, and figural environments, much the same problem addressed by Marx (commodity fetishism), Lukacs (reification), and the Frankfurt School (eclipse of reason).[3] I am not saying that the dispersal and degradation of authorial signification is new but only that it is qualitatively intensified in a stage of domination more than ever requiring writing not to be read but simply lived. Thus, I approach critical theory from the perspective of discourse theory.[4]

The structuring sign systems of western culture have depicted a social nature so entangling it is difficult to trace the boundaries between these structuring texts and the topics and objects to which they refer, namely the social world. The world is not only a text, but every text intends a world constituted in the reader-writer relationship. By implanting text in things the world attempts to script certain behaviors that readers believe unavoidable, necessary, naturelike. Domination today uniquely blurs the boundaries of text and world precisely to provoke the enactment of its "fate" without engaging anything but the reader's autonomic nervous system—television advertisements assimilated and then enacted in the flash of an instant, science textbooks approached in the attitude of unhesitating reception and acquisition. Texts *disguise* their textuality, becoming as much like the "realities" they describe as possible by *suggesting* them to readers resigned to their textual incompetence, a facet of their overall dependence.[5]

These tendencies sound mystical. Indeed, it is extremely difficult to demonstrate the eclipse of textuality in a book. But positivist culture degrades significance in a host of subtle ways, notably including the tendency of writing itself to become a slogan. The Frankfurt School faced much the same problem where they tried to demonstrate the eclipse of reason (Horkheimer 1974b) or one-dimensionality (Marcuse 1964). Critics noted with glee that Marcuse exempted himself from his general analysis of the public loss of mind in late capitalism. On this basis they said he was both elitist and a bad scientist, damning charges in a liberal-positivist world. He responded that one could learn as much as necessary about one-dimensionality by watching an hour of television. I would hold with that. But epistemologically it may not win the day, especially with people who watch public television.

I resolve the problem of evidence at least by acknowledging that it exists. It is difficult to demonstrate the absence of something, here book culture. It is made more difficult where we *forget* (Jacoby 1975b) that we used to enjoy a public culture in which ideas stood at one remove from the world they address and thus defy. Saying that risks a left notion of a golden age (Agger 1983a). Yet the appeal to memory is a way of revealing the existence of historical tendencies otherwise unnoticed. The Frankfurt theorists implicitly challenged others to show them wrong in demonstrating the plenitude of two-dimensional critique and corresponding political openness of managed capitalism. Instead, positivist critics dismiss their thesis about the demise of the public sphere and of critique within it on methodological grounds, notably the lack of evidence. At that level the argument is circular. At least *we* do not lose it.

Poststructuralists have tried to broaden the notion of textuality from writing per se to all varieties of cultural expression; they recognize that many texts are not really written by a narratively self-conscious writer or, if they are, that they are deauthorized as mere social nature. Much of the inert landscape has been carefully authored to encode messages intending thoughtlessly to provoke behavior. The risk inherent in this crucial poststructuralist broadening of the meaning of textuality, similar to the risk implied in the Frankfurt expansion of Marx's exploitation/alienation into the broader concept of domination, is losing sight of the specificity of language. *Text becomes a broad landscape that then swallows textuality into the various semio-textual/ideo-ontological levels of hidden persuasion.* I want to keep in mind the narrative nature of this swallowed textuality; deconstructive reading intends less to restore the pristineness of writing than to decode and thus deconstruct the swallowed versions virtually corporealized into the landscape as second nature.

This descends to methodologism quickly if everything in the inert landscape is subject to "reading"—buildings, highways, and clothing as much as videos, television, magazines, and science.[6] Indeed, much American deconstruction, mesmerized by Derridean pyrotechnics and committed to the cultivation of the literary, fetishizes itself as method, losing sight of the politics of significance.[7] This outcome of Derrida's ambivalent relationship to politics is virtually unavoidable; even less than Adorno he couches the implied social criticisms of "grammatology" (1976) in unfocused readings of philosophy and literature. Yet we can avoid this apolitical outcome when we expand a notion of literary practice beyond high texts per se but not so far that we try to "read" all material practice. Only in fast capitalism do books become things and things books.

This is not a middle position between high textuality and what one might call hypertextuality, where every artifice enmeshes some discursive code. In effectively deprivileging text, both overnarrow and overbroad notions of reading fail to understand discursive practices in sufficiently political terms. What Marx called ideology as a dominant power center *works its way outward by saturating nondiscursive practices, products, and processes with a surfeit of overdetermined, fatalizing, moronizing, and robotizing "meaning";* ideology presses outward to disguise itself in objectified forms. In fast capitalism textuality is swallowed in its own objectifications and thus is so quickly received that it cannot be remembered. Such instantaneity utterly overwhelms the capacity to remember, let alone rewrite, what one has read.

Material structure here, then, might be conceived as the ability of language to organize reality in a way that the real is then self-reified, played out, enacted. The problematic duality of western civilization in these terms is imposed on the recalcitrant particulars of an essentially meaningless past. Writing imparts structure to things confronting us as the essentially inert particulars of a destined history. Structure gives meaning to what we have forgotten had meaning in the first place— people struggling to survive, love, and reproduce themselves in body and culture. The structuring dualities of western civilization emanate outward from a grounding textual practice through which a fast capitalism reproduces itself seemingly beyond the discursive mediation of deconstructible claims.[8]

Marx's physicalism (e.g., base/superstructure) obstructed a sufficiently deep understanding of the ties binding desire to the objectified world in which desire is located and to which it all too frequently submits. In fast capitalism the ideal/material differentiation conceals its hierarchy, ever the problem with subject/object dualism. Marxism for too long has labored under the heavy weight of Marx's epistemological mechanism,[9] in Habermas's (1971) terms precluding a communicatively rational basis for social change by modeling mind and speech on instrumental action. The emerging corpus of Habermas's work only continues the earlier attempts by Horkheimer, Adorno, and Marcuse to rethink classical Marxism in terms of the increasing interpenetration of cultural and material systems, given most recent voice in Habermas's (1984, 1987) two-volume study *The Theory of Communicative Action*.

I do not want to be read only as an expositor. I want to explore critical theory deconstructively for *words that make better sense* of the domination of reproduction than have other critical traditions, even Frankfurt theory itself. Of course, there is no single or simple "Frankfurt theory" but only elaborative versions as often as not differing on crucial issues of substance, even (especially!) on the question of fidelity to Marx. Words fail because thought has been so reduced to terms of reflection, of *representation;* it is difficult to put distance between concepts and the realities they are meant to convey and thus transform. My work acknowledges its own contribution to the traditions of thought and practice whose meanings I presuppose by talking about them in the first place, the notion of the hermeneutic circle haunting writing as well as the reading it occasions. My version of critical theory says something about me as well as about my topic, thus changing both of us and, more important, taking the reader to a different place.

I write this book with an ear open to the text's echo of itself, its desire leading me to say what I do and then to advocate that subtext in a committed way.[10] This opens my writing to community—the political telos of every version in spite of the positivist pretension merely to represent presuppositionlessly. Representation constitutes; it divides subject and object, inferiorizing the subject by setting up the mute object world as a resource to be plundered—ironically provoking its vengeful return. If the meaning of words is not fixed, then writing can either conceal or make thematic its constitutive contribution to "what" it represents, thus taking into account its own political force. The metaphysic of representation, secretly subordinating representation to what Adorno called the "preponderant object," has made it incredibly difficult to think Marxism itself without objectifying it beyond the compass of the text discussing and thereby transforming it.

Although every text reifies itself, only some are able to recoup that self-alienation in a frenzied capitalism dispersing textuality—thought —into an exterior world no longer susceptible to easy reading. Considered reading requires slowing the speed at which images, signs, and symbols flash by us, making it nearly impossible for us to "read" and thus reformulate their authorship. Fast capitalism can be slowed only if writing, provoking the labored reconstruction of its intentionality, makes itself available to other versions of itself. Neither digressive where necessary nor merely "personal" in its mode of presentation, the self-referencing text defies representationality at every turn if representationality is taken to mean the process by which thought's distance from reality is canceled under sway of methodology. Writing makes strange what ordinarily is understood (by it), not simply shocking but using its occasion of textuality to *empower itself and thus to model empowering for others;* self-referencing writing proudly acknowledges the constitutiveness of text as an occasion for transforming the world.

I cannot simply give examples of this (*that* was such an "example") as if my text was clearly disassociable from its reflexive margins usually relegated to endnotes, preface, dedication, afterword. Instead, I can only write straight ahead through the thickets of confusion and oppression inhabiting language as much as language encodes and thus transforms the world it makes its topic, echoing in Adorno's (1973a) terms the notion that the only way "out" is "from within."[11] This requires me to use text's words (e.g., subject and object) in a way quite alien to what they originally intended; their deconstruction adds a kind of dialectical spin to them, showing their traces of narrative presence and thus reformulating them to read what they initially intended to say—their subtexts laid bare for new versions. An apolitical deconstruction would simply assign new meanings to old terms, thus proliferating philosophical glossaries. Notions like subject/object have the meaning encoded within them, even if that meaning has been occluded by their overdetermined development into the various levels

47

of narrative in fast capitalism; Pepsi/Coke taste tests reprise while reducing Descartes's reflections on duality, thus requiring movement outward from them only by thinking them at least initially in their own terms.

The discomfort this may cause readers inured to their own domination by positivist culture is fortuitous, if initially widely resisted, for it thematizes the discomfort they experience in fast capitalism. This model offers a literary version of what Brecht differently called estrangement between readers and a text whose authorial play is written into it *as its central topic;* [12] at first discomfiting to readers trained to want so-called plain language to do their thinking for them, this model of self-referencing narrative is intended to model all transformatively empowering relations between subjects and objects. Deconstruction is thus both an ideal and material process; critique refuses a more explicitly ideologizing text lest it be read circularly as false, implicitly prefiguring a deideologized world. The question of what such a world would look "like" is unanswerable in its own terms; such a world has never existed. Yet the question begs response lest the transformative process only crush people under its millennial insensitivity to their concrete particularity.

Where Adorno (1973b, 1984) developed an essentially musical version of critical theory, arguing that language has been so adminstered that we can only project images of a better future through art and especially music, I want to broaden the notion of art in his terms to include prose unashamed of its literary nature. A textual-practical imagery of a different society can be developed in much the same spirit as Habermas's notion of a communicative ethics; it can comprise Adorno's aesthetic version of critical theory in addressing dramatically the textual overdetermination, structuration, and administration of life in fast capitalism.

Habermas (1971, 1984, 1987) in his own communication-theoretic reformulation of original critical theory relinquishes too much of Adorno's, Horkheimer's, and particularly Marcuse's original "romanticism" about a different society, resisting their optimism about "erotizing" capitalism.[13] Habermas reintroduces the reproduction of domination in his (1971) split between instrumental and self-reflective rationalities, resonating in his later (1984 and 1987) forays in communication theory per se. Habermas, as I (1983b) have written elsewhere, is right to rethink Frankfurt particularly where later Adorno seems to freeze the notion of administration but wrong *thereby to truncate the emancipatory agenda;* for example, in his *Negative Dialectics* (1973a) Adorno seems to portray the irrevocability of revolutionary defeat as the starting point of any future critical theory—but to what end, if the circle of totalization has really been closed? Adorno and Marcuse did not aim too high and thereby lose all hope when political struggle went badly. Yet the historicization of critical theory must continue beyond and beneath any local excrescence of domination, whether Auschwitz, Cambodia, or Siberia, if only because *history is open*.[14]

Adorno knew that history is always vulnerable to its own transformation. Why else write? Yet he poetized domination in order to estrange concepts from the world precisely to subvert the hold of the latter over the former—for example, the notion that in Vietnam we "liberated" villages by burning them to the ground. I am not against poetization in general for I agree that the "reality" we construct in its obdurateness escapes its identity with the words we use to describe it. I agree with Adorno's overdrawn depiction of a world without exit; such imagery snaps us out of our doldrums. Yet I would narrate domination differently precisely because I agree. The more language overdetermines, the more we must attend to its overdetermination—"from within," to use Adorno's own decidedly non-Leninist terms. This is not a question of one's optimism or lack of it; temperament does not decide issues of political theory. The prevailing pragmatism enjoins pessimism on utilitarian grounds. Although critical theory can be read as Schopenhauerian resentment, this misses its attempt to understand and thus overcome the intellectual and political failures of Marxism as a way of keeping faith with Marx's dialectical optimism. I have written (1983b) that critical theory as empirical theory continually revises itself in response to political context and, as such, with self-conscious reference to its own prehistory as a version of Marxism, the first and most important revolutionary philosophy in a modernist age.[15]

Critical theory addresses the supposedly postmodern world with its orgy of intellectual and political eclecticism by kindling the millennial optimism of Marx. It keeps faith by having the temerity to appear apostate where biblical exegesis only reinforces the dominion of left-wing elites hagiographically. Frankfurt thought diverges from Marx's revolutionary theory and practice by rethinking what it means to be practical. Its conclusion that the practical is too frequently defined by the structuring discourses of accommodation and adaptation does not mean they eschewed practice as such[16] but only that they interrogated the notion of political adequacy *as part of the transformative process*. This interrogation in itself bears "positive" fruit; it forces us to reformulate the bifurcation between the ideal and material as a practical accomplishment of an unashamedly revisionist politics.

Where the original Frankfurt theory derived from classic Marxism it intended a version of Marx's ideology-critique laying bare and then learning from invalid claims the world makes about itself. Today these claims read nowhere and everywhere at once reproduce falsehood, lived out by the billions of disempowered, disillusioned, depressed agents of the seemingly ontological. But from its genesis in the 1920s, Frankfurt theory quickly put distance between itself and Marx's theory of ideology precisely because in Marcuse's (1964) later terms the Frankfurt thinkers realized that these clear-cut validity claims about a reflected reality had been "introjected" by people who act them out unthinkingly, without reference to their representational validity. I build on this tradition where I attempt to deepen this deepening of Marxism in a more self-consciously communication-theoretic direction, albeit without abandoning Frankfurt aesthetic theory or endorsing the Kantian/Cartesian echoes in Habermas's (1971) truncation of the emancipatory agenda.

Thus Marx's original critique of ideology becomes a critique of, and thus dialectical response to, the onto-ideologies detextualizing themselves as a condition of their validity in fast capitalism. Text detextualized as a condition of its immediating reading, retinal reception issuing instantly in the enactment of the symbol's injunctions, is best addressed by unburying authorial intentionality repressed deep beneath the surface of fast prose or figure; thus, a deconstructive version of critical theory both *puts subtext into words* and *engages it in dialogue, frequently in dispute.* I want to remove critical resistance further from the orbital pull of the powerful centering forces of reproduction's domination, reducing all intention to the fungible and operational. Initially, this may seem like an abstraction if abstraction is understood as an antonym of affirmation,[17] reduction of thought to terms of dominant imagery. Yet if abstraction is understood differently as the necessary effort to make dispersed language speak for itself thus opening dialogic lines of communication and community, then my deepening of critical theory with a literary agenda will not invite the charge of post-Marxism.

This issue of political apostasy is not to be dismissed with unexplicated assertions of one's good intentions; the posture of post-Marxism (let alone non-Marxism) itself capitulates to the dominant construction of Marxism as a lifeless object, a litany of received truths.[18] I will explore this issue further in Ch. 6. By insisting on my own Marxism, I open up the question of the political; I refuse to acquiesce to its conventionalization by the powers who prefer to have Marxism stand for economic determinism, parliamentary socialism, or the Gulag rather than allow it to interrogate its own politics as a substantive theoretical topic. And even if most self-named Marxists refuse to grant me the

appellation Marxist, I cannot abandon the name Marxism; that need-
lessly gives up yet another word to the mind police. Marxists endorse
intellectual fashion, notably decentering postmodernisms, at the risk
of submitting themselves to the same criterion of marginal utility—is
it "worth" anything?—thus inviting their own devaluation as fashions
change.

In fast capitalism text disperses into objects to be read and enacted
instantaneously. Mind is bypassed as text is engulfed by the "reality" it
secretly, subliminally constructs. Thus, Marxism's traditional attempt
to demystify a distorted reality founders if it neglects its own susceptibility to becoming a thing, a piece of nature—even a voice of
affirmation unwittingly validating production's primacy over reproduction, fatefully including its own text. In reading money Marx is
wrongly read to imply that money is the most important arena of the
political in capitalism; in fact it is only one among many. I read Marx
as a reader able to read text where before only figure had been, an
author of critique in different terms.

Today texts are things because they thing-ify, congealing into nature
as a mirror reflecting the ontologically unalterable. Positivism conceals
the mirror as a constitutive part of the nature it pretends presuppositionlessly to reflect. But the mirror, textuality, not only belongs to the
world but also reproduces it by concealing itself. Far from overestimat-
ing the power of positivism generalized into a global language game,
I treat positivism as a source of discipline encoded into the exterior
environment as its own reading. Where for Marx ideology stood at
one remove from the world and thus could be read as an autonomous,
if inaccurate, account, today ideology conceals itself in texts that in
effect read themselves by appearing only to reflect frozen social nature.
Marx did not understand his own reading of money as the ideology-
critique it was; money thingified itself into an exterior environment
in a way concealing the social relations it both represented and thus
reproduced.

Money is both thing and text. As a text dispersed into the world,
money congeals the dominated labor given over to its production,
realized in exchange. As a thing, money is an object of accumulation
itself; as such, it only deepens the hierarchical relations of capital
and labor that make money money in the first place. In other words,
money both embodies exchange value and directly has use value, the
double character of dispersed texts in fast capitalism. Marx's analysis
of ideology in the case of religion and bourgeois political economy
treated ideology too much as an autonomous account. Although not
wrong, ideology in its more effective stage—that is, speeded up—is

51

both text and thing at once, in the case of money embodying the social relations comprising it; ideology can thus be read to show a whole social structure propped by money *and at once* constituting a thing to be acquired in its own right. Text is social relation and thing; once authorized, it can be read to be an account of its own role in occlusion. As well, it can be seen to possess both economic and talismanic value in a world in which degraded significance has enormous utility (use value) as a source of meaning.

Marx's exemplary analysis of money rewrites his own overly dualist theory of ideology once we hear his account of money's simultaneous textuality and utility; it both offers an account of a world reified in it and *as such* is prized for its own sake, thus only reproducing the world reflected in it. Money's falsehood lies in the truth it conceals about capital/labor relations, namely that money is possible only if workers are robbed of surplus value. But money is not simply a text to be read against an external standard of validity, namely that of critique. It is also a "thing itself" whose value lies in its measure of value, reified capital/labor relations.

Texts are valuable in capitalism because they provoke the world whose account they already conceal. Money has utility. It also tells the truth in its reified social relation dispersed into the exterior environment. Its utility lies precisely in its defiance of easy readings. The more money is not read but simply acquired the less it appears to be a text; yet for all that it is even more important to read it as one. As things whose textuality is suppressed, texts in fast capitalism powerfully compel the behavior they represent as ontologically unalterable. The less we can read "things" as authored accounts, the more they author us and our social arrangements, as in the case of money. They impose a standard of value defying critical scrutiny; they are simply there, a plenitude of existence. Try to tell people that money ought not matter, indeed is not only matter but text. Better to read money to the people it already oppresses.

I (1989) read science much the way Marx read money, hearing its account of the world it provokes by appearing not to be an account at all. Money still matters, but now it shares the stage with science as main texts of domination. Science ensures that we do not read money, the fundamental shift between slow and fast capitalism—a dialectical continuity and not a rupture. Although labor still loses itself in the money medium, science dispersed into nature ensures we do not read money as the text it is. But nothing prevents science from being read as a dispersed account that brings itself about in effect by reading itself.

52

Critique cracks science's code and thus authorizes the whole built and figural environment.

Science's text compels the world it already ontologizes as naturelike. Thus, we could say that science in ontologizing also reproduces an order of social being. Critique cracked the code of money, and now it must read science as a dominant form of life oppressing imagination. Then it will read edifice and figure as texts that, in concealing their literary artifice, provoke a world fashioned in their own frozen images. Ideology makes history seem like nature; virtually every account of the world today in losing its distance only succumbs. As Jacoby suggests (1987), no one writes books bridging public and private; instead, bookness disperses into an exterior world undifferentiated from the mediating thought—critique—required to understand it as an authored accomplishment. In fast capitalism books are things written by no one. And things compel readings in the unthinking routines of the everyday. Money, science, edifice, and figure all dictate an order of value in which everything is subordinate to productive labor, including their own representations that do the important work of protecting capital against its own aporetic shortcomings. The seeming weakness of text is really its strength at a time when the world does not want us to write but instead to live—to adjust. Watching television, getting money, acquiring education all produce the hierarchy of value subordinating reproduction to production. Television moronizes and diverts at once. Money justifies wage slavery as it reproduces it. Science is proved in the world it provokes.

Books and things exist in this sort of ironic relationship. At times books achieve enough distance from things to be able to criticize and thus reformulate. Today books are too close to the world of which they purport to be accounts, dispersed into the codes of an exterior world defying authorizing reading. Critique puts the public world into words by historicizing what appear to be naturelike social arrangements. It reformulates the public environment in its own account joining negation and new construction. Critique slows the process in which text disperses and degrades into things, compelling the reiteration of their veiled accounts; it authorizes what otherwise appears not to be text at all. It gives voice to the political agendas encoded in money, science, edifice, and figure, deconstructively authorizing text-objects as the orders of value they recommend.

Money, science, edifice, and figure are not value-free. Nor are they simply representations whose semiotic force is concealed in the worlds they would become. They are texts passionately arguing for certain hierarchical orders of value in which they are superior to an otherness they only imply. Money implies a difference from and thus reproduces its hierarchy over symbols, enjoying no fungible value. Science intends superiority to nonscience, especially art. Edifice in its imposing obdurateness connotes a permanence denied life outside it—shelters for the homeless, tent cities, trailer parks. Figure ontologizes the rule of number over concept, monetarizing the social world and thus social policies. Our task deconstructively—*politically*—is to hear these silent texts for the polemics they are and then to argue with them once we reclaim significance for ourselves.

What is politics, then?[19] In fast capitalism the realm of the political is eclipsed where political agendas are concealed in things appearing not to encode political passion or the intent to persuade. The Greek *polis* is empty where in fast capitalism the colonizing forces of administration penetrate heretofore "private" realms of culture, sexuality, and personality in order to encode everyday life with the thoughtless routines of political imitation. Traditional politics phrased discursively in argument is ineffective where politics is dispersed into the objectified texts provoking our reproduction of the world. Politics resides in what seems to be least political, social nature. The literary constitution of political argument reserves for politics the right to stand apart from the world in appraising it. Thus, its literariness must be occluded where the world defies thought to stand apart from it in critical mediation.

The private has become public and the public private. The Greek ideal of public speech gives way to the privatized consumption of administrative imperative encoded in the invisible texts of culture defying authorization and thus critical evaluation. Shared by Marx, the Greek conception of politics made argument itself a norm by which the good polity would be constituted. Marxists and feminists deepen the Greek concept of politics by arguing that everyone should be admitted to the *polis*, not simply male land-owners. In fast capitalism politics is shunned as corrupt; the end-of-ideology is celebrated as millennial advance over the fruitless venality and passion of the *polis*. But ideology does not end,[20] it simply takes new and unforeseen forms, dispersed into money, science, edifice, and figure as invisible entreaties for themselves—for the given. The world today advocates by appearing bipartisan; more than that, any agenda is read to be illegitimate in a postmodern age.

Thought opposes a purely technical reason reducing intellectual judgments to matters of sheer utility.[21] Reasonableness becomes an ontology where writing cannot effectively resist its dispersion into things. The fact/value distinction is meant not simply to distinguish the two but to elevate factual existence over evaluation. Weber's technical rationality with which he proposed to organize bureaucratic capitalism without reference to larger axial questions of truth and justice eclipses reason altogether. The Greeks, Hegel, and Marx all presupposed a vantage outside the phenomenal present with which to evaluate social arrangements. Marx added that reason would decide political questions without losing touch with history. Yet Weber's theory of rationality effectively severs private judgment from public policy in a way that augurs the eclipse of mediation altogether. Although Weber was not against books, his notion of technical reason heralded a mode of text in which writing would decide fundamental questions with reference only to the factual—*positivist culture*.[22]

Today books disperse into things so that we do not read and thus rethink our relation to the world. In fast capitalism technical reason intends to replace old-fashioned speculative judgment as a basis of norm. Yet as Marcuse (1964) has argued, technical reason is itself replete with ontological and political preferences, notably for the world as it is. Weber's presumption that organizational problems could be resolved value neutrally conceals technical reason's deep investment in capitalism; thus, bureaucratic rationality is the rationality of capitalist business organizations. In fast capitalism writing itself becomes technique where it merely copies the world; of course, it does so only with aid of ontological and political desire, notably the desire to reproduce the given as a plenitude of possibility.

Technique overtakes textuality where the mediating role of writing is lost; instead, text becomes thing the more it intends only technically to copy—and thus reproduce. Although there is no purely presuppositionless writing, versions that claim presuppositionlessness encode a certain agenda to keep the world the way it is or appears to be. Text mediating thought and world becomes a world itself where it refuses to interrogate its own political commitment to a certain state of affairs. Money, science, edifice, and figure are features of Weber's rationalization where he tried to purge reason of mediation and constitution. This is not to say that Weber opposed books as they stand apart from the world they address, for he lived in slow capitalism where ideology still took more discursive forms—Protestantism, state socialism, militarism. Yet Weber's standard of a purely technical reason accelerates the dispersal of mediating thought—text—into an exterior environment in which authorship is concealed under the illusion of ontological neutrality. And literary commitment to the interest of one's own version is in some ways the deepest political affiliation, the bane of positivist culture.

The epochal dilemma of vanguard knowledge, of educating the educator, is easily resolved where we install reason in the midst of history, recognizing, even celebrating, its perspectivity.[23] Interest sullies reason only if we imagine a standard of knowledge absolutely devoid of pretension or presupposition. Weber ontologizes technical reason in opposition to the caprice of speculative philosophy and theology. If we could not decide absolutely what people ought to do, at least Weber could get the job done, whatever it might be. Yet there are other alternatives. Marx's historical materialism and later the Frankfurt School retain Hegel's Greek notion of a world-historical rationality without reference to an Archimedean standpoint from which sullying perspective is washed with the clarity of absolute knowledge. Instead, Marx said that people *make* the truth. Reason is the standard by which we judge the equity of social relations as well as the process by which we get "there." The failure to secure absolute values need not issue in a retreat from evaluation; there is no such thing. The posture of disinterestedness today is the most impregnable interest because it conceals its own literary desire behind the cloak of technique. But writing never simply copies; it always constitutes.

Authorial constitution proceeds from the vantage of interest (Habermas 1971). Yet interest need not sully writing if we understand the corrigibility of all representation done from the viewpoint of political passion. Science as fiction differs from literature only in that it methodically claims validity for itself. Otherwise it is no different—simply an account of the world that would bring that world into being by reflecting it as desirable. Both are narrative. We shun interest only because we believe that absolute knowledge can be attained disinterestedly, notably for Weberians through the operationism of intellectual reasonableness, really intellectual conformity. Dispersed texts of money, science, edifice, and figure are desirable today because they seem to have abandoned the infantile passions of polemic antithetical to the mien of the skeptical realist—Weber's culture hero. They do not read like anything but copies, authorial commitment having gone the way of other useless passions.[24]

It is facile to say that people do not like to read. It is more important to observe that they do not want to read, and often cannot, where reading sparks awareness of the world's insufficiency. We can live with an authored world swallowing old-fashioned narrative where reading otherwise creates anxiety. Texts do not become things mysteriously;

their dispersal facilitates power and also soothes the sentiments of those who refuse to totalize, theorize, *think*, where to do that would exact too high a toll in psychic turmoil. Jacoby (1987) argues that there are no more intellectuals; as well, there are few readers. The two arguments condition each other and make it harder to write in a way that intends a different world in which difference persists as a guarantee of the possibility of critique. Yet some try. We cannot guarantee our reception because we are not sure what chords we will strike by wild claims that no one writes or reads books. After all, what am I doing here?[25]

The totality swallows mere tendencies as they freeze into the hard-and-fast. Thus, I say that no one writes or reads. I do not want it to be so; I do not really believe that "no one" does. I know that is untrue. Yet to dwell on the exceptions to thoughtlessness only exaggerates their importance when compared to the overwhelming tendency not to think or criticize. Adorno wrote so intelligently because he could sum up the totality without neglecting the difference he made to it, however miniscule. In any case, the ontology of figure itself guarantees that discussions within its own frame of reference about the "extent" of autonomy divert us from honest evaluation. I do not have to measure resistance to know there is not much of it; dulled readers are produced by, and in turn produce, a bookless world in which the real books appear not to be versions at all but simply pieces of nature. If I am wrong, exactly where is the active intellectuality giving the lie to my monochromatic portrait of a dumb world? As Jacoby (1987) suggests, it is certainly not in the university.

The demise of book culture is checked by its announcement. The orthodox left would require critique already to know its audience and have a strategy. Some of us know better. In registering critique's eclipse, critique reverses it in an initially slow and halting process. But no one knows exactly how many defiances the world can contain before they irrupt in system-wrenching change. I am safe as long as I do not claim a lot for critique; moreover, I should not claim nothing, for it is only work like this that educates imagination to its blockages and possibilities. Of course, some will read me to say that "critique is writing books" where I contend that bookishness is threatened in fast capitalism. Thought seems to reduce itself to slogans, distorting what was really said. Writing books is not enough; they must be certain books, reversing textuality's tendency to degrade into thought-objects unable to gain distance from the world under address.

Positivist culture is as solid as the whole material infrastructure of world capitalism; yet it is as fragile as the everyday lives comprising it.

Both are true. How we move back and forth between the two is an empirical problem, not one of speculative construction. Certain things we can say. Above all, we must treat everyday life as a materially entwining circuitry reflecting and thus reproducing the organization of desire. Domination is done to people, and then they do it to themselves. It is difficult to separate these things temporally once the fateful cycle of production and reproduction gets underway. For this reason the base/superstructure problem ceases to be a problem. Everything is material; everything produces; everything reproduces, including textuality. Not to see this is a conceit of a peculiar species of historical materialism. In avoiding the fetish of the textual we detextualize domination too much. Although domination is not only a text, sometimes it is textual —especially in fast capitalism.

My empirical problem is how the world stays the same. It does so by changing—deepening ideology, moronizing everyday life, suppressing critique. By the same token "text" is never constant. Sometimes it is found in covers; we then call it book. Today it is increasingly found in the embedded codes of money, science, edifice, and figure. Text is that which compels or liberates behavior. What is a book is an empirical question. We cannot assume we know the answer.

CHAPTER 4

The Degradation of Signification

FAST CAPITALISM WHITTLES down and otherwise so reduces opposition that it is difficult even to pose the problem of the degradation of signification. The stronger the center, the more it marginalizes dissent; and the more dissent is coopted, the stronger the center becomes. The fateful circuitry exists through which it is so difficult to think another society without borrowing so much from its fast texts that they reduce the dissenting writing merely to terms of given discourse. Critique wants to *slow* capitalism. It does so both by breaking the commodifying webs of exchange value colonizing virtually the whole social terrain and by narrating the dispersed codes written quickly into certain cultural and natural objects the better to be relived instantaneously, without mediating reflection. Deconstruction helps critical theory articulate its critique of the instantaneity of a world rushing from page to act without detour through mind, broadening the notion of textuality into a politically fruitful concept of material practice.

Signification in fast capitalism is degraded as discourse is dispersed into the inert environment so as not to be read as a text at all. If the ontologizing versions of science, culture, and politics were to be read as texts standing at one remove from the reality they addressed, they could be reformulated. Critique in fast capitalism is forestalled in order to protect the world from its reformulation by people who would write and live it differently. Texts signify without being seen to do so, thus reproducing the world they tell in the ontologically frozen frames of science and culture.

Ideology used to possess a more overtly literary form where it was written into accounts in effect turning the world upside down, portraying the bad as good and making us want it badly. We could thus criticize ideologizing texts and tomes in slow capitalism because they were available in their obvious difference from the world they addressed, albeit in mystifying ways. Marx could undo the bourgeois world by undoing the political economy veiling it in the illusion of harmony, as he demonstrated in the relentless prose of *Capital*. Indeed, *Capital*, as much as anything, was a book about books and through them a book about the world that the texts of bourgeois political economy only entrenched ideologically.[1] By the same token, religion narcotizes by promising an afterlife. As text, it purposely stands at one remove from the world of faithful subjects it wants to bring into being.

The Marxian theory of ideology under sway of scientism and economism reiterates the bourgeois subordination of textuality to a seemingly more important material order of being. Although in capitalism valued activity matters more than unvalued—production more than poetry—Marxists have too frequently adopted exactly the same standard of value in relegating ideology to the realm of the merely derivative, thus opposing it with a representational concept of science. Unfortunately ideology is deeper than the pages on which it is inscribed, defying critique to penetrate its surface to the interstitial social relations encoding and embodying it. It is and always has been insufficient to pierce positivist political economy with positivist Marxism. As Habermas (1971) showed, Marx lacked an epistemological foundation for his own activity of critique, thus giving license to subsequent economisms that could not adequately understand and thus oppose the deep hold of ideology.

In this way Marxism has been prevented from understanding and thus opposing the material nature of signification, preferring to view ideology simply as bad science. The Frankfurt School and people who have made inroads in various theories of interpretation offer Marxism a better grasp on the literary nature of ideology, thus affording a means of critique to combat it. The domination of reproduction ironically degrades thought and language through which critique gains voice. Theory is subordinate to the practice it is supposed to abet instead of being seen and lived as a mode of practice itself—a vitally prefigurative one at that.[2]

Fast capitalism reproduces itself through this circuitry between the realms of valued and valueless activity—work and home, public and private, men and women, science and fiction, practice and theory. The domination of reproduction, degraded into mere intellection, text, superstructure, reproduces domination by providing a reserve army of labor and unpaid houseworkers through which a capitalist lifeworld perpetuates itself. The irony of textuality's degradation today is that text is more than ever required to prop a material world in which what Marx called contradictions threaten to irrupt at every turn. Ideology occludes material forces straining against each other to burst forth from dominant structures. Marx through Hegel recognized brilliantly that the supposed laws of the capitalist market would eventually erode through their very success in colonizing both the exterior and interior lives of the world's many. This could be prevented only through the narrative inculcation of lives dedicated to their own powerlessness in face of the nearly ontological imperatives of bourgeois duty, work, home, religion.

In this sense the degradation of signification conceals aporetically its heightened significance in a stage of capitalism when the overwhelming structures of capital/labor and public/private threaten to topple with the support of texts that provoke their reproduction. The more texts are dispersed into an external environment in which they are not recognized as such and thus only enacted immediately as the agendas they really are—work, consume, marry, procreate, kill: GIVE IN—the more textuality, formerly Marx's ideology, gains material force. Texts in Wittgenstein's (1953) terms are life forms, nucleic units of social structure connecting ideal and material nature. Whether bourgeois or Marxist, productivism degrades discourse as a valueless realm comprising a host of merely reproductive practices, including sexuality, housework, and culture.

The feminist critique of productivism revalorizes unwaged labor by understanding its economic and sociocultural contribution to the reproduction of male waged labor.[3] My version of critical theory joining deconstruction and feminism interrogates the public/private split as a hierarchy through which a host of these unwaged activities reproduce their own degradation by acquiescing to an economism and productivism gauging value only with reference to marketplace standards.[4] This is not to say that women are solely responsible for their degradation but rather to criticize the formulation of a better world that would simply free women to work alongside men in the paid labor force; this strategy is advocated by both corporate feminists and orthodox Marxists inspired by Engels. A more thoroughgoing imagery of liberation would address the hierarchy of public and private in revaluing the realm of the putatively valueless—home, sex, poetry, theory: TEXT.

But feminist theory, even in its most explicitly socialist versions, has

61

not succeeded in offering a full version of critical theory. Instead, it has hemmed itself in with a sectarian strategic agenda. I insist that feminism is about women only in the trivial sense that women histori-cally have borne primary responsibility for the realm of the valueless. It could have been different; biology does not determine valuelessness. Today we can make use of feminist insight where we read feminist theory as the theory of ideology largely missing from Marxism. More than a theory of sexual politics, although it is that too, feminism is a theory of textual politics, addressing text's own self-subordination to the more valued realm of public production and politics. This is not to ignore women's oppression as a unique valence of modern capitalism but to understand the degradation of women in terms of the larger domination of reproduction, as I called it in Ch. 2. Therefore, we can link the particular oppressions suffered by people simply because they do not participate in the mainstream—labor, women, people of color, inanimate nature, thought. Feminism in its best sense is a critique of value's subordination of valuelessness.

Signification is the process by which meanings are made public in an exterior environment of architecture, text, and figure. In this way cities, books, and number all signify inasmuch as they congeal au-thorial intentions that in themselves become social relations. In fast capitalism signification is increasingly degraded the less we can hear or see authorial voice behind the public objectifications of building, book, and figure—the more, in other words, the public environment does not read like a narrated act. Ironically the privatization of mean-ing is accelerated by its public objectification, a process I understand in terms of the dispersal of textuality into an external environment.

Now there is nothing ontologically inevitable about the dispersal of signification in things requiring significance to degrade when scru-tinized for signs of an absent author. We can build buildings, write books, and create designs that do not degrade authorial intention-ality and thus defy their ready reading as well as readerly reformu-lation, ever the opportunity of social change. The degradation of significance is a historical process associated with the structural over-reliance on texts—ideologies, superstructures, cultures, lifeworlds—to buttress an increasingly fragile material world otherwise threatening to shatter into a diversity of decentered margins. Marx's "contra-dictions," his Hegelian word, are only checked in fast capitalism by dispersed texts compelling system-serving behavior with a minimum of mediation by critique. Marcuse (1964) characterized this as a one-dimensionalization of public experience, where we lose the ability to transcend mere appearances to a higher level of critique along which we can make qualitative judgments about the proper direction of world history.

I twist this Frankfurt thesis of administered, one-dimensionalized reason as a reformulation of Marx's old concept of ideology into a literary framework because I want to understand how significance dispersed into naturelike objects degrades and thus loses the ability to refuse and oppose. Textuality matters less the more it is matter, an irony occasioning a politicized deconstruction excavating authorial meaning from text-objects dispersed like land-mines across the public landscape. By excavating meaning from its degraded form we can "read" buildings, books, and design as the intentional products of human imagination and thus oppose instances of imagination that enslave and entwine, a program of a radicalized hermeneutics I will elaborate in Ch. 5. The built environment conceals its own textuality precisely because buildings encode meaning and thus provoke adaptive behavior in a fast capitalism threatening to dissolve if read as such.

These dispersed texts, degrading when confronted with deconstructive readings, compel political adjustment. Significance dispersed into a public world ontologizes where it presents itself as an invariant piece of social nature, provoking forms of life otherwise impossible. This happens in all sorts of ways. The built environment structures privatized action where we are warehoused into office buildings and factories fragmenting us into cells, spaces, and corridors only reflecting and thus reproducing the Taylorized division of labor. Foucault (1979) has written about how domination technologizes itself particularly in the criminal justice system, a telling oxymoron of the modern period. Buildings imprison in giving substance to form and figure. Although all architecture crystallizes imagination, the peculiar characteristic of the modern city fragments and further estranges social experience *the better to administer it;* a "rationalized" public environment serves the interest of rational corporate and state control, Weber's quintessence of modernity.

Books compel adjustment where they appear not to have been written at all but are merely divine copies of an invariant cosmos. I have written about how this happens over a whole discipline (1989), thus modeling disciplining as a whole. In this sense positivism penetrates a whole culture in which we read as if writing reflects an invariant state of affairs, thus only reproducing it within the accepted framework of the metaphysically possible. In my study of sociology I excavated authorial intent from disciplinary prose apparently cleaned of authorial desire to bring a certain order of value into being. For example, the claim that "all Americans want to get married" only provokes its own validity by appearing to reflect unalterable fact. In this way, fact becomes fate reproduced through the nearly autonomic circuitries of so-called everyday life.

Figure and number compel adjustment where they monetarize social experience and thus disqualify other literary approaches to the human condition. Number and currency are nearly inseparable in fast capitalism. In my own university quantitative method and funded research are about equally valorized, figure's form and substance fatefully intermingling. In addition, figure's form acquires substance where mathematization drives out thought, an especially likely event in the human studies. Although against Heidegger and other humanist critics of mathematics I do not reject figure, symbol, and number as such, the mathematization of the world plays a political role of some significance in disqualifying thoughtful prose. Method has historical significance where it degrades textual significance in appearing to solve intellectual and hence political problems by itself. Today we are to believe that number means.

Marxism misses the point if it weighs texts and codes on a scale of mere verisimilitude. Significations do not only dissemble and misrepresent, although they surely do that, too. Rather the textualized world appears not to signify *at all* in its naturelike unalterability, defying radical imagination and thus reformulation. Degraded signification must be made to signify once again so we can engage it in argument. In itself, the deconstructive narration of dispersed prose —reading buildings, books, and number as the constitutive thought they originally were—does nothing more than expose pernicious desire to the political light of day. Ethnomethodology as a version of a larger social phenomenology fails to historicize and thus politicize the social construction of reality (Berger and Luckmann 1967). Social construction is a hierarchized practice, including some and excluding others from the act of constitution. Thus, the deconstruction of construction empowers those left out of the originary sense-making of history—most everyone denied power.

Texts dispersed into the exterior environment in effect enact themselves in the practices they provoke. Reading is nothing more than the reception of imperatives suggested by a fatalizing version of the world. Positivist knowledge exhausts metaphysical possibility: What "is" cannot be other, the coda of "everyday life" in fast capitalism. The obdurate rationality of the real is reproduced in everyday lives habituated to work, family, and consumption within the dominant modes of administration. Foucault's (1979) Panopticon, a seamless prison in which the eye of surveillance is at once everywhere and nowhere, is a social technology in which physical and social space combine to circumscribe metaphysical possibility—in the case of prisons, the possibility of freedom. The prison is a text that does not read like one. By imagining that we are always being watched we watch ourselves.

Foucault reads prison as an archetype of rational administration in which people curtail themselves as they are curtailed by more powerful others. In reading prisons this way, the Foucaultdian reader undoes rational administration by revealing rationality to be nothing more than one literary possibility among many. In fast capitalism domination cannot be sustained without the props of the built and figural environment like Panopticon, circumscribing freedom indirectly. Sociology calls this social control, allegedly a generic of all civilization. Yet Foucault's archaeology of texts dispersed into social nature as the requirement of total administration reveals social control to be a contingent feature of social orders, as such subject to reformulation.

That the built environment encodes meaning does not suggest that we cannot rebuild it or rewrite the implacable tomes naming eternity in the solemnities of social science. The degradation of signification varies with the political requirement of social control. The more mind wanders from its assigned responsibilities, the more it must be short-circuited into duties and releases reducing the pain of alienation. Marcuse (1955) crucially argues that the development of capitalist technology *increases* the requirement of self-imposed social control, "surplus repression," lest desire experience the possibility of a release from toil altogether, threatening a qualitatively different social order. Advances in technology require self-technologies of social control like Foucault's Panopticon. Otherwise we may recognize that the prison has no walls: we are doing this to ourselves.

Of course, the prison does have walls. Texts provoking the world they tell are real in their consequences. Resignifying the external environment as an authored accomplishment does not reformulate them in themselves but only politicizes the apparently apolitical. In seeing how things became the way they are, especially what they say to us, *we realize that they are only versions* and can be redone, relived. Whether or not we reformulate them ultimately depends on the extent of our social power. But in the beginning we must read the environment enmeshing us as a corrigible literary text, a narrative construction of artifice that in concealing itself contains powerful meaning.

Marx revised Hegel to show that human self-objectification in nature only alienates itself under certain historical conditions.[5] Similarly, significance is degraded only where texts' dispersal into nature serves the interest of power, order, and administration. That signification

65

does not signify is as important a "content" as what it signifies—indeed, its self-concealment is part of its meaning, as Foucault showed with respect to Panopticon. A prison appearing to be other imprisons in a different, deeper way than a prison naming itself as such. As a Marxist I believe in writing texts as a means of vital self-expression without losing the aura of textuality, inviting readers to respond in gentle correction and community. Socialism is a book endlessly formulating itself across the readerly relations conceiving it differently but respecting others' versions, indeed requiring other versions as our humanizing recognition.

Authorial excavation is a socialist agenda only if we can then engage the surfaced author in political debate, breaking the prison by showing it to be a prison. It is not enough to narrate signification concealing itself in the artifacts it becomes; through critique we rewrite and thus prefigure a better world in which significance remains at one remove from the world it addresses, the inevitability of what Adorno (1973a) called the nonidentity of word and thing.[6] Textuality is an essential mode of being in the sense that through it we both connect with and mark our difference from the world bearing our embodiment in the first place. Critique, the activity of signification, comprehends its own difference from the world it suffers; indeed, critique celebrates that difference as the distance required for thought.

Text publishes mind, connecting it to others through the language games constituting nucleic units of social structure. Writing is meant not only to be read; under positivism discourse disperses text directly into the things it describes—thus bringing them about. Writers write writing as a way of bringing being into being; the lie is that history is exhausted by the present. Text solicits readings confirming its own claims about the eternity of a certain world order. In naming the universality of family Parsons and Bales (1955) want to provoke familied lives; "text" here is the positivist account of universal family that breaks through the thin membrane separating itself from the world by being lived as such. Parsons's text practices by appearing unalterable in its own right, vouchsafed in the positivist protocol of writing only appearing to copy, not to construct. Here sociology's literariness is suppressed methodically in order to reproduce the family produced in writing as an unavoidable situation of differential gender relations, with men working and women nurturing.[7]

This claims a lot for dispersed textuality in a fast capitalism degrading significance. Texts live as the lives they provoke; the thin membrane separating word and thing bursts under pressure of positivist versions that become pieces of nature themselves, losing the imprint

66

of their own literary corrigibility. Books naming the universality of certain social relations *become* them by concealing their narrative authority. If men's and women's natures are fixed in text, writing provokes them out of readers who understand and thus recreate themselves in those terms. Parsons's masculinity derives from a masculine version of social nature addressing male readers who already recognize their difference from the feminine in those terms.

Texts do their fatalizing work in the midst of history. Parsons does not create masculine and feminine roles; he only reproduces them in the interface between his version and the world it names and thus provokes. Ideology only deepens what we already knew to be true; the behavior it compels is precisely the *absence* of defiance and, as such, cannot be detected with the methodical tools of social research. I can show the material efficacy of Parsons's version of family only by showing how family continues to prevail after 1955, his year of publication. He did not create skewed gender relations but only added to their implacability in his small way, failing to undo them by challenging their earlier ontologization. Parsons affirms family by seeming only to reflect its universality. In this, he produces and reproduces it; his positivist account is dispersed into the world to which it bears the secret affiliation of advocacy. Methodology in describing also recommends.

Duality is so deep a tendency in western civilization, even within Marxism, that we feel compelled to choose between accounts of texts' degradation emphasizing either economic or ideological features. I regard them as complementary logics of domination. On the one hand, capitalism in its latest stage degrades significance as quickly as possible to prompt frenetic consumer behavior. Texts sunk into commodities as their alluring auras degrade rapidly to stimulate new acquisition. On the other hand, the immediating dispersal of meaning into naturelike things prevents us from reconstructing their authorship and thus reformulating them. The degradation of significance degrades the aura of commodities and imagination equally,[8] indeed the one through the other. Lives dedicated to shopping as a reprieve from the structurally damaged life both reproduce profit and cause the rate of intelligence to fall. Profit requires intelligence's diversion from its proper object— its own alienation into things.

Marxist periodization fails to distinguish slow from fast modes of signs' degradation, just as Frankfurt's domination was present in Marx's concept of alienation from the beginning. Capitalism always bore the tendency for ideology to scatter into things themselves as ideologizing tomes pierced the thin membrane separating them from nature. Today we call this everyday life, ironically understanding that

67

it is less than a full life. The tendency is brought to fruition in fast capitalism, requiring us to rethink ideology narratively in order to grasp its full extent. At stake is not simply empirical adequacy in our address to the fast-capitalist world but imagination itself. Strategically socialism fails to excite the western mind for which it has either been degraded into safe social democracy, a quantitative improvement at most, or demonized as Soviet practice. Either way, the left must derive a more exciting imagery of qualitative difference by fighting the tendency of its own significances to disperse into extant practices and regimes claiming Marxist names for themselves. The falling rate of intelligence affects all of us.[9] The critique of signification's degradation in fast capitalism is a materialist project if we understand textuality at once as a productive and reproductive force. Marxism's hierarchizing dualism subordinating the valueless to valued tends to degrade textuality into the merely epiphenomenal, a realm of strategic interest. But ideology dispersed into things themselves is more than that, especially where texts pierce the membrane between concept and thing and thus enact themselves in everyday life as the fatalized existences they recommend and provoke.[10]

Fast capitalism degrades significances quickly both to stimulate production and consumption and to conceal the constitutiveness of its own textual reproductions—that, as such, become productions themselves. I do not suspend the analysis of the theft of surplus value, but I do understand commodity fetishism underlying surplus value and Lukacs's reification as special cases of semiotic dispersal. This does not deeconomize Marxism so much as materialize the theory of ideology;[11] after all, Marx was the one who understood commodity fetishism as the objectification of social relations into seeming relations between naturelike things—for me, his deepest insight into capitalist administration.

Today commodity fetishism continues apace as people regard the social relations of their labor as thinglike in their seeming necessity. Capital and labor are abstractions because the working process remains abstract for most people. Feminism adds to Marxism a concern for sociosexual fetishism played out in the hierarchical relation between public and private spheres; gender relations are also commodified and objectified into pieces of nature, exactly the desideratum of those who hierarchize masculinity and femininity. An adequate critical theory comprehends the public nature of private alienation in suggesting that there is *no such thing* as private space in a colonizing social world.[12] We name these colonizing imperatives differently, and yet they refer to the same thing: commodification, reification, textual dispersal.

The public world invades privacy in a way that we cannot think their difference—indeed, in fast capitalism we can barely think at all. Signification degrades where it is dispersed into things swallowing the signifying marks otherwise standing at one remove from the topics and world they address. What Habermas calls colonization involves the dispersal of texts in seemingly nondiscursive forms that then provoke their own accounts of an unalterable social nature, ever the goal of rational administration. In fast capitalism textual degradation is a type of administration that literally loses its mind *into* things no longer signified but signifying.

Qualitative judgment is diminished where thought loses its ability to stand apart from the topic or object it names. Writing that would normally refuse to abandon its meditative distance from its topic ironically loses itself into things where its significations are dispersed and ultimately self-alienated. But that is only half the story. Significations lost into things then take on social power where they compel readers to follow routines against their best interests. In positivist culture texts mean for themselves to be enacted as the alleged fate they encode. Administration administers everything equally; both writer and reader fall victim to the degraded significances dispersed into the exterior world compelling conformity, adjustment, adaptation.

Positivism loses its text in things that then become compelling versions in their own right.[13] Texts dispersed into the built and figural environments do not have to be intended as such for their effects to be the same. They all comprise a positivist world in which thought and talk degrade into the things they address and thus become things themselves, no longer having the potential to be reasoned. Text in a positivist world degrades into the various tableaus of the built, textual, and figural environments, thus precluding its own reformulation. This is not to say that every text keeping its distance from the vortex of degradation is dialectically enlivening; after all, positivism eschews its own constitutional narrativeness as a methodological requirement of its validity. Society is not generically a "text," nor is every text liberating. Textuality must be historicized in light of its political possibility.[14] Today textuality dominates itself by dispersing itself into things defying authorizing readings, instead ontologizing a world they would provoke. This need not be so. Necessity is a discourse.

Science today can be read much like Marx read money. For Marx, money concealed hierarchical relations between capital and labor that produced money and in turn were reproduced by it; today science both reflects and provokes an inert world. Money and science both signify, yet they are hard to read as texts—precisely their talismanic power. As texts that become things, they compel a world they only seem to reflect, the essence of a fast capitalism in which meaning is elusive. We need not choose between money and science as modes of significance's erosion because they both matter. Indeed, science allows money to continue to reflect and thus reproduce labor's theft. Ordinary Marxists mistrust ideological analysis because it fails to understand Marx's own contribution to the critique of fast capitalism in his analysis of money. Instead they follow Marx where he suggested that ideology as false consciousness was a *camera obscura*, merely bad reflection, and not a more material form of practice producing and thus reproducing production's dominance over reproduction—labor's dominance of thought.

Ideology-critique is only one form of political practice; yet ideology is simultaneously a mode of production and reproduction. The critique of consciousness materializes consciousness where texts are dispersed into things themselves. The confusion can be traced to Marx himself where he offered two quite different models of ideology: first, in *The German Ideology* (Marx and Engels 1949) he viewed ideology simply as a false text inverting the real in its image; second, in his analysis of money he understood money as a text that matters because in concealing its textuality it is matter. If we follow Marx's first model, it is possible to understand the left's frequent frustration with analysis diverting into issues of consciousness, thus ignoring the bond between lifeworld and structure. But if we follow Marx's second model, as I do here, ideology is traced in the palimpsest of the dispersed texts complexly entwining everyday life. Significance dispersed into things robs thought of constitutiveness, an occasion not of false consciousness, strictly speaking, but of the absence of consciousness, Horkheimer's (1974b) eclipse of reason. In fast capitalism the split between the ideal and material is further reduced as textuality subsists in its naturelike expressions defying ready reformulation.

At least "false" consciousness could be rectified, educated, elevated. *Capital* gave the lie to bourgeois political economy as *The Holy Family* gave the lie to religion. But money and science dispersed into naturelike obdurateness cannot be falsified in the same way. Who would think that money and science lie? Indeed, the truths they embody ironically teach more than any course in political education delivered to the faithful. Marx required *Capital* to reveal the labor contract to be a "*fictio juris*"; as well, I needed *Socio(onto)logy: A Disciplinary Reading* (1989) to read positivist social science as a purposeful falsehood provoking its own validity. It is incredibly hard to fight text with text where text and thing blur—money, science's tomes, buildings, number, and figure. Critique exhausts itself authorizing versions appearing merely to be pieces of nature and thus unalterable.

Marx did not need the many pages of *Capital* to undo bourgeois political economy and the world it propped any more than I needed nearly 500 pages to undo disciplinary positivism. We could have synopsized the arguments in a few pages.[15] Capital exploits labor under the guise of the market's naturelike harmony and equity; positivist sociology freezes domination in order to provoke it. But deauthored texts like money and science must be authorized, put into words, in order for us to deal convincingly with them. Critique must be relentless lest it fail to bring the objectified world to life and then reformulate it in better terms. The degradation of signification dehistoricizes writing merely as copy, the essence of every affirmative ontology. We do not think twice that money, science, building, figure, and number talk to us; they are not between covers in the usual sense. They appear intimate with what they address.

Significance's degradation closes distance, overcoming what Adorno (1973a) called nonidentity. Text and thing melt into one, making it hard to read either of them and thus to defy the codes of adjustment they imply. Capitalism temporalizes the text/world relationship in quickening the approach of text to thing, thus precluding a distancing critique. In a positivist culture prose *enters* the thing it addresses without having to claim validity elaborately in the way writing used to do. Even science dispenses with elaborate methodological ritual where prose immediately gives way to number and figure as adequate reflections, and thus ontologies, of the given—thus giving it again. Capitalism quickens the metabolism between text and thing in order to stimulate consumption of economic and cultural commodities.[16] Television has the dual problem of not only selling advertising but also simply filling the viewing hours in order that viewers are filled in turn —both stimulated to buy and diverted from the bigger picture.

Capitalism degrades significance in order to deny us signifying power. Reading is not to be contemplative and reconstitutive but receptive, stimulating both acquisition and adjustment. The faster images move from mind and voice into thing, the less chance we have to decode things and images as the texts they are and thus to reformulate them. Image gathers substance precisely in order for it not to be read as an authored act. Instantaneity is the enemy of distance, reflection, critique—indeed, a norm of social organization where defiance

71

hinders efficiency. Constitution degrades into the images and things congealing it, a tendency first found in the case of money. German idealism, especially Weber and Nietzsche, conceptualizes alienation as a product and process of the "loss of meaning." But the real loss is meaning *constitution,* the ability to rethink and relive. Indeed most of the world's billions never possessed "meaning" as a sufficient reprieve from a damaged life. Only intellectuals could lament its loss, especially where the alternative was a Marxist one, threatening the very privilege of the disengaged.

It is a thoroughly Marxist agenda to restore disengagement as a powerful political aim. This is possible only by reinterpreting money, science, edifice, and figure as the hortatory texts they are, recommending themselves as versions of an incontrovertible world. Books are things. Yet when books become things concealing their authoriality, their *bookness,* they compel "readings" enacting various forms of life—adjustment, adaptation, acquiescence, affirmation. Significance is the terrain of the political today especially where politics is concealed in an inert exterior world in which no one seems to be making ontological claims. Things do not "stand" for other things or claims but simply compel worlds out of readers *by being worlds themselves.* Few read money as the text it is; likewise, few people read science as literary artifice, as false—and thus as true—as fiction.

But as the sign atrophies, signification becomes all the more rampant. The world's deficit requires the inculcation of obedience; sociology suggests social control as an inevitable feature of the power of the social. Text must still intervene to quiet metaphysical anxieties about why we are doing this to ourselves in the name of seeming "necessity." Texts are not to be read as such but instead merely copied in what they recommend about a singular state of affairs. Money recommends its acquisition just as edifice recommends that we inhabit it as a piece of nature, accepting and thus perpetuating the social relations it implies. Number provokes us to believe in number as a source of unmediated significance, resolving disputes and conceptualizing problems in terms of the rule of mathematical difference. Science reflects a world and thus compels us to relive it thoughtlessly.

Today significance is implanted in "things themselves." Although people still write, they write technical recipes, news, description; all defy interrogative work and thus fail to suggest imaginative reformulation. Yes, books still exist—many of them. But they merely copy their subjects in biography, journalism, and shallow, diverting fiction. Text does not put distance between us and reality but realizes itself in its commodification and consumption. Books are a good read, not epochal challenges to the world as we know it. Books as signs lose the capacity to signify, that is, to recommend meaning; books as things dispersed into a naturelike social world take over signifying authority. Both versions are available today, but only the latter really do significant work in plugging the gaps of the world's deficit. Traditional books merely affirm and entertain, keeping us busy. The books we cannot read easily as texts—money, science, edifice, figure—are the real texts, the more so the more difficult it is to read them as literary versions.

In fast capitalism, then, books become things and things books, reversing the ideal/material relationships of antiquity and early industrial capitalism. Of course, this sort of construction is not absolute; people still manage to distance their writing from the world it addresses and thus escape the machine of administration. Similarly, people like Marx do read money as texts signifying and thus reproducing a whole social structure. Indeed, I write because I trust that my writing will neither divert harmlessly nor disperse itself into an exterior world as a thing compelling thoughtless behavior. Fast capitalism as slogan degrades whatever insights it originally offers. Critique opposes the degradation of significance as a resignifying mode of address to text-objects otherwise defying easy interpretation. Thought tries to recoup its dispersal into things whose obdurateness—implicit ontological force of presence—suppresses thought.

Against Hegel ideas need not lose themselves in things. Beyond Marx ideas are not simply epiphenomena propping or undermining given social orders. A variety of developments in theories of interpretation since WWII help us think more adequately about what I call the degradation of significance, indeed about ideas' materiality.[17] Marxism does not reverse itself back to Hegel by theorizing the detextualization of significance as if ideas are somehow superior to the material forms they sometimes take. The ideal/material relationship varies historically and must be reassessed by Marxists in this era when it is harder than ever to grasp the distinction between texts and things.

Against poststructuralism, I am not arguing that everything is text; that decenters political critique into a mode of cultivation, of aesthetic sensibility.[18] Only texts are texts, ideologies ideologies, and yet it is hard to grasp the site of significance in fast capitalism. Critique pursues concealed signs for the work they do in provoking a given order of being; it recognizes that capitalism is not naturelike but only pretends to be. Increasingly we do what we do not "because" we are told to do so by texts but because money, science, edifice, and figure structure thought and action into seemingly unalterable patterns appearing not to be historical variations at all. Things do our thinking for us where they conceal authored meanings compelling a certain state of affairs. Only fools do not want money or disbelieve scientific evidence. Yet it takes much more than foolishness to read money and science as telling expressions of a social order that needs them to reproduce it in fact. Things concealing writing and thus compelling certain lives tell important stories about why we fail to read them for what they are—literature.

I leave critique to read books as things and things as books. Critique writes the book of books and things in deciphering the palimpsests of significance in the material forms versions have become. Critique is science; it learns from things their narrative nature and thus susceptibility to narrating anew. Yet it also rewrites them directly in authorizing what has lost the aura of literary work. Money, science, edifice, and figure are challenged to be different by readings addressing their artifice, their bookness. They are opened to a community of versions refusing the inertness of texts that would speak to us monologically, compelling a singular world fashioned in their own image. Critique in undoing writing's dispersal remakes the political world.

At stake, as always, is the survival of the public sphere. Cultural conservatives since Plato have suggested that a healthy society needs a public forum in which citizens gather for their mutual edification. Conversation is praxis that simultaneously gratifies and orders. The public person has been an emblem of the good polity from the Greeks through Marx. Although not wrong in itself—for without a public sphere we are depressingly privatized and thus administered by the secret political agendas of the time—the conservative critique of the demise of the public sphere, shared even by the Frankfurt School,[19] Lasch,[20] Sennett,[21] and Jacoby,[22] misses the point. The public sphere never really disappears; public imperatives of control and censure invade heretofore "private" realms of household, body, mind.[23] Traditional political speech is largely silenced in the mass representative democracy of late capitalism. Yet it is not enough to restore that public sphere without understanding that all public/private distinctions since the Greeks have devalued privacy to the benefit of public action.

In Greek thought this was transparent. People with citizenship in the *polis* existed off the labors of slaves and women. Similarly, today, even orthodox Marxism narrows politics into what happens in the public realm of the labor market; it ignores sexual politics almost entirely, except when Engels advocates the entry of women into an egalitarian labor force. The problem with public/private distinctions is that nothing is really private anymore; what Habermas calls colonization has penetrated into regions of existence heretofore ignored by political and social philosophy. Indeed, I would argue that to the extent to which privacy has traditionally been the domain of women and slaves it is good that privacy is no longer shielded from critical scrutiny as if it somehow "did not matter" politically. Men who defined the public sphere have defended it from private challenges precisely because whole groups of people responsible for "private" labor have made possible the prerogatives of male and class public life.

This is not to confuse the problem with the solution. Administered capitalism in which nothing goes untouched by dominant imperatives of control is not a desirable state of affairs; now we have lost even the traditionally inviolate realm of public life in which the Greeks and Marx wanted us to formulate challenges to the dominant order. But the lack of public conversation (e.g., Lasch 1979; Jacoby 1987) is only symptomatic of deeper administration. To restore publicity without addressing the way public subordinates private only slows capitalism; it does not halt it.

In fast capitalism the public is at once everywhere and nowhere. The dispersal of texts into the exterior world compels adjustment and acquiescence, and yet no one seems to write these texts in private time. The public culture of books has eroded, and yet there is no strictly private sphere in which people can meditate on political issues. There are *neither* public nor private spheres in fast capitalism but only undifferentiated administration spanning all sorts of material practices comprising "everyday life." In this I risk a Marxist deus ex machina in the same way that Adorno seemed to contradict himself when he said that opposition is impossible—after all, he was opposing (Adorno 1973a). *Someone* writes the books that congeal into social nature in constituting a positivist culture in which few think. The point is that *we do not know who the authors are* for money, science, edifice, and figure bear no literary aura, no trace of having been crafted by design.

Critique must exhume authorship when significance degrades into an exterior world that is neither strictly public nor private. Critique hears the scratch-scratch of the pen where "texts" seem to have fallen from the sky. This way of rethinking the concept of the political includes activities and oppressions carried out in what has traditionally been called both public and private. The social problem of most immediate moment here is not the lack of publicity but an inability to trace thought to what thought has authored. Even if we did write the accessible books of earlier times, when intellectuals were not crushed by the administrative pressures of university discipline, no one would read them for there is no reading public anymore. People read different things—television, popular magazines, money, science, edifice, figure. These texts become the lives filled by them. It is not enough to say that people have simply lost literary skills, the claim of cultural conservatives like Allan Bloom (1987). The very concept of the text has changed as the pace of capitalism quickens.

Instantaneity rushes thought to "read" things instead of books. Mediation takes too long. Of course, this is a dialectical problem: if people wrote public books, perhaps a readership would be cultivated; if a readership existed outside the narrow academic disciplines, perhaps people could write public books. Yet books traditionally defined as public acts have changed their material nature under the pressures of economy and culture. Fast capitalism diverts mind from mediation and meditation in order to occupy mind with text-objects like money, science, edifice, and figure both to stimulate consumption and to maximize control. Books have degenerated into literary fast food—quick, cheap, insubstantial. It is not enough to write books about how people do not write public books but to write about what is happening theoretically and politically. Of course, that assumes publishers will publish versions like this as "trade" books (for a large market of unspecialized readers) and then that readers will read them—big assumptions indeed. What are my chances of publishing *this* book by a trade house and not a university publisher? One in a million? And if I did get published, would I be read?

All one can say is that sometimes it happens. Marx probably did not sit down to write a best seller anymore than Plato realized he would be required reading in philosophy courses for the next two thousand years. Critique responds to its object, not to the predilections or abilities of its audience. If I am right and people do not engage in mediation at all, preferring to "read" the "texts" dispersed as social nature into the exterior world, then I would seem to be engaging in a self-defeating labor—writing for an audience I say does not exist in a form that cannot exist. Although an "audience" may not exist, people do—they fall through the cracks and can be addressed. We never know how writing will fare in the world, and we cannot be too concerned about it. The only way to guarantee a reception is to duplicate other versions, precisely what happens in academia where journal and monograph publication is channeled by external "readers" who domesticate defiance into versions of the ever-the-same—scholarship, as it is called.

Having said this, though, I must add that critique cannot afford to neglect the possibility it might be read. Care must be taken to address an imaginary reader, if not the "real" readers standing next to us on the bus or sitting in our classrooms. While that sounds obvious, even a cursory perusal of poststructuralist criticism reveals that some versions are not addressed *to* readers at all but are written only to please themselves; for example, Barthes's (1975) notion of the pleasure of the text obscures any public dimension writing ought to have—indeed must have—to be political. The alternative to a pacifying positivism is not the orgy of authorial subjectivities in which people like Derrida (see his *Glas* 1987) engage. A social and material world exists outside the text, even if we must also add that text is part of the world in the first place and crucially reproduces it. Poststructuralist writing does not anticipate an imaginary reader because it does not view itself as political work, regarding politics as yet another excrescence of the Enlightenment's will to power. That is both empirically and politically wrong. Writing matters, and writing ought to matter. Thus, critique must imagine a utopian reader even if it is reasonably certain that such readers are hard to find. The refusal to go public only ensures its demise.

Critique wants to produce the ideal readership in reality by joining a community in which dialogue opportunities as well as competences are democratically distributed. Derrida does not recognize the political responsibility of critique in reformulating the public world. It is not enough to talk as if no one should read it, even if that talk derails the linearity and false closure of positivist culture. Neither Derrida nor Adorno will make it on the trade shelves in contemporary America. Yet Adorno was driven by the political intent to create a community of writers committed to dialogical and thus political equality. His ideal reader, able to master all of German idealism plus Marxism, may be rare. Yet Adorno understood the political intentionality of his work in a way that made his writing different than it would have been had he been the only reader.[24]

Perhaps this is the most fundamental difference between science and art. Although I have said that all writing is narratively crafted and thus can be considered a type of fiction, science serving political ends wants to comprehend difficult truths about the extant world and then to make them available to a community as a way of building community. Art does not intend its duplication in a community; it intends to disclose the truth directly. This is the gulf between Adorno and Derrida, Marxism and poststructuralism. I use them as examples because they pose different interpretive challenges. Adorno wants to be understood to be talking, however indirectly, about the empirical world and thus to change to it; Derrida makes his work available for aesthetic consideration but not political education. He says he is a

Marxist, but his work does not show it. It cannot, given its inattention to imagined or ideal readers, thus an absent public.

Finally, critique becomes cultic where, like biblical exegesis, it requires long study as an act of faith. But text has no claim on the body politic except in the way it constitutes it. Abstruseness in itself is no more a viable political stragegy than is cynicism. Postmodernism only affirms the modern in its refusal to make qualitative distinctions and judgments. This is not the same as wanting unproblematic clarity for that assumes the world is clear and can be communicated linearly. Difficulty educates where it grasps the totality in its complex circuitries of desire and structure. Positivism has never solved the philosophical problem of how subjects can know objects except to say that this is not a problem. Methodology is to quiet metaphysical anxieties—epistemological Valium. Historical materialism suggests that subjects can only know objects once they understand the objectivity of their own subjectivity and then work outward from there.[25]

Poststructuralism is not simply conservative.[26] In refusing to grasp the object world in prose it only avoids positivism but does not exemplify its alternative. The world remains uncomprehended and thus stays the same. Not only does Derrida not inspire revolutionaries; he refuses to think the possibility of social change because most such attempts have failed before. Some still cling to notions of reason guiding social betterment without forgetting that reason fragilely inserts itself in history and thus cannot be absolute. Poststructuralism rejects reason because it has been betrayed so many times before. Thus, it attempts to constitute a self-sufficient world in which the play of signifiers—sheer writing—stills politics as a useless passion. Yet reason's betrayal is no more absolute than the false rationalism announced in the Enlightenment. History moves on. Someday we may meet, even educate, the ideal reader who can join community with us. In the meantime, critique accepts its own insufficiency without giving up.

CHAPTER 5

Thinking Otherwise: Radical Hermeneutics as Critical Theory

THE ONLY WAY to address the degrading forces turning our prose into pieces of nature provoking their reenactment is in a different literary practice, revealing authorial artifice where before only figure had been. Disclosing narrative narrates anew; thus it is political practice. We must trace the palimpsest of versions of the world that have become the world itself. First, we reveal them to be corrigibly literary products; then we reformulate them in politically different terms. Actually, these twin projects of authorial excavation and reformulation belong together in the generic practice of deconstructive reading, prefiguring a whole new order in which reproduction is revalorized as a form of creative activity itself. One might call this interpretive strategy a radicalized hermeneutics[1] if one understands that understanding is directly a mode of political reconstruction and not an ancillary activity somehow less important than economic production. Interpretation directly constructs, suggesting new versions of old texts degraded into naturelike obtrusions in the built and figural environments. Radical hermeneutics is more radical than hermeneutic. It emphasizes that reading is writing itself, thus politics.

I do not ignore power by suggesting an interpretive political strategy. Reading stimulates imagination and prefigures nucleic forms of life joining writers in gentle correction. Interpretation is not all politics, even though it is political. Marxists have had this problem with Marx's critique of ideology. Diverse structural thinkers resist the concept of ideology because it seems to imply spontaneist and idealist approaches to social change; "to be a Marxist" seems to require the assumption that the motor of history is the clash of large-scale social and economic structures. I agree. But Marx also suggested that there has to be an electric moment when people realize they have only their chains to lose. At that instant the preponderant weight of structure would begin to lessen as people replace historians as the authors of history. As members of a dualist civilization, many Marxists view the problem as either/or—either structure or consciousness. This is a mistake especially where we understand the material nature of consciousness as well as the textuality of structure.

Nevertheless power endures, silencing some and privileging others. Critique does not ignore this; it suggests a view of power refusing simple mechanism. Power is both imposed and self-imposed. To the extent of its self-imposition it can be undone, especially (Marcuse 1955) in an advanced industrial society close to eliminating what Marx called necessary labor time. The preponderance of the capitalist totality is not invariant, as left structuralists imply. Indeed it cannot be undone without theorizing it as an historical artifice, even a "text" compelling adjustment in its seeming ontological obdurateness. In any case social change can only be fashioned in concert. Nothing guarantees a good end, even for Marx. *Capital* plots the likely crisis points of an unfettered economic order. The expropriation of the expropriators always depended on the tenacity and organizational skills of revolutionaries. That is, at some level socialism depends on *texts*, be they *The Communist Manifesto* or other modes of radical invigoration and critique. This does not dissolve history into consciousness, as if given a choice; it merely recognizes that narrative is a kind of power in its own right. Foucault said that power is everywhere; Marx said that power is nowhere but on Wall Street. Both are correct.

Critique prefigures a utopian order addressed differently in Habermas' image of an ideal speech situation[2] in which the process of discussion among equal dialogue partners is also the product; socialism in Marx's original terms is not simply a library but a literary intersubjectivity in which writing solicits its gentle correction by other versions. In this chapter I consider how to slow down the degradation of signification in a way that hears its own critique at once as a mode of new construction. The model for this kind of work remains Marx's critique of bourgeois political economy; he simultaneously demystified by historicizing the naturelike patterns of the bourgeois marketplace and prefigured a new economic order in which capital and labor would cease to be opposing terms of value.[3]

Yet the critique of ideology in its more traditional tone is insufficient to address ideologizing texts dispersed deeply into nature itself. It is no longer clear at all what is ideological and what is not. Opposition is too readily coopted in affirmative ways. By the same token, ideology does not self-consciously programmatize a certain state of affairs, refusing baldly to exhort or admonish. Rather ideology—the mystification of the possible—is concealed in nature's seeming reflection in versions provoking themselves, ever the aim of social ontologies engendering our plight as fate. We must trace ideological claims into the degraded significances that they have become in order to undo their compelling hold on thought. Imagination is stimulated by a critique addressing ontology dispersed into things themselves, even if these things appear not to be texts narrated with a transformative intent.

Fast capitalism speeds up mind so much that imagination takes too long. The radical agenda is foreshortened in this way by limiting it to local causes—the usual reformist agendas of interest group politics, if not to unequivocally affirmative behavior notably including consumption. Thus, the goal of a radical hermeneutics is to *historicize* textuality in a way that shows the temporality of its conception as a process of authorial artifice. Marx historicized the categories of bourgeois political economy by showing the historicity of the bourgeois world it conveyed. Similarly, critique would defuse and delay the instantaneity of dispersed texts that do not admit of meditative readings because they pulsate with the concealed authoriality of social nature. Reading would slow the degradation of signification so that things were not allowed to become identical with the signifiers covering them with names and senses. Instead, language would reclaim for itself the right to speculate, meditate, mediate—and thus reconstruct.

The historicity of texts opens the possibility of their reformulation among communities of coequal speakers. This reformulation would follow a critique showing author where before only figure had been. The built, textual, and figural environment must be reauthorized where texts have dispersed into things that provoke their own accounts in a positivist world. Buildings, books, and number can be read narratively once they are narrated deconstructively as the driven fictions they really are. The excavation of writing's historical character shows the act of authorial artifice that made self-conscious choices about design and discourse. In this sense, reauthorizing readings would allow us to glimpse the possibility of reformulation as both literary and political work.

This narration of dispersed texts recoups their self-alienation into an exterior world. It takes back text from things where it restores the methodically suppressed traces of authorial signification from its identity with its topics. Deconstructive reading is not enough, however, to undo the disciplining effects of texts concealing their own drive to identify with the given order. A positivist world read narratively still dominates. A radical hermeneutics must also engage the reauthorized version in dispute about social possibilities, refusing the ontologizing accounts congealed in sociology, cities, and sentience that then reproduce those accounts in actual states of affairs. Power is ever at issue in the effort to overcome texts' self-alienation in things; the dominant order defies versions of literature opening science and technology to radical self-management; Habermas's ideal speech situation opposes positivist social being.

Thus, an interpretive approach to fast capitalism necessarily comprehends its own political purpose and passion not only to trace the palimpsest of authorial significance but also to open authoriality to a general community of equal speakers. The problem in western civilization is that writing remains an elite activity, restricting constitution to those competent to draw blueprints, write prose, and do math. This is a tiny fraction of the world's people, but it need not remain so. Freire's (1970) pedagogy of the oppressed teaching literacy as a tool of political liberation inspires a pedagogy of expertise empowering people to use heretofore esoteric languages of planning, the professions, and science.

These elite argots must not only be open to outsiders; they must also be reformulated in ways admitting their own literary corrigibility, thus soliciting gentle correction by other versions. New science and technology (Marcuse 1969; Agger 1976) prefigure a good political community in the openness of talk to its own correction, another way of suggesting Habermas's communicative ethic as a political methodology of socialism. It is not enough to learn positivist languages of administration but to reformulate these languages reflexively so that their unabashed narrativeness humbles their efforts to control nature and other people. In any case, radical hermeneutics cannot simply dent the elite monopoly of text while accepting its positivist intentionality without losing its own mind. Positivist text drives toward its own dispersal into social nature and thus positivist codes must be rewritten, not simply learned and used democratically.

Domination not only resists its authorization but also defies other versions of it. Authorial excavation does not require that surfaced author concede dialogue chances to other versions of it, challenging its ontological world with the possibility of other, different ones. Dialogue silences where monologue overwhelms. Thus, at bottom the politics of interpretation, like every other politics, depends on persuasion, coercion, coalition, mobilization. Positivism will not concede science to other versions defying a positivist account of frozen social nature. The purpose of authorization is not to convert those who perpetuate and profit from domination's eternity but to lay bare our own authorial possibilities where heretofore they were occluded. Radical hermeneutics raises consciousness to the level at which it can recognize its own nonidentity to the world engulfing it.

From that point, people who propose different, nonrepresentational versions can only prefigure a better world in the hurly-burly of power and persuasion. Positivism will not be undone in its own terms, nor will the built environment suddenly melt into air (Berman 1982) upon deconstructive critique. Reading radicalizes but must also be relived as the possibility of new community.[4] An authorized world remains the same unless we all talk and live it differently—the agenda of any political movement that wants to win converts and thus redistribute power. A politics of textuality must move outside itself in reconfiguring the whole material world of which textuality is only a part, albeit a pivotal one.

Radical hermeneutics suggests, indeed embodies, transformative lives in all sorts of public and private realms. Critique addresses many dominations, not simply those of dispersed textuality—of intellection, ideation, so-called superstructure. Critical theory written under the auspices of Adorno and a political version of deconstruction refuses axial reductions to a single master narrative replacing labor with text as an archetype of generic human activity and thus domination.[5] Critique decenters itself while keeping analytic principles of domination and liberation firmly in mind. Although my critique of fast capitalism suggests some overall tendencies, it does not apply itself ruthlessly to local contexts in which my analysis of textual dispersal may be less than adequate. Radical hermeneutics reads author into narrativeless texts, rewrites them, persuades others of the possibility of other versions, and then interrogates itself in asking itself the question of its answer.

In this way we resist being swallowed by our own slogans—surplus value, organic composition of capital, reification, total administration, ideal speech, fast capitalism, dispersed textuality, authorization. As slogans they cease to do any analytic and thus political work, a crucial weakness checked only by what Communist cells call self-criticism. Critique flattens into affirmation and thus apologia where it uses concepts to do the work of mediation and negation. The irony of a dialectical materialism is that we must use concepts to understand the degradation of these concepts into things, swallowing the attempt to criticize them. Word play does not do all of the analytic work available, and yet it cannot be avoided in favor of a Derridean relativism sticking so close to the world's names for itself that it refuses to think new practices for fear of being harmlessly constructive, thus irrelevant.

Fast capitalism degrades every concept quickly, celebrating its novelty and then dispersing it to name things that live as a parody of what concept was initially meant to criticize.[6] Freedom becomes freedom to buy, park, borrow. Justice embodies in police, army, prison, missile silo. Criticism becomes interpretation and explication. Repressive tolerance (Marcuse et al. 1965) goes farther than that, turning critique into its opposite in naming and thus reproducing practices it initially opposed. Marxism is the Soviet Union and democracy capitalism. This does not tolerate any number of Marxist versions but singles out the one that will do the most system-serving work, disqualifying the left by Sovietizing it.

In this sense critique must resist its own deauthorization into lazy concepts substituting for thought. Critical theory is not a body of received truths but a literary strategy. Opposition to texts' degradation takes the temporal form of slowing down the signifying process, halting the proliferation of names and labels only bound to dissolve into their own othernesses. Calling domination something else only degrades another word; yet language cannot transcend constitution and still communicate the energy of transformation driving it. Indeed, critique drives less to be science than to create community out of mutually provocative and respectful versions, refusing definitiveness as a conceit of Promethean mind—how Marxism got into trouble in the first place. This does not mean that we have to abandon rigor, especially if rigor's opposite is the mushy method of humanist subjectivism, a problem for much of women's studies eschewing abstraction as male projection. Opposition to positivism does not have to renounce any language of figure, especially where we can reauthorize mathematics as a literature in its own right and thus use it to comprehend the mathematizing forces of fast-capitalist administration turning us all into number.

Critique, a powerful political force in its own right, must be revalorized by those under the sway of a mechanistic version of the relation between ideal and material. Textuality materially intervenes in history where texts as matter provoke or compel certain enactments of its version of metaphysical possibility. In fast capitalism this process of provocation both accelerates under the imperative of capital reproduction and takes nondiscursive forms where writing no longer enjoys its previous distance from the world it addresses and thus can no longer be easily read—hence criticized. Critique both slows down and reauthorizes text acts as a mode of political resistance and reconfiguration; we need not apologize for this. The region of the political is both smaller and bigger than it once was—smaller in that nothing much of importance seems to take place in the sphere of public debate, bigger in that politics disperses itself into things as these things provoke their own reading and thus reproduction.

A radical hermeneutics politicizes what appears to be only nature. My critique of sociology (1989) models a critique of all disciplining, blending Habermas and Foucault through a literary-theoretic version of Adorno's negative dialectics. These names matter only as autobibliographical signs of my own engagements. As such, if taken too literally as pedigrees, they risk the inertia of all names given to things that are then swallowed in the names themselves. The sign must possess some distance from the reality it addresses lest it take on a concealed reality of its own and thus substitute for the thought thinking it in the first place. I avoid the congealing tendencies of my own thought without pretending an originary intellect that, in the fashion of Madison Avenue, promises wholly "new and different" products—this time, social theory. By saying the names Adorno, Foucault, and Habermas to describe some of my beginnings, I suggest a version of them that elucidates all—me through my reading of them, them through the invitation to read them en route to understanding me.

Radical hermeneutics reads discipline as a politics of signification's degradation. When names dispersed into nature as pregiven objects do our constitutive work for us we need new names to give to things. Before that, though, we need to read social nature as an authorial achievement concealed in the reifications of a positivist culture. Sociology as a positivist discipline was important to me only because it represents a generalized fact-fetishism dulling historical imagination.[7] Sociology's names—family, institution, role, stratification—swallow the realities they originally meant to describe, in particular rendering oppressions ontological as a generic social nature.[8] In turn, science's text reproduces the contingent family, institution, role, and stratification named by sociology to be invariant features in its discourse of the power of the social. It does this by copying them into its pages, ironically proving itself by reading family off social nature once it has provoked it as fate.

Now I know that sociology does not count for much. Yet it helps me model a critique of discipline; I unearth it from the way academics let names work as the essence of disciplinary advancement, today the apology for text's forced identity with the world it addresses. In particular I read sociology as a modal positivism, concealing its own

85

political agendas written into its presuppositionless representation-ality. Description is more than an ontology; it risks becoming a world when published as a definitive account. Critique reads discipline in the texts enforced as discipline on disempowered readers. Thus, critique aims to turn readers into writers. As a story, methodology can have a different ending.

Any text disciplining imagination by appearing not to be writing at all—the essence of fast capitalism—requires narration; it narrates itself storylessly. Domination has been regionalized not to be traced easily to a single axial principle that can be opposed as such. Disci-pline happens in numerous local settings and must be opposed there. Domination can neither be reduced simply to a regime, country, or conspiracy nor to what some call dominant structure. Instead, power-lessness corrupts heterogeneously, requiring dedisciplining readings with nuanced tones and textures. Although the nature of discipline today is common—history concealed as the authored version it is and might be again—disciplining proceeds locally according to principles of rational administration. Damage control requires that the world order not come undone through a single powerful thrust, whether Marx's *Manifesto* or a missile.

Critique theorizes implicitly by authorizing discipline suppressing not only theory but all thought. It suggests a better world in a com-municative ethic of many speakers. Critique by authorizing dispersed texts not only opens the possibility of other versions; it also refuses to canonize a single definitive version, ever the corruption of apodictic knowledge. Deconstructive reading goes still further. Not only does it narrate social nature and then open it to possible reformulations but it also refuses to play off these reformulations in an epistemological or moral marketplace, preferring to *criticize as a political way of being human;* strong reading addresses disciplining monologue in the voice it recommends. Critique and construction blend where authorization purposely provokes other versions directly as a form of community itself.

Critique sharply demystifies by showing author where before only figure had been. At the same time, it gently provokes other versions as a way of implanting intertextuality in a living community of literary mutuality. The critic must balance negative and positive passions here, vigorously opposing versions that hide themselves behind the appear-ance of social nature while at the same time challenging concealed discourse to voice itself in a dialogical way. In this way critique hates oppression but loves the oppressor, charity strategically indispensable if we are to avoid the ascendant left's own ossification. Concealing its authorship in order to monopolize authorial authority, bad text contains within it the possibility of its own reformulation. In any case, we must believe that closed versions can be opened and made part of dialogue itself lest we arrogate to ourselves the right to name. The left's right is no less wrong than the right itself.[9]

Is this adequate politics? It depends on how we intend adequacy as well as politics. It is adequate if we read politics in places where it is not usually sought, notably in signs and codes dispersed into nature as its own reproduction. Debunking slogans is today political work. A positivist culture transvalues the political into virtual ontology, albeit found in "things themselves"—material culture—and not in abstracted metaphysical tomes. Positivism exists precisely to replace the speculative metaphysical construction of the Greeks that at least preserved a distance between itself and the world. Positivism disqualifies utopia on grounds that it cannot be perceived, measured, operationalized. Method in replacing metaphysics becomes metaphysics. Critique reads the metaphysics hidden in scientism's allegedly ontologyless account of the given world as a version that can be opposed. Critique then engages with science in inviting it to be different from the world it surreptitiously narrates. Ontology *itself* prefigures good community; nothing is better than the conversation about what "better" ought to mean—theory's praxis.

By finding politics encoded in dispersed codes we live a new politics. Positivists temporally separate theory and practice in order to postpone theory's practice indefinitely. In the meantime, scientific fetishism precludes deeper speculation about the good. And now in fast capitalism fetishes become texts in their own right, especially with regard to the mathematics that has virtually replaced speculative construction in the human studies. Number is the ultimate dispersal of sense into a sentient world, defying its other versions by seeming not to signify at all. I can think of few more effective political strategies today than to replace math with metaphysics especially where we read math as the secret metaphysic it is and would become—absolute fungibility made a principle of social organization.

I do not simply propose a better metaphysic than sheer representation; metaphysical construction itself is good because it cannot avoid inviting its own correction, thus joining community. Plato's good defies other versions to best it even if Plato would reject those versions as inadequate. At least he gets us talking, *doing socialism* in the interplay of versions tolerant of each other—indeed, needing each other as reciprocal audiences. Greek truth is the time and trouble it takes to get there, not simply truth objects found pregiven to philosophy's

87

lens. Dialectic thus connoted dialogue for Plato; ironically his apodictic sketch of the good life in *Republic*, the original perpetualization of domination, belied his implication that the good life was the time spent together arguing it. A Marxist version of Plato would use Plato's own dialectic and especially its simultaneity of theory and practice to undo the explicit Plato of *Republic*.

But this is neither a Platonist treatise nor against Plato. For better or worse Greek metaphysics at least augurs an intellectual constitution of utopia resisting the degradations of positivist culture, where non-science is dismissed literally as nonsense.[10] But critique today does not have the luxury of *de novo* construction of Plato's type; the weight of positivist writing is nearly preponderant. We must reverse the direction of the textual so as to prise mind free to think a different world. Politics is ontological construction where today ontology resides in building, tome, and figure, thus precluding other versions both of it and the world it provokes. Where Plato meant for people to live the *Republic* directly, the positivist banishment of constitutive metaphysics is no less metaphysical for all that. The extirpation of ontology is itself a political agenda—adaptation, acquiescence, adjustment. We oppose it by revealing it as agenda, now so deeply buried as to be virtually invisible in the things into which it has been dispersed.[11]

Hermeneutics is a way of life where all reading is a version of writing. Derrida's poststructuralism makes us think differently about the activity of reading, dehierarchizing the traditional positivist relationship between authorial construction and a subordinate interpretiveness. Critique constructs where it reveals the narrativeness of versions not heard as stories. By insisting on the world's textuality, reading offers new versions. Critique refuses its subordination to the weight of the given by "giving" it differently. The world's textuality is political because, after all, the world is present to us as the untranscendable horizon of human possibilities. Existentialism continues to educate where it compels us to stick within the worldliness of metaphysical questioning; historicity is not flattened with the aid of method but celebrated as the occasion of new histories.[12]

Fast capitalism replaces knowledge constitution with positivist representation now projected into technique itself. The mirror supposedly reflecting the world becomes a world itself, producing behavior it supposedly only records phenomenally. Where critique questioned the possibilities of all knowledge and history for German idealism, today critique is reduced to commentary, explication of text, a narrow interpretive accounting. Even deconstruction becomes methodology. The denigration of reading as derivative and dependent reflects the overall domination of reproduction addressed in Ch. 2. This does not mean that we can suddenly empower critique as if its denigration did not occur, writing marginally, epigrammatically and playfully in the way Derrida does. To be critical reading must address its marginality while insisting on its centrality—a process of becoming in which reproduction struggles to produce, not simply buttress. In this sense critique expands the sense of available constitutive work.

The critic acts politically when he or she refuses the dominating western order of value—production over reproduction, capital over labor, men over women, text over commentary. As Marx indicated, value is the real battleground of the political. Indeed, the transformation of use value into exchange value is one of the best examples of textual dispersal in fast capitalism, a process only accelerated since the mid-19th century. Commodities conceal the social relations that make them valuable by becoming enmeshed in the cash nexus assigning them significance only to the extent of their cost and self-reproduction as exchange value. Marxism criticizes the degradation of use value's significance in a money economy, arguing not for the abolition of money itself but for the social relations concealed in transforming use value into exchange value. Marx was for utility and against the dispersal of utility into its money representation, especially where that dispersal empowers some and immiserates others.[13]

In capitalism money encodes the hierarchical social relations that brought them about in the first place. By concealing its own textuality in this sense, money is accepted immediately as a legitimate standard of value and thus reproduced in monied practices. Money mathematizes domination once read as a text concealing its own textuality—historicity. Marx did no more than read money in *Capital*;[14] here I am trying to read readings that money would provoke, thus to rewrite it as an example of a more general type of oppression—our oppression by the books we write and then forget how to read. Today everybody writes but nobody reads. In reading money Marx explicitly challenged the naturelike account of money offered by British political economy; in reading positivist culture I challenge the accounts of the mathematizing social sciences like sociology.

Not only is my account more fundamental than Marx's because I try to generalize his own particular reading; I could not read writing not meant to be read without Marx having already read money as a dispersed and thus self-reproducing text. In this sense I call my account Marxist. In a similar sense I call myself feminist because my version presupposes the feminist reading of sexuality as a text of gender.[15] I read Marx's politics as an urge to reprivilege use value over its money transformation, thus suggesting all sorts of institutional changes across the economic system and polity—and, feminism would add, the realm of intimacy. Marx suggested more than that, too, where he implies that money is the most fundamental form of domination in capitalism. I do not disagree, although the strategic priority is not to assign priority to one or another level of domination but to figure out how to read domination not meant to be read at all. In this I look to Marx for guidance. But it is impossible in the late 20th century to endorse Marx's own unexamined hierarchy of productive over reproductive activity (e.g., the implication that only commodities bear use value, not also children, sexuality, intimacy) in the way of most economisms. For me, Marx's reading of money is his most fundamental contribution to an enduring critical theory.

In reading money for the world it both represents and reproduces, we reduce its fetish character. I (1989) have tried to read science the same way, listening for the world it conceals and thus provokes. In fast capitalism significance is lost as text becomes thing; reading recoups it and at the same time learns from it. Marx in reading money opened a whole social theory around which money pivoted both as text and thing. In reading sociology as a modal form of positivist science I continued that reading. Here I want to understand better what Marx's reading of money and my reading of positivist culture have in common beyond a certain political intent. They both pursue sign into the things that signify today. As such, they learn from the texts dispersed and concealed in the exterior environment and also refuse their accounts of an unalterable social nature.

Indeed critique goes one step further. In authorizing hidden texts as they have become compelling things, reading's account models a different world. By refusing bourgeois political economy's nonsemiotic understanding of money, Marx suggested a world in which money's phony equivalences did not rule human behavior. By refusing positivism's world I suggest a world in which meaning does not have to erode into things that take over the monopolistic and monologic process of constitution. And by reversing the erosion of signification I open signification to a democratic community of writers, a powerful political strategy in its own right.

In presupposing the incorrigibility and infinity of interpretation radical hermeneutics forestalls its own methodologization. Utopia oppresses where it only inverts the old; Marxist positivism is still positivism, just as left and right oligarchies subordinate. Critique must check its tendency to install a new absolute and thus short-circuit the spiral of writing and reading guaranteeing the identity of epistemological and political democracy.[16] Although domination is wrong absolutely, dissent is not for that reason absolutely correct. By resisting versions disqualifying all contest, critique must read itself as another corrigible version lest it canonize into another inert order of being.

This is not a plea for tolerance; tolerance today only tolerates the horrible.[17] Critique by authorizing hidden texts wants to vanquish their accounts in order to change the world entirely. Yet a dialectical spin must be put on a different version of versions refusing to arrogate all moral authority to itself. My version of critical theory will doubtless provoke alternative formulations, as it should. The point is that the good society, whether named socialism or ideal speech situation, is the *talk it takes to resolve the babel of tongues*—realizing that we cannot achieve a definitive resolution. It is one thing to beat back counter-revolutionary versions, as we must attempt. It is another to refuse all talk that challenges and corrects. The good is in getting there, even if "there" always eludes us.[18] Or if the good does not materialize en route, at least we can avoid the bad by institutionalizing communicative democracy.

Critique realizes that it will be criticized itself. It should be defensive only where it realizes that criticism is not meant to open the world to many versions but would establish itself as an enduring version. It should be open to criticism where critique is playfully and dialogically intended—where the point of criticism is to start or refresh human relationships and not simply to scold or punish.[19] Positivist habits of mind run so deep that we can barely refrain from turning our defensiveness on those who need it least—our comrades. The left competes with itself in a self-destructive way because its scientism frequently gets the better of its transformative desire. Too many Marxists forget Marx's passionate opposition to capitalist being; instead, by doing their own positivist version of versions they ironically reinforce positivism's hegemony. This has been said often, but it must be said again. Marxist validity is not theory but practice, better a practice that theorizes itself circularly.

Radical hermeneutics reads the world against itself. Where things authorized to be read as texts seem to defy utopia, reading historicizes and thus reformulates history. Smith and Ricardo, Davis and Moore, Parsons and Bales are thus read to express ironic dialectical truth: they depict a frozen world including their accounts as buttress. The world, in its need to be written, reveals its own deficit of obedience. Thus, critique takes advantage of the world's openness as an opportunity to write and live differently, what Foucault called thinking otherwise. There is no more profound political agenda than to reformulate formulation's own role in reproducing the given—thus revealing the "given" to be only one among a number of narrative possibilities suppressed by methodology.

Thus, critique utopianizes even where it avoids construction. In resisting ontology the critique of ontology suggests a different order of being to which it contributes its own example. Unlike positivism, though, it accounts for its own role in bringing being into being. Critique's utopia lies in the norm of democratic speech it exemplifies in its ability to be simultaneously radical and tentative. It drives to change the world, and it recognizes its historicity as a mortal account requiring other versions to complete its humanity.[20] But left critique fears challenges where it realizes that the world too frequently crushes negation. It must get beyond this, however, if its utopian norm is really to become a constitutive principle of social order. Irony and radicalism belong together if radicalism is to avoid its own eclipse.

Few Marxists or feminists admit irony where any sign of weakness could be exploited by the dominant discourse. It is easy to understand left fascism as a response, albeit totally inadequate, to the liberal fascism of money and science. In this sense the Frankfurt School understood the tendency of Marxism to degenerate into a repetition of dominant categories of value. Marxist economism only repeats the economism of the world at large; it fails to think itself contributing to the problem it addresses with the perverse passion of the canonical. For its part mainstream feminism rejects the politics of production because Marxism traditionally missed the importance of reproduction as a region of important human experience. In this way left feminism fades into a liberal version economizing women's public exploitation and familizing gender relations.

Opposition epochally finds itself at a disadvantage where it opposes an order that would control the meaning of value. Critique must simultaneously address mystification in its own terms and yet rise above it by insisting on a new order of being. Language must both refuse old meaning and yet engage old meaning in terms clarifying its deceptions. Marx read money not because he wanted money himself but because he opposed the way money encodes and thus reproduces value in capitalism. By the same token feminism reads pornography as a sign of what happens to women under patriarchy and thus risks giving women's objectification an undue ontological significance—as if pornography, like money for Marxists, were here to stay.

Critique must struggle toward a new language in which to reorder and thus reflect a new order of being. Western language split between subject and predicate conceals hierarchy under what appears mere differentiation. Language authorizes domination, and then it is dispersed into things that talk to us and compel us to enact their fateful codes. Thus, we need a new language in which to convey and contribute to a new order of being—one alive to the aporias of language and yet willing for all that to dwell within talk's circularity in gentle and reciprocal dialogue.[21] Deconstruction suggests that language uses us; yet it can also augur a mode of being in which language's structuring tendencies are checked deconstructively—by thought, reason, imagination. A radical hermeneutics traces the oppressions of language in order to undo them. In this sense "new" language will trade on past meanings and yet in so doing will say something else, thus allowing lives to be lived through it.

A future society, dispensing with money's concealment and thus the reproduction of skewed exchange relations, will not do without symbolic media of exchange. Money can still represent, if not falsely. In reading money, Marx opens the possibility of a world in which money tells its own story unproblematically and in which people acquire sufficient amounts of it. Similarly, a feminist society need not dispense with imageries of sexuality, especially where sexuality has been freed from its representation as the violence men do to women. It is hard to foretell the future language games of a free society without knowing exactly how present ones structure thought and life into unacceptably confined possibilities. The only way out of bad talk is through more talk, trading on but transcending past meaning.

Critique undoes constraining language repeating self-destructive behaviors by recognizing that language itself is a form of behavior. Meaning cannot subsist beyond language, and thus the Marxist search for apodicticity is as futile as the Enlightenment's pursuit of eternal laws of social motion. We can only live within systems of meaning structuring the pregiven grammars of rhetoric. Yet by opening closed texts to readings we necessarily change meaning. Money encodes and thus reproduces an order of value peculiar to exchange economies. By reading money Marx suggests an alternative order of value in which money does not stand for and thus deepen the theft of surplus value; Marx thinks money otherwise by reading it for what it tells about a social order. Critique at once stays within the circle of meaning already established and then suggests different meanings, playing off the sense of the old. Marx's "value" is certainly not the same as capitalist value, and yet to suggest its possibility he must read capitalist value for its aporias.

Critique constructs by thinking text otherwise. It makes deception reveal itself and thus bespeaks a social order in which deception facilitates domination. My concern with domination's text is materialist and not aestheticist. I do not want to read literature for its insight—although as a pastime that is certainly work many of us already do—but to read science, money, edifice, and figure as literary artifices that by concealing their narrativeness provoke worlds of which they pretend only to be disinterested accounts. Where Marxist aestheticians read literature for its class truths and feminist critics read for gender truths, they do not realize that their own sciences are fictions concealing authorial commitment and desire. Concealing its literary auspices in this way, deconstructive reading pretends an indubitable account that in turn deauthorizes into the cant of political correctness, thus risking its own hierarchy over other accounts. Although hierarchy over the false is certainly an acceptable political goal, critique inattentive to its own literariness risks oppressing companion versions, thus turning itself into yet another arrogant architecture.

Otherwise critique thinks falsehood not to establish an eternity of truth but to turn truth into a corrigible accomplishment of many speakers, precisely what we ought to mean by socialism. Not only do dispersed texts of science, money, edifice, and figure misrepresent; they seem not to represent at all and thus only reproduce the world encoded in them as ontologically unalterable. Thus, reading is difficult in fast capitalism. We do not know exactly what is text and what is thing; better, it is hard to discern where text's thinghood conceals its authorial artifice in a way that it could have been written differently. Yet there seem to be many books out there, especially works intending critique. They almost inevitably are swallowed in the maw of administration; their textuality fails to become a thing having a prominent place in the public world. Instead, the real texts today defy easy reading, dispersed into things compelling "readings" of adjustment, adaptation, acquiescence.

Books do not look like texts, and texts are things in fast capitalism. In this situation critique risks obscurity by standing apart. Yet there is no real alternative lest critique reduce itself to dominant discourse as method. It is said that the critical theory of the Frankfurt School, indeed Marxism generally, has had translation problems in the New World where the original thinkers presupposed sophisticated knowledge of European philosophy and high culture.[22] True, but translation in the sense of popularization would not have helped. Adorno is not a television show, popular magazine, or board game anymore than he can be "mainstreamed" as a sociological theorist once reduced to simple English. *Negative Dialectics* opposes common sense with the irony of dialectical allusion; today clarity obfuscates. Thought must labor to think the categories of German idealism differently, deconstructively. Adorno did not write straightforward social theory, whatever that is, because administration defies straightforwardness to understand its complexities.[23]

Positivist academic disciplines want simplicity in order to divert thought from comprehending its complex object, the totality of domination in which discipline itself plays a part. Critique must wrestle with the mystifications of ordinary and disciplinary language in order to wrest language from its straitjacket in the straightforward. This requires Promethean deconstructive work, especially where authorial figure virtually has been erased from the text of science and must be interpolatively replaced as if it had been there all along. Critical theory cannot simply read and rebut books because it must instead read money, science, edifice, and figure as the real texts of the time. *Negative Dialectics*, like this work, struggles to become a thing when things are books and books nonentities. Adorno wants to be read for his reading of other discourses concealing domination; I want to be read for my reading of text/things compelling adjustment. Yet I realize that even within academic fields this sort of critique goes largely unread because it does little fungible or productive disciplinary work.

I do not produce hypotheses, contribute to a literature, or suggest ways of "applying" my version to the world in remediating it. It is far too late for that. And if academics do not read books appearing to do little disciplinary work—that are not disciplined—how can we expect anyone else to read? But writing cannot account for its reception, and thus it ought not try to ensure its comprehensibility to readers it thinks it knows. Writing relying too much on a sense of its audience only reiterates. I do not counsel a studied obscurantism; I simply think the dilemma of trying to write about administration in an overly administered world. We risk succumbing to the same fate as everyone else. Writing's auspices must be sought elsewhere; for me, they exist in a notion of critique that radically plumbs writing for echoes of thought methodically kept concealed so as not to invite its rejoinder. Popularity is not a measure of truth but, today, of unconsciousness.

The standard critique of critical theory is that it writes obscurely in order not to *have to* join the fray, exhibiting the intellectual's usual disdain for the rabble. But what is the virtue of being sucked in and thus under, apart from having done one's political duty? Critique distances itself to be as direct as possible about the way ideation entwines us materially, subverting even the words we use to express our rage and then formulate alternative living arrangements. Obscurity educates and liberates where it resists banalization, reduction into platitude, and thus affirmation. Positivist culture degrades signification by denying imagination the ability to think beyond the categories covering the present in ontological amber. Critique addresses this reduction of imagination as a way of understanding how all sorts of marginality are disciplined.

Deconstructive reading politicizes interpretation where it recognizes how books that become things defy interrogative responses and thus new social arrangements. Critique insists on the right to interpret texts littering the exterior landscape with their dispersed and thus suppressed significances, opening them to reformulating readings as a way of taking back the word. Recognizing that many books have become things and are thus unreadable as the acts of authorial mediation and constitution they originally were, books insist on their distance from things. This is a way of being direct, not evasive, in spite of doctrinaire caricatures to the contrary. Today it is not at all clear what is political, allowing for all sorts of sectarian disputes about strategy. I view politics as the region in which the least political things provoke the most political behavior—the area in which money, science, edifice, and figure compel their own "readings" as nucleic forms of life. Critique insists on the right to name the political, especially where politics hides behind the label of ontology, mere representation of what "must" be. Politics and ontology are separated by history, although in fast capitalism politics uses ontology well as a way of concealing its historicity and thus susceptibility to reformulation.

Radical hermeneutics politicizes by opening things to narration. This is inadequate strategy where not all things encode an ontology of adjustment and affirmation. Yet it is a beginning; it is unavoidable where we no longer know what it means to read or even *what* to read in the way of arguments constructed by apparent authors. The world argues for itself without the seeming need of ideological buttress. But this is false. Falsehood must still insist on itself with the aid of versions of what must be. Critique in penetrating falsehood imagines the possibility of different worlds and thereby helps them come to be.

The name radical hermeneutics is a problem, as are all slogans announcing their political sufficiency. "Radical" recognizes that hermeneutics is typically conservative. But why do it, then, if its disengagement requires politicization from the outside? Although labels are risky for what they claim for themselves—always too much, for example, historical materialism or communication theory—we cannot strategize without them. Perhaps I should simply say that I am doing, and propose, critique; at least it is a shorter name than radical hermeneutics. But critique intends things I do not mean as well. For example, it connotes a foundationlessness forever avoiding the work of positive architecture. And hermeneutics suggests reading strategy, which becomes political strategy when I add the adjective radical.

We do different sorts of work in opposing domination. All the things we do are material because they matter and are matter. Cultural criticism, another self-limiting slogan, is my version of politics today, and thus I politicize reading where I believe empirically and politically that reading and writing are at stake in fast capitalism. The problem is not only that there is no public anymore for whom one can write but also that there are no more books to be written that can stand outside the world they address and thus oppose. This is politically serious, given a certain perspective on how capitalism complexly administers mind and thus inhibits resistance. We feel we must apologize for "merely reading" where orthodox Marxism makes us feel guilty about not doing ostensibly more political things like organizing unions. Not to apologize is a good political beginning in its own right for it says something about how we must revalue public and private activities. That economics matters does not require us to be economistic—thus dualist, sexist, stupid.

Radical reading not only undoes ideology, appearing not to be, but in doing so helps us think differently about its possibilities. Critique, if successful in authorizing dispersed texts of money, science, edifice, and figure, recreates a public world in which people write and read together as a dialogical norm of community. If that is to happen, critique must think about the way it wants to relate itself to other versions and to readers and incorporate that desire into its critical approach to texts and things. The rhetoric of negation bears within it a glimpse of the possible. Thus, difficult writing imagines a historical situation in which it becomes clear—and understands its own responsibility for narrating that history. Perhaps this is only to say that negation is not enough; I offer this caution to textual fetishists who conflate the material and textual worlds so thoroughly that text seems to have no outside, thus losing the specificity of a critique of ideology addressing discourse as a medium of domination.

The lament that no one reads or writes—that there is no viable public sphere—must recognize that in saying that it already models a better public world. Critique suggests itself as a norm where it understands its opposition as the implication of a possible positive to which it contributes through its own version. Critique builds community by understanding how positivist culture vitiates community, making texts things and things texts. In thinking the complex totality, critique inevitably thinks it otherwise, measuring it against a standard of his-

97

torical possibility giving sense to its angry opposition. The challenge for criticism is to understand this about itself. Reading presupposes a standard of otherness grounding anger in the possibility of happiness.[24] It needs to articulate the imagery of this otherness in order to provoke negation toward new construction. If it does not, it tends to be swallowed, domesticated, academicized, professionalized, precisely the fate of much thought today.

Critique is not method but historical intervention prising imagination free from the exterior world enmeshing it in the tautology of itself.[25] Once critique develops into an interpretive rule it disciplines attempts to use it differently, passionately, wildly. Yet without some discipline critique peters out in the endless play of signifiers—whatever that means politically. The challenge is to theorize without being ruled by theoretical abstraction. Without theory, critique fails to think the structural properties of its topic and thus goes nowhere politically. Too much obedience to the rule of concepts in architectonic rigor stills the passion of politics; critique becomes another academic specialty to be applied anywhere and everywhere. Deconstruction in itself suffers both fates, neither developing a social theory within which we can understand and thus oppose language's structuring domination of mind nor resisting its own methodologization in English departments. It is telling that "critical theory" in the American university describes both a version of Marxism of the kind I am doing here *and* an approach to literary interpretation—again, the problem of two cultures.

Who can we read to find out how to criticize alert to the way critique intends itself as a norm of a better society? Who "thinks otherwise" without being idealist? The list is very short. I would include Marx, Adorno, Marcuse, John O'Neill, Russell Jacoby, and a few others. These people all resist the reduction of their critiques into method even if some have been unsuccessful, notably Marx. We are never fully responsible for how we are read. Yet we have some control over our reception the more we are clear about the implications of our mode of talk for a new society. That way we resist becoming either high theorists (Marx) or cherished celebrities (Derrida, Foucault). Habermas is sometimes treated as both. In any case, precious few examples exist. Academia disciplines. Thus, we ought not look there for many examples of intellectuality. And the world of letters confines thought by fashion in refusing politics as dirty work unsuited to people who would live the life of the mind.

A prominent critical theorist once told me that we need heroes, not only people to explicate but people to whom to appeal for moral energy. At the time I thought he was justifying idolatry. Having thought more about it, I am now convinced he was right. We need heroes to help us imagine the audience to whom we write, to sustain us as dialogue partners. Without heroes we are too isolated and thus too frequently beaten down when things go wrong—we cannot get published, obtain decent work, enjoy hospitable colleagues, sustain imagination. The heroes need not oppress us if we can avoid reading them methodologically but only as people who complete our speech by gently correcting it.[26] Political community must start somewhere, even between two or three people. The point is to begin.

It is by now a truism among those who teach writing that getting started is the hardest thing.[27] Critique disciplined by the rule of method reads too much for fear that the community of scholarship will reject the argument as unstudied. This is especially rampant on the left where scientism and professionalism prevail like never before. Critique in going public refuses to be ruled by authority structures. In the process, it will be corrected in a way prefiguratively modeling a good polity. Today writing risks being overeducated not uneducated, so obedient to tradition it loses its voice. This will not be corrected superficially by scrapping some of the accoutrements of scholarship like footnotes, bibliographies, and third-person voice, although none of those is essential. It will only be corrected by writing self-confidently unafraid to risk criticism, disapprobation, even oblivion. Those who truculently chastise critical theory for its political aloofness are less courageous. They frequently do not even write but spend endless hours studying *Capital* or other modern masters of left scholarship. Hermeneutics done by radicals is no less conservative than Bible study.

CHAPTER 6

Avoiding the Fetish
of the Textual

IN MY DISCUSSION of fast capitalism I suggested a radical hermeneutics that forcefully rescripts degraded texts compelling behavior as a way of short-circuiting meditative construction; this is indeed a Marxist project if we understand Marxism broadly as a literary version of social criticism.[1] In this chapter I address the concern that in authorizing domination I neglect economic and political issues central to the historic Marxist tradition. Much as Habermas suggests, a literary version of critical theory reformulates Marxism as a special case of a more generic theory of communicative competence and blockage. This only deprivileges Marxism if Marxism arrogates to itself the right to speak for all varieties of domination, no matter how complexly mediated through the circuitries of world history.[2]

The decentering of Marxism vitiates Marxism only if it cannot translate itself into other rhetorical modes and media. The concerns of Marxism and feminism are the same if Marxism can understand its critique of capital/labor contradictions in terms of a larger critique of the hierarchy of public and private, waged and unwaged, male and female, valued and valueless. This does not require it to lose its specificity but to learn from other critical traditions about its own blindspots and thus to reformulate itself. The Marxism/feminism convergence is not only strategically necessary; it offers Marxism insights into its own aporias in terms fundamentally continuous with its own dialectical logic.[3] This does not integrate feminism mechanically; it allows Marxists to speak feminist words by giving them a Marxist twist, thus

100

opening the Marxist mind to traditions of critique outside itself that refresh its own catechism empirically and politically.

Feminism's particular contribution to Marxism lies in its politicization of the realm of reproduction, heretofore disregarded simply as the realm of valueless, unwaged, private activity. For its part Marxism contributes to feminism a structural intent, raising what risks being a voice of special interest into a universal critique. Whether this is a fair exchange is not my concern. In any case, feminism does not supplant Marxism even if it politicizes the relation between public and private, productive and reproductive. Too many feminisms simply reverse the male/Marxist hierarchy of public and private in the other direction; women's suffering is now on top. This is the old story of how dominant discourse dominates everything equally.[4]

Marxism needs feminism where feminism, like deconstruction and other approaches to discourse theory, interrogates the hierarchy of value on which western civilization rests and which Marxism too frequently reproduces. The realm of the textual is no less important than the realm of work and organized politics precisely because the public/private hierarchy suppresses the realm of "private" reproduction *in its own interest*. Production claims ontological superiority to reproduction so that reproduction will reproduce that superiority in devalued, unwaged, degraded ways. Public creates a marginal realm of the private in arrogating value to itself. No matter that privacy does not exist in administered society; it must be invented.[5]

Marxists who resist literary theory only perpetuate productivism in spite of their opposition to capital's rule of social production for private profit. Politics connects public and private, compelling private to reproduce its own subordination to public. Thus, domination happens twice—first, by force, and second, by the victim's choice. The first cannot be undone without lessening the burden of the second; in this case the compulsive power of texts that become things thus dictate an order of being without being read at all. Marxism ignores the duality of domination because it understands and thinks it opposes ideation's function in propping a public order with sheer misrepresentation. Thus, it degrades ideation into a mere utility of real politics, failing to understand and hence oppose the historicity of the ideal/material hierarchy in the first place. Ideas mystify material oppression and then become material in their own right, especially where capitalism needs to suppress all textuality as an occasion of mediating reformulation. Texts produce as well as reproduce where books become things. In particular, by appearing not to be authorial accomplishments in fast capitalism texts produce reproduction's own subordination to pro-

101

duction, a circuitry fatefully replenishing domination with unwitting victims.

Consider the charge that in reading feminism for Marxist purposes I do what all men have done—use women. True, *if* feminism is a women's study in its nature. But for me feminism interrogates the hierarchy of valued and valueless activity, public and private spheres. It is only contingently about women to the extent to which women have historically been responsible for tending the realm of the valueless. Feminism is no more about women than Marxism is about the working class. Of course, many on the left disagree. But theory is not simply agitational; it comprehends the totality within which dominations are pitted against each other in diverting them from their real enemy. In any case I want to question what it means to be feminist and Marxist without assuming the answers. Fast capitalism robs left words of meaning no less than it robs other words.

Critique politicizes where we recognize that the very notion of the political is at stake today. Timeworn strategies of class resistance have failed largely because they were not thoroughgoing enough: they missed women, ideology, world systems. Reproduction's devaluation is a political topic, especially where ignoring the devalorized will only devalue it still further. In fast capitalism there is no mere writing but a blend of text and thing, occluding the world's use of writing to re-inforce social control. Ideology continues to be a political moment, albeit it takes subtler forms than it did for Marx. And ideology is not mere thought but practice that thinks for us; this makes so-called cultural analysis so crucial. As Horkheimer knew much earlier (1972b), in advanced capitalism base and superstructure become indistinguishable as reproduction produces its own subordination and thus vital contribution to productivism's dominion.

The usual charge that critical theory evades political work (e.g., Slater 1977 and my response, Agger 1983b) depends on what is political today.[6] My point is that the realm and scope of the political changes in response to volcanic pressures pushing upward from capital's structural core. Today virtually everything is political except, perhaps, politics itself. Critique seeks the political in its least obvious manifestations; it does so not out of aestheticist preciousness but simply because the political has displaced itself into realms seemingly defying political readings. Reading politicizes where it reveals the realm of reproduction, including textuality, to be structured by imperatives of capital, patriarchy, racism, and the domination of nature. Western Marxism as a whole pursues hierarchy in a myriad of manifestations scarcely imagined by Marx. It is not his fault; yet it is our fault if we continue to seek the political either in bourgeois-parliamentary processes or in the class struggle traditionally defined.

The left fears idealism and with good reason. Theoretical innovation tempts us with its methodologization. But critical theory is not a method if that means it can be applied anywhere or to anything. Yet at least critical theory has a direct link to the Marxism that bore it fitfully. Other theories of interpretation on which I draw were never politically driven and thus too readily succumb to methodism. For example, deconstruction has value for the left project only inasmuch as it sheds light on the complex circuitry of domination and thus becomes critique. Deconstruction, as intended by Derrida and others, is otherwise merely an intellectual fad drawn from a Nietzschean irrationalism anathema to critical theory's modernist faith in reason. This is not an issue of self-identity for anyone can claim Marxism. Rather intellectual innovations only bear political fruit if they illuminate and thus oppose domination manifested in heterodox ways. Derrida educates Marxism only because Marx could not foresee fast capitalism. In itself, Derrida's deconstruction is simply word play.

In the best sense Derrida exemplifies free mental labor in a different order. But process and product are inseparable. His form is good but content bad. Critique must be able to play with words and things, and yet it politicizes discourses and practices suppressing play out of a certain ontological/political investment.[7] Critique can only prefigure utopia by attacking contemporary dystopias, particularly, as I do here, opening language to its own ironic reversals where language becomes a thing and things talk. The fetish of the textual beckons in an age when intellectuals are dispossessed of their words; words in the meantime have been dispersed into the exterior environment of money, science, edifice, and figure. Derrida's language strategy is provoked by the archaic nature of books themselves and thus of traditional interpretive approaches to them.

Where writing no longer mediates, Derrida's word play might be read as a kind of protest. Where books are things compelling a world through unconscious "readings"—really, assimilation—and thus where books no longer retain distance from their topics, a decentering deconstruction defies the linear mien of the positivist. That is good. But critique must formulate dissent within a larger conception of the structuring forces marginalizing thought in the first place. Old-fashioned thinkers would say that critique aspires to be science. Remaining acutely sensitive to the way positivism claims all scientificity for itself, I would endorse the project of science as a way of structuring critique politically. Defiance is Nietzsche without Marx, and thus it affirms by failing to hit the correct political target. Language no longer *means* in the absence of absolutes. Notions like reason and justice have no historicity; as regulative ideas, they endure. Language is degraded only in service to world-historical forces diminishing defiance—what I call fast capitalism. Derrida and others methodologize the degradation of signification into poststructuralism. But structures have not disappeared;[8] rather, they evade critique by dispersing themselves into local regions of experience. Centerlessness conceals its structural continuity, whether as capitalism or the dialectic of enlightenment. To call the world situation "capitalism" or "sexism" barely scratches the surface of what is wrong. And yet we still need names to address the large structuring pressures bearing down on us and eroding our ability to mean and thus oppose.

Deconstruction only defies. It does not oppose. Although Derrida privately calls himself a Marxist, Marxism's universalizing tone does not echo in his interpretive work. Derrida affords insight; he models a mode of literary being suggesting a new order of value—beyond subject/object hierarchies only reproducing domination. Yet as method deconstruction fetishizes itself. Not only is there a world beyond the text; deconstruction locates textuality in the wrong place, notably between covers. It does not understand the dispersal of discourse as the eclipse of reason. Poststructuralism wants to restore significance, but it does not understand how it has been eroded in the first place. Thus, Derrideans read intensely, immersing themselves in word. But *they read the wrong things*—books having an old-fashioned distance from the world and not the world itself that has become a book and thus resists political narration.

The poststructuralist fetish of textuality misses the degradation of text in fast capitalism. They are right to oppose the distinction between original text and derivative critique, exemplifying reading that is strongly constitutive in itself. They prefigure a writerly world but do not understand how a deauthorized world must be opposed in authorizing writing, even risking being read as hopeful. They lack analysis. Indeed, deconstruction eschews analysis as positivist linearity. Yet as I have tried to demonstrate, analysis need not proceed representationally where it narrates its own narrativeness. Science need not dumbly copy a dumb world but can understand its structural tendencies and aporias. Of course, poststructuralists reject structural analysis. But they cannot rightly deny that structures are real, if not the invariantly self-enclosing ones traced by Lévi-Strauss[9] and Foucault.[10] Structure can be reconstituted without being structuralism, especially where structures are historicized into the merely typical patterns they are. Indeed, structure appears immutable where its structuring sign-systems are occluded as pieces of nature itself, precisely the role played by money in a market economy. Structures need texts, albeit unreadable ones, to conceal their political impermanence.

Language degrades where it becomes a piece of nature. The solution is not simply word play but a caprice of concepts at once reauthorizing dead matter as literary productions and in itself prefiguring a nonpositivist, nondualist culture. Critique ironically must pierce dualism by using dualist language, separating concept and thing in order eventually to unite them. Analysis distances itself from the world, thus risking the concealment of its driving desire to bring about a different order of being in which we could not think of analysis apart from the processual word play encoding it. But critique must live with its ironic nature in this regard. Expressive extravagance can only be indulged once hegemonic forces and forms have been put to rest, a distant prospect at best.

Deconstruction pretends that its time has come. But the pleasure of the text must await the liberation of textuality—thought, mediation —from its objectification. Critique authorizes and analyzes at once, poetizing dispersed texts of money, science, edifice, and figure and simultaneously providing a different account of the possible. Properly deconstructive reading seeks utopia by thinking otherwise, recognizing that we "get there" only by being able to think and then talk about "somewhere else." In reading money and science we reinvent their possibilities. Critique communicates by engaging monologue in dialogue, thus piercing monologue's implacable hegemony and modeling a dialogical social order. Deconstruction rises above ideology and domination by talking in the voice it recommends. Yet this is not enough; we must confront the thoughtlessness of the time in structural terms, not as a result simply of authorial inadequacy or moral failure of nerve.[11]

Marxist and textual fetishist converge where they miss the really political. Marxist repeats the litany of class analysis where textualist would dissolve politics into a decentering orgy of multiple signifiers. But politics subsists in the appearances of its eclipse, which we can read and learn from by reformulating a discourse refusing subject/ object hierarchies. Science and poetry blend in critique where critique must understand and prefigure at once. But at least critique politicizes, recognizing ideology in things and practices typically passed over by Marxists as epiphenomenal and by poststructuralists as materially obdurate. Text is neither all nor nothing today. Writing politically depoliticizes where it transcends narrative and thus provokes the world as a reading. Politics thus is *reading differently,* prising open the world portraying itself seamlessly and thus deceiving. I call this different reading a radical hermeneutics or simply critique, and I suggest it is a political strategy without disqualifying other strategies and struggles.

It is Archimedean to legislate a process through which to attain a benign world ruled unironically by a single concept. We only do what we can to rage against our bondage and then to think our world differently. Critique simply takes the world to hand and turns it into an account compelling its repetition, thus suggesting different versions of it that would change its order of being and value. Rage thus prefigures by talking in the voice it recommends without having the audacity to rule out prefigurations in different, even exotic locales. Strategy heterogeneously arrays itself into what it needs to be; or it does not and fails. My world is the world of ideas no long penetrating their objects, indeed losing themselves in the things they automatically become. Books today are everywhere but in the library. Thus, I deconstruct hidden texts by formulating a nonpositivist language through which to create a nonpositivist world signified by dialogue and epistemological openness. But there are a million other worlds in which the colonizations of administration play out differently.[12]

Liberations are both different and the same: they struggle against different particulars, but they aim to speak for themselves and invite other speakers. That much is basic. They might name themselves differently as long as they locate utopia's norm in a critique receptive to other versions of itself. We are all strange to each other, the more so the more dissent is marginalized as the raving of lunatics. To be human means to be available to sameness experienced in people's differences. This is not a metaphysic or morality as much as an anthropological universal. People talk different languages and yet sometimes understand each other. Not only does every speech act intend consensus, as Habermas[13] suggested, but also every utterance would change the world into a place in which talk is only an act of friendship requiring its reciprocation.

Marx (Marx and Engels 1949) meant something when he suggested that in socialism people would sit around and criticize after dinner. He imagined his own version of Republic, although he would have allowed anyone to be a critic; Habermas (1984, 1987) might require everyone to be a critic. I add that criticism takes any number of rhetorical forms; the most political ones are sometimes the least overtly political, especially where we understand politics only as another mode of human concourse. Thus, we do not have to say that we are engaging in undistorted and unconstrained speech when we launch into text.

Habermas's words for utopia become true by outliving their utility as fighting words—slogans.

We need to put the world into words in order to say how it could be different. Thinking and speaking it otherwise are only possible once we have made it read as an account—*of itself* in the case of fast capitalism. The objectified environment encoding meaning and thus compelling acquiescence is only a text contingently, not in every possible manifestation of it. A better world proceeding from our authorization of and opposition to the present bad one would not be a text but would include textuality as a moment of its self-consciousness. I do not want the world to be a text; it is a text only because textuality's suppression suppresses thought. Deconstructive methodology is turned on its head: in a better world deconstructive critique would dwell within any writing able to distance itself sufficiently from things that it could mediate and meditate without fear of being sucked in; critique would not have to be applied from the outside.

I do not suggest that beyond domination language will suddenly lose the silt of oppression that makes it so difficult to speak of oppression without oppressing. The complex circuitries of world history make history by mystifying. Language will not be complicit in its own neutralization as it disperses into things defying mediative reading. If the deconstructive project is to show author where before only figure had been, in an authorized world wherein we knew clearly the difference between text and thing deconstruction would be unnecessary. Rather, every account would acknowledge and celebrate its literary corrigibility as a way of soliciting other versions and thus joining community —Marx's community of permanent critique. Deconstructive method is useful only where positivist method suppresses the narrativeness of money, science, edifice, and figure in forestalling responses—political action.

This is not to say that aesthetic interpretation will be an illegitimate mode of self-expression under a different order but only that it will be *self-expressive work* and not definitive exegesis. Interpretation is fine as long as we understand, with Derrida, that reading writes. The hierarchy of text and commentary only reflects and then reproduces the hierarchy of western being; few doubt that some activity has more inherent value than other activity. Once hierarchy is overcome historically, interpretation will be free to play with the significances it finds in texts, art, music, and theater. But we will not extend that mode of critical interpretation and appreciation to all the social world; presumably we put sufficient distance between text and thing that we will know what to read as authorial artifice. Interpretation's methodologization apolitically assumes that everything is text where, in fact, text is a historical process and product of signification. When we put significance back into books and take it away from things secretly enforcing their meanings on us, we can enjoy the luxury of textual interpretation again. In the meantime interpretation is nothing less than the building of critical social theory addressing significance's degradation in fast capitalism.

The fetish of the textual beckons not as some on the left would have it because literary intellectuals revel in their distance but because textuality represents a life instinct (Marcuse 1955). We want text where it has been dispersed into unreadable talismans of the exterior world. No one reads books, but everyone reads—currency, science, building, and figure.[14] Text's eclipse in fast capitalism provokes text's fetishism, understandably. Dour Marxist condemnation of literary intellectuality misses the point that we want the same thing—to be able to read and write the world and not to have it read and write us and things. The left vitiation of literary interpretation for its alleged lack of engagement misses our common concern for the eclipse of thoughtful mediation.

Where a literary intellectuality risks methodologizing interpretation, the orthodox left denigrates textuality still further as a mere excrescence of the productive base. For their part, many feminists regard text as important only if it is women's text, that is, done by women or about women. But text itself is a woman where it reproduces its own unnecessary subordination to the rule of male value, notably wage labor. The truth is not in the middle but somewhere else. I use discourse-theoretic phrasings because orthodox Marxism threatens to drown out all culture-critical concerns with a canonically mindless economism. Indeed, from the beginning critical theory put distance between itself and orthodox Marxism not because as Lukacs said the original Frankfurt crew inhabited "Grand Hotel Abyss" but because they *were Marxists* and wanted to save Marxism from itself.

I claim Marxism just as I claim science; deconstructive theories of interpretation help me understand empirically how fast capitalism ingests textuality and thus the possibility of critique as a text of difference. Positivist culture wrecks on the shoals of authorizing versions of it. This is not a matter merely of either "ideology," as the dualist left would have it, or "consciousness," as the idealist left and feminists contend. Ideas as matter matter, the more so the more writing loses its ability to stand apart. Distance seems like the wrong political strategy when so much seems to be going wrong. Yet the alternative, particularizing immersion in facticity, lacks a language with which to make itself heard above the din of the everyday. Just because critique seems an unlikely political strategy does not mean that economism is better; indeed, economism is worse. A fetish is a fetish. The weight of dualism deludes us that there *must* be a correct life to live, that we have only to find it. But there are no guarantees because history is not a narrative. It is only the lives wasted by it.

Marxists require absolutes because they rightly see that relativism is the most absolute worldview of all.[15] But because liberalism is a sham does not mean that other absolutes are available to us—except the notion that "absolute" is a literary artifact. Better to vest truth in an ideal speech situation of coequal speakers than in an elite, whether philosophers or Party officials. The relativity of truth does not mean we cannot try to achieve consensus, indeed to change the world, with every speech act. Without trying to do so, we can never achieve fundamental social change. In any case, we do not have the opportunity to indulge ourselves, especially today, for thought cannot deny what it finds, notably a world increasingly closed to books in which thought reposes as the negation of things. The Marxist dismissal of culture as a realm of struggle is wishful thinking. The colonizing forces of administration penetrate *everywhere*, requiring us to reformulate Marx's literal base/superstructure in historically and politically adequate terms.

We do not have the luxury of avoiding discussions of the text in a time when books—*thoughts*—are things. This does not mean such discussions must methodologize themselves in the fashion of deconstruction or provoke consciousness raising as in feminism. We focus on consciousness and text strategically not because we do not want to dirty our hands with material practices but because they have been politicized. Politics is where we find it—today everywhere but in the political. Some say that with class compromise, relative affluence, and the seeming end of ideology, the traditional arena of Marxist practice —work—has been largely depoliticized. But we know better; labor is increasingly proletarianized, women increasingly constitute both a reserve army for deskilled labor and a housework force, and ideology takes less discursive forms. Yet depoliticization is an empirical process as Habermas [16] has suggested in his reformulation of historical materialism. The realm of the political is where we find it, not necessarily where we want it to be. Positivist culture politicizes the seemingly apolitical—privacy, sexuality, textuality. Thus, critique cannot afford to decide intellectual and political agendas with reference to sacred texts especially where textuality is degraded methodologically into mere representation.

The crisis of Marxism reflects Marxism's failure to understand the displacement of crises into seemingly non-Marxist realms. Similarly, feminism fails to transcend its perspectivity if it cannot address women's oppression in larger structural terms, notably in light of production's hierarchy over reproduction as an axial theme of western civilization. I do not hyphenate myself as a Marxist-feminist because that assumes Marxism and feminism can stand alone and then converge tactically. Better, they integrate into a larger critical theory in which the modalities of oppression are addressed in a totalizing way. Thus, we do not ride roughshod over cultural particularities. We try to *reason* the world in making seeming differences similar, tracing domination to certain modal principles of hierarchy yet without effacing difference altogether; difference defines the good society where it embodies our human particularity as well as the nonidentity between mind and the world it would master and enlighten.

Deconstruction seems to give the lie to an imperial reason of intellect. It recoups Nietzsche by defying both liberal and left versions of mind's arrogant mastery of otherness. Yet reason deconstructively tempers itself by understanding what Habermas called the "universal pragmatics" of discursive competence and thus social life in a nontranscendental framework.[17] This means that we need not abandon absolute notions of truth, freedom, and justice even as we oppose prevailing standards of the absolute as projections of an unhappy consciousness. Critical theory, including Marxism and feminism, cannot do without an orienting notion of the truth with which to evaluate the empirical present and prefigure future possibilities. Yet critical theory's "truth" in recognizing its corrigible narrativeness—the fact that it could have told its story differently—*makes truth out of the community of versions approximating it.* I do not say that truth can be summed in a marketplace of ideas in which the most popular survive unscathed. Bourgeois scholarship modeled on marketplace equivalence fails to solve the metaphysical problem of truth; or rather, it solves it in a peculiarly self-serving way.

Instead, truth is the time it takes to trace its fiction back to a constituting authoriality, which in claiming it vigorously realizes that truth emerges out of contestation, discussion, gentle correction. Truth is not an object as opposed to a subject but subject's address to its own objectivity. We objectify truth because we realize that texts have become things, orders of nature, and not fluxes of sense and sentience. Marxist truth is the way we get to a new order of being as well as that order "itself." Ultimately we need a different language to describe their simultaneity, yet we will never get language to do all our philosophical and political work for us.[18] Text will ever be different from the world it addresses, and thus our social arrangements will need to be revivified through new accounts of themselves; our aims will always be defied by the world they create and then name. Thus, the good society will never see itself that way; it will need to reinvent goodness in democratic talk. The good will be *both* unconstrained talk and the order of being it creates.

We cannot specify the good ahead of the talk it takes to name it. On this basis Nietzscheans would abandon attempts to attain metaphysical finality mainly because the good has been viewed as a representation of nature and not the language through which we talk about social nature and thus reformulate it. Philosophy since Plato has viewed the good in terms of utopia, the image of a future order used as a guide to getting there. Thus, utopian thought has busied itself with social architecture, depicting the particular features of desirable social arrangements and then trying to approximate them in practice. But we must hear the double sense of practice—the Greek *praxis*, creative activity, and the sense of trial-and-error—in order to understand that practice cannot be established before the fact without ensuring its failure to precipitate original intentions.

Practice ensures that others will correct the original version, especially where that version requires practice to check tyranny. The only way to do good architecture is to incorporate revisionist principles themselves constituting the good—discussion, debate, correction. Anyone knows that things are made this way, buildings, houses, paintings. Creativity defies the original design and thus shows it was a good one, an inspiring imagination of what could be. Similarly, the good is talk requiring itself. It cannot be brought about punctually and then left standing without the revisions and different versions giving it life. That the Soviets declared socialism in one country does not mean it has arrived. By monetarizing and militarizing their notion of the good, the Soviets effectively precluded dialogical means of revising what Marx and Lenin first foresaw. Marx's commune and Lenin's soviets are now merely icons; they are as integral to Soviet practice as democracy is to American politics.

I do not say that the good is talk and all talk is good. Positivist talk silences other versions just as Derridean word play does little political work apart from showing the empirical possibilities of free mind. The good is a world in which talk discusses the world dialogically and thus prevents us from distinguishing between good things and the talk enmeshing them in their sense. In itself talk is a liberal diversion from real political work, although real political work is not a closed issue. Liberal talk separates itself temporally from the action following it.

111

But talk is practice even if all practices are not talk or text. Although political talk would solicit its correction as an essential feature of what it means by goodness, it would silence bad talk—positivist talk itself silencing metaphysical and thus political dissent as cosmically impossible. The recommendation of conversation is not Marxist if it supposes that all differences can be resolved merely through liberal democracy. The power of the strongest argument is only a regulative principle; today it fails because no argument is as powerful as guns and money. Conversation is a Marxist desideratum only if we add that conversation between unequals is impossible, frequently amounting to political suicide.

Positivist versions of the world will not give up their ghosts even if authorized as literary accomplishments. They will say "who cares?" and carry on. Talk addresses power by trying to convince people not to respond to bad accounts only reproducing seemingly unalterable social arrangements. We need not listen to the deceptive rhetorics of persuasion embodied in money, science, edifice, and figure. They will always be false because they foreshorten dialectical imagination. And we need not play the positivist game, trying to prove why socialism or feminism is possible with reference to so-called "evidence," for evidence is only a text intended to persuade those already convinced. After all, the standard argument against Marxism is that so far it has not worked—people do not want it, capitalism endures, inequality is ameliorated. But the future cannot be captured in a definitive account of what it is certain to bring. Unlike that of Hegel, Marx's dialectic, with existentialism, accepted history as the determinate horizon of many possibilities to neglect or actualize.

Critique criticizes while wanting everyone to become a critic, that is, an author. Yet it realizes that positivist writers would silence them against a rule of metaphysical indubitability, and thus critique addresses positivism only as an account to be opened up, not engaged in a reciprocating pursuit of common reason. Although a generous critique allows for the possibility of conversion, there is no reason to expect the world's custodians to be different. Tolerance is repressive where we must tolerate them but they not us (Marcuse et al 1965). The concept of tolerance could only have been formulated in an unjust order where interpersonal civility was problematic to begin with. In the war of all against all truce is equivalent to peace, if not real peace. A better order would make tolerance elemental, yet it would refuse to offer its courtesy to accounts failing to be tolerant in their own right.

Talk is only good where it builds community out of literary respect for other versions or vanquishes accounts intending to silence it on specious metaphysical/political grounds. Critique ironically loves humanity and hates certain humans, without apology. Rage and love combine in the passion of talk to change the world. Humanism mistakenly views a flawed world as a product of flawed human beings, for which it prescribes religion, rehabilitation, concern. Sometimes that works, but usually it does not. Negation cannot risk its own negation by those who are not sick or flawed but merely invested in a particular structure of being. Humanism also uses talk to change things, but in believing in the power of its reason it only repeats the arrogance of positivism to bring about a certain pregiven order. Scratch humanism, and you find corroded idealism veiled in the imperialism of good intentions. Humanism fails to comprehend the world situation in a sufficiently materialist way, preferring to understand social problems in terms of human corrigibility. But there is no question that people are flawed; the discovery of venality only surprises religion. Changing people in isolation from the world they reproduce and that reproduces them is less than futile; it is a waste of time and effort. Help is the indulgence of those complicit in structures they would not address as such. That is why American liberals historically care more about injustice in distant lands than at home; changing foreign policy is seen to be easier than changing whole structures in which foreign policy is only a minor moment.

Fast capitalism is both quick in its erosion of significance and lasting in the resistance it presents to negation. "Fast" like practice should be heard both in terms of time and solidity. We can see it either way: the world order is flimsily held up by the codes of money, science, edifice, and figure, and yet the world order seems to defy correction. Material practice enlists language to short-circuit thought, thus reproducing itself. Realizing this does not give comfort, especially where few would agree. But the failure to understand the structural force of significance's degradation only reinforces the given. We must realize that the "best" thing to do today is avoid the worst alternatives if we can. Although that may not be much, history compels an honest appraisal.

Too frequently the demand for practice, strategy, organization forgets its own reason for being. Sometimes it never had one. Critique without analysis expends itself harmlessly. The left schizophrenically studies Marx closely, seeking the key to unlock political blockages, and at the same time the left requires an undifferentiated commitment to "politics." Over time Marxist study groups become the sublimation of political action without seeing themselves for what they are. Reading Marx is important, but the left, wanting both science and politics, separates and thus confuses them. Bible study does not necessarily evidence faith but only a certain technical acquaintance with holy words. Marx is not a more appropriate object of study than Adorno in the absence of more direct political avenues. Few of us know what to do; indeed, critical theory tries to *theorize* its own inactivity in learning from it. It does not pretend that negative dialectics is a harbinger of social change but knows that without understanding the complex totality we will be duped by it.[19]

These are unacceptable alternatives: poststructuralism or orthodox Marxism. One fetishizes the textual, the other certain sacred texts. Neither understands its inability to capture a public world in theoretical terms for neither theorizes. They have both become method, suppressing thought. Ryan (1982) has tried to put them together but only ironically shows their peculiar disengagement. My own disengagement is only less peculiar, not less disengaged; I am disengaged on the evidence. Accordingly, I try to theorize the absence of publics and books in a way that I can understand and thus help overcome the predicament of what Jacoby (1987) calls last intellectuality. He is absolutely right: in the United States we have lost a whole generation of critical thinkers. In his terms, who under 45 has public purchase the way earlier generations of writers did? He blames the academization of critique among other things, and I fully agree. Scholarship has become thought minus the Dionysian; discipline is a force of crippling social control, especially for a sectarian left already disciplined enough. Critique hides within technical academic prose in order to survive (academic jobs, publication, tenure—the new holy trinity) as well as to find an audience no matter how forbiddingly small. Indeed the community of critical theorists, if such a notion makes any sense, is not bigger than the 50 academics Martin Jay (1984b) named.

Jacoby tries to be charitable in refusing to point the finger at those among us under 45 who do not write the public book—whether Mills's *The Power Elite* (1956) or Baran and Sweezy's (1966) *Monopoly Capital*. He succeeds not least, I suspect, because he is not much more a publicist than the rest of us. His writing for *Telos* will not sell in bus stations alongside the books of his teacher, Christopher Lasch, even if his recent (1987) *The Last Intellectuals* may conceivably become a left companion to Allan Bloom's (1987) *The Closing of the American Mind*. Yet Jacoby is right: critique must break out of its hermetic self-enclosure in a few inspiring books. That is the other side of what I characterized earlier as necessary intellectual heroism. Eventually we simply have to write in a way addressing the world, not only other

114

versions of it. I have tried to do that here even though I contend the world is increasingly bookified, textualized—thus preventing us from writing the kind of book Jacoby recommends. Thus, explaining why I cannot write the big book in accessible terms, I have my cake and eat it too. At least I know that the likely obscurity of this book *tells me something important about the empirical world*, namely how thought is either disciplined (if I do not get published) or (if I do) doomed to obscurity.

Nevertheless, whatever we want to believe, the options are few. My point is that we must learn from that in order to increase them. This requires plundering apolitical intellectual traditions like deconstruction in order to fertilize an ossified Marxism successfully vanquishing deconstruction as the useless passion it is. Although I agree with Jacoby that the loss of a critical intellectual generation is owed to the academization of thought as well as the suburbanization of the city, I have tried to argue here that something else is involved, too. Not only do we not write for an educated but generalist audience but *no one can,* given the way the boundary between text and world has blurred in fast capitalism. The things people read today are things, not books. They imitate the world from which they pretend to have autonomy and thus only reproduce it. Money, science, edifice, and figure are the ideologies today, as well as matter itself. Jacoby writes eloquently about the technical nature of Jameson's reading of a Los Angeles hotel as a "text"; I do not disagree. Yet the fact that things have become texts helps explain why books no longer enjoy a critical distance from the world, as they once did. Capitalism changes as it remains the same. That people do not read or write is a crucial empirical datum, explaining the trouble we of the last generation have in getting across to a politically recalcitrant but troubled public. No one gets across anymore, whether they are over or under 45. All generations are lost.

I suspect that Jacoby agrees. He admits that the generation of American publicists (McCarthy, Trilling, Bell, Howe) against which he judges the absence of his and my generation is hardly intellectually promethean especially by European standards. Edmund Wilson is not Karl Kraus, let alone Adorno or Benjamin.[20] But for those of us who are North American it is extremely troubling that we have not been able to sustain an indigenous critical tradition through which to make sense of our debts to Europeans and others within our own context of history and culture. Mark Kann has considered the absence of an authentic American left and decided it had a lot to do with our liberal-Lockean political culture precluding the Europeanization of our emancipatory imagery. In a later book on the takeover of city hall in Santa Monica by some Yuppie socialists, he approaches the problem from a more practical point of view.

This matters so much because the American brand of colonizing capitalism, sexism, and racism sets the world standard for oppression. Where we read Derrida and Habermas the French and Germans are protected under our nuclear umbrella, eat American food, and increasingly follow Reagan's political model of economic and social retrenchment. It is fine to read Habermas, indeed I would suggest we must, yet we still must address Americans in a regional tone, with unthreateningly popular proposals for a better social order. Jacoby largely ignores Michael Harrington,[21] yet Harrington is one of the few who has tried to write above the heads of academics about American socialism. That he has not been very successful in reaching the public world is partly his fault, especially where he has not learned enough from the European theorists.

In order to resist its own academization critique must keep its political desire clearly in mind. In order to resist its own trendiness it must understand itself and the world historically. That is no solution, but it does head off the typical impasses of criticism in an age swallowing negation. Even if we cannot change the world this time at least we avoid being wrong. In the meantime, one never knows how his or her version will be received, reciprocated, corrected. Not to take the risk of writing in an age suppressing text with its dispersal into things is unjustified, especially where we already understand what happens to writing such as this. The world is not seamless; how far from seamlessness is another question, important but not decisive. Adorno never meant that the world was totally administered.[22] He said that to provoke other defiant versions. Against positivism, which declaims harmony in order to produce it, critical theory names totality in order to decenter it, scaring us into prose and politics that would undo it.

The cliche that critical theory is resignatory is wrong.[23] It is pessimistic, yet it justifies pessimism on the evidence and thus learns from it. Marxist Bible study embodies the real fatalism captured in the notion that the revolution is bound to happen. Deconstruction, too, resigns itself to the unreal world of pure textuality, having given up on politics, really on history. The left says this about critical theory because its politics is unfamiliar, especially to pragmatic American radicals. Just as I said that critical theory must be Americanized in its way, so the American left must learn different styles of radical thought and dissent from critical theory, enriching its own practice in the process. That Adorno, Horkheimer, and Marcuse are "difficult" or "abstract"

116

is exactly the point. They are difficult because the world is difficult. Only thought that understands its public nature can make it less so, albeit not easily given the power of opposition.

That is what the orthodox left forgets. Critical theory looks power in the face by reformulating Marx's temporary optimism. By recognizing the miniscule opportunities for penetrating the haze of mystification critical theory is empirical theory, as I (1983b) argued. The charge tendered by mainstream social science positivists that critical theory avoids the empirical is simply wrong. We attend to the shifting bedrock of late capitalism precisely because we want to fulfill Marx's apocalyptic optimism, albeit in different terms. 1987 is not 1867, *Capital's* year of publication. Thought must think the differences between then and now, reassessing political possibilities including the proper stance of theory itself. Total administration only completely totalizes when we ignore it. By opposing the indirection of critical theory as political treason orthodox Marxists are the real idealists, avoiding empirical changes as well as structural continuities in capitalism. They avoid the empirical because they do not want a changed historical circumstance to shake their faith.

Critique survives as political action because it has to. Fast capitalism integrates ordinary political opposition, forcing politics to take indirect forms like the work here. I would prefer to have more direct political purchase; to understand why I do not I must look at the world and theorize it. I am trying to do that. As such, I commit a political act. Of course, it is not enough.

CHAPTER 7

Avoiding the Fetish
of the Sexual

MY ARGUMENT HAS been framed largely within the rhetoric and political problematics of Marxism, yet I have addressed feminist thought where I argue for a revalorization of the entire realm of reproduction, including both sexuality and textuality. In doing so we could better understand how textuality in positivist culture acquires a thoroughly productive role by provoking a world it pretends only to freeze in edifice and figure. In this way feminist theory has done much important analytical and political work helping me address fast capitalism. But for most feminists that will not be sufficient.[1] I will only have "used" feminism in much the way I say that mainstream social scientists "use" Marxism—in order to vitiate it.

Marxism has been largely oblivious to the specificity of women's oppression because it has accepted the capitalist standard of value in waged public work. In defense Marxists would say they must address capitalist alienation of labor in its own terms as Marx did when he unraveled bourgeois political economy in *Capital*. Engels then appended (1948) *The Origin of Family, Private Property and the State* as an afterthought. Although Marx was certainly justified in attacking the capitalist labor contract as a vehicle of worker's public oppression, his obliviousness to the private sphere in which women bear the brunt of unwaged reproductive responsibility, in addition to suffering exploitation in the public sphere, is rightly a topic of feminist critique. The question is how best to combine Marxism and feminism without being stymied by parochially territorial issues—not only who will educate the educator but what will the educator's sex be.

My own response to the problem has been to rethink women's op-

pression in terms of the larger hierarchy of reproduction and production, so-called private and public spheres.[2] Civilization, in splitting public and private, has privileged the one over the other. Greek
philosophers could inhabit the *polis* only because women and slaves
did the necessary labor. I have made this notion of reproduction's
domination thematic (see Ch. 2) because it helps me explain how textuality, like sexuality, props the dominant public order. In fact, far
from being secondary or derivative, reproduction including sexuality,
textuality, psyche, and culture *produces* social control where the public
order threatens to fissure and explode. Where the state manages economic crisis, culture manages psychic crisis especially where culture—
textuality, here—does not stand apart from the material world but is
deceptively dispersed into it.

Marcuse (1955) argues that sexuality has been dispersed in much
the same way. What he calls "repressive desublimation" in my terms
suggests that objects are sexualized precisely to divert people from
their own erotic and thus potentially political and economic alienation.
It is clear how public things have been sexualized in fast capitalism
such that authentic sexuality and intimacy suffer as a result. I have
tried to make the similar argument that we no longer write and read
books because books have become things that we prefer to "read," thus
reproducing the world of which they profess to be presuppositionless
accounts.

I do not collapse sex and text, but I theorize their dual subordination to the requirements of the male-dominated labor market. These
are more than economic requirements; what is at stake is an order of
being. Reproduction, including text and sex, is devalued precisely to
the extent to which production is valued, perpetuating an order in
which duality conceals deeper hierarchy. *It is only accident that women
are largely responsible for maintaining the realm of reproduction.*[3] This does
not mean that women's exploitation is not structurally crucial in fast
capitalism, for it is. But in broadening sexism into a larger understanding of western hierarchy in which realms of existence are split
and thus subtly hierarchized—like male/female—we can better understand parallel dualities like that of text and world together reproducing the given.

The women's movement is only a special interest group where it
does not theorize the oppression of women in larger terms. Feminists
will respond that I rob women of their specificity, a typical male-
Marxist posture. But no one has any specificity, and thus no nobility
of suffering, where total administration administers virtually everyone
and everything totally. The mainstream American women's movement

119

suffers from the sin of pride. Although the domination of women is crucial for fast capitalism, there are other equally important levels of hierarchy like text/world, nature/society, colored/white, and labor/capital. It is not enough to say only that. All these hierarchies have common roots in western dualism, and thus they must be theorized together, even if their particularities differ in their concrete manifestations. This book is largely about the text/world relationship and not about labor/capital or women/men because economic and sexual domination are not mysteries in the late 1980s. I do not forget them, but I want to relate them to other cultural phenomena like the eclipse of textuality only deepening them.

Feminists fetishize the sexual where they trace all dominations to originary male domination of women. This is especially tempting where Marxists neglect the sexual. But this temptation has gotten the better of the women's movement and even of large parts of feminist theory (Jaggar 1983; Donovan 1985) where feminism somehow stands apart from, even opposed to, Marxism. True, gender and class are different ostensible bases of differential treatment, of subjugation. Yet gender and class are only names differentiating the same process, the epochal subordination of valueless to valued activity couched in metaphysical dualism. That unwaged houseworkers and waged workers do valueless and devalued activity must be theorized as the historical contingency it is. Men did not have to oppress women or capital labor; it just worked out that way in history.[4] Marxists and feminists essentialize their oppression where they allow names like gender and class to do analytical and political work in *splitting apart the world's dominations,* then orchestrating them strategically—always too little, too late.

The world is a totality and must be grasped as such. We are all workers just as we are all women because our activity is devalued. While devaluation itself is a differential process, truth is not decided by a calculus of the greatest suffering for the greatest good. That men, even leftist men, have exploited women does not make feminism as the voice of a special interest group correct any more than working-class art is somehow truer than high culture because it is proletarian. Feminists understandably fear male hegemony, not only in the household but also in social movements. Yet that does not excuse ignoring, even advancing, sectarianism. Once we agree on the structured nature of a range of dominations, we must theorize them in a way that understands their common source, for they all have one. Here I call it fast capitalism, although others might call it patriarchal capitalism. Although names are important for the distinctions and hierarchies they suggest, they cannot do our thinking for us.

120

In this chapter I discuss two particular features of feminism ironically strengthening fast capitalism: first, so-called feminist methodology, and second, the feminist aversion to economism. While understandable, both weaken feminism. More than that, they strengthen the order feminism opposes by affirming its axial principles. Marxists have the opposite problems, scientism and economism, as I have suggested in the preceding chapter. The truth is not somewhere in the middle but on an altogether different plane of understanding.

Feminist methodology[5] rejects abstraction and quantification as male power trips. Instead it prizes direct experience and intuition, especially that of women, as bases of phenomenal knowledge. Feminist method in this respect closely resembles social phenomenology and ethnomethodology, [6] eschewing structuralist theories deemphasizing human experience and initiative. Feminist method's aversion to quantification is similar to its denial of abstraction. Number dominates, especially women. Furthermore, feminist researchers in this genre believe that anonymous survey research is immoral where the researcher does not form empathetic and political ties with her research subjects, even sharing her findings with them as a mode of consciousness raising.

Now much of the thrust of feminist method is obviously compatible with some of my earlier arguments for a deconstructive reading of number and figure. I also oppose the methodologization and mathematization of the world. Yet feminist method makes two mistakes. First, it implies that men are more abstracting than women in their nature as men; this only reinforces the biologistic bases of sexism feminism opposes. Second, feminist method fails to address the world in its own terms where it refuses on moral-political grounds to theorize or count. Concept and number are not essentially male tools but ways of understanding the duplicity of concept and number dispersed into the exterior world as self-sufficient texts in their own right. This book is highly abstract in places because it must understand the complex circuitries of material and ideal today. Similarly, only someone sophisticated in the metaphysic of social statistics and research methodology can understand the complicity of these intellectual apparatuses in veiling and thus reinforcing a metaphysical—thus political—account of the world. Science and number *tell* where they are read as texts narrated and thus narrating. Marx read money in highly abstract prose in order to unlock the political-economic secrets it concealed as well as to propose a different standard of value for socialism.

Feminist method is morally affirmative in a world that wants women to cultivate the realm of spirit and thus to be better nurturers, poets, "people."[7] Many women who work and write in women's studies departments exhibit a deep personal commitment to "womensculture" and "women's perspective" as a way of building a decent women's community and an alternative discipline. Although understandable, especially in a world that seeks out and then colonizes such pockets of defiance, this commitment to avoid the "world" of men, including their intellectual tools, only acquiesces to it by accepting the hierarchy of soft and hard methods. If intelligence is not biologically distributed, nor soft and hard modes of intelligence, then the subculture of women's studies in which quantitative method and theorizing are eschewed only allows men to continue to monopolize number and concept. Although not every scholar in women's studies eschews "male" method and concept formation, most women scholars who count and theorize work in more traditional social science disciplines.

Similarly, feminist method tends to apply itself only to women's subjects of inquiry, women studying women.[8] This marginalizes women's inquiry, ceding the rest of inquiry to men by default. More fatally, it makes the study of gender legitimate only in women's studies departments and not in the more traditional disciplines except where women study women's behavior in various subfields of a discipline (e.g., in sociology: family and sex roles). Although important for the study of women's experience and history to be legitimated, people who use feminist method tend to make the study of women their exclusive research focus and thus deny the validity of gender studies in traditional disciplines. By opposing the marginalization of women's scholarship, feminist methodology only increases its marginalization and strengthens the hegemony of positivist discourse as male discourse.

Positivism is not a male mode of knowledge but a historical development only contingently correlated with patriarchy and capitalism. Methodological humanism, whether ethnomethodology or women's studies, refuses to read positivist text on moral-political grounds; yet it fails to learn from science, concept, figure, money.[9] The monetarization of value in fast capitalism compels us to read money as a mode of signification and thus domination. The study of seemingly "hard" issues like income differences by sex not only discloses the world but also challenges the economization and monetarization of value—a directly political agenda. These difficulties raise at least two issues for feminist scholars: female exclusivity in the discipline and cultural fetishism.

Some feminist methodologists would concede that theoretical and quantitative approaches are legitimate in their own right but must be leavened by ethnographic attention to women's unmediated experience. Thus, survey research must be followed (or preceded) by qualitative interviews, even consciousness raising, in balancing soft and hard methods. Yet some people are "better" in counting, theorizing, interviewing, organizing—by sensibility and socialization. Nothing compels despecialization where intellectual-political strategy is concerned, especially where it requires considerable work to do adequate social history, ethnography, quantitative analysis, theory formation. Women to be politically apposite need not pay any methodological deference to soft method as if that method somehow essentializes women's intuitive, poetic being—a being forced on women historically to keep them down and dumb.

Nothing benefits the powers more than the monopoly and hegemony of scientific and technical expertise (Habermas 1970b; Mueller 1973). Political pedagogy, refusing to address issues of technical and communicative competence, does so at its own peril; these issues are crucial in fast capitalism. Admittedly, in the women's studies program at the State University of New York at Buffalo, where I work in sociology, women are offered courses in auto mechanics and statistics. Yet the foundational course in women's studies requires intensive cultivation of "women's spirituality," clearly the dominant epistemological motif in their undergraduate curriculum. Their students are taught that theory, concept, and number are male power trips, challenged best by humanities-based qualitative methodology. As a result, women's studies students learn virtually nothing about either social theory or social science research method. They may take "feminist theory," but it is taught by a historian.

Feminist method is supposed to be democratic; anyone can do it with the right amount of care for their research subjects. The democratic tenor of feminist method taught in the context of women's studies programs accompanies feminist valorization of "process" and group decision making. Indeed, women's studies courses at SUNY-Buffalo are advertised as "student-centered" (as opposed to the other kind) with collective decision making about "grading contracts." Yet a seminar was recently offered on the political and power problematics between women teachers and students. New Left lingo buttresses seeming epistemological democracy where in fact many women's studies programs are every bit as authoritarian as traditional departments, sometimes more so. Feminist pedagogy is often a power trip, as it is for many Marxists, the tragic outcome of lives spoiled by a corrosively authoritarian social order. Yet it advertises itself as something else, a conceit no better than the myth of consumer and worker sovereignty.

123

Thus, authoritarian women use touchy-feely methods to cultivate a women's culture. Although, unlike regular Marxist authoritarianism, this pretends methodologically to be better in its refusal of male abstraction and quantification, it is Habermas's "left fascism." Men on the left cower before the moral authority of women's studies because in correctly understanding their sex's historical investment in the hierarchy of production over reproduction they do not want to repeat it. Fine. But, as a result, critical work on sex-based oppression is further marginalized and loses connection with the theoretical and political totality required to give it local meaning. Although rape is bad, rape crisis centers are no more adequate politics than is this book or those by Adorno; they are necessary but insufficient. The cultivation of women's spirituality has exactly the same political outcome as Yuppie cocaine use—none, or worse.

Second, feminist method fetishizes culture, rejecting economic and political analysis—again—as male. With no concept of the totality, largely upper-middle class American feminists inflate the political importance of their own lives including their cultural participation—women's theater, music, film, pedagogy. Although no iron law, in a fragmented world devilishly difficult to conceptualize as a totality, it is tempting to project one's own version of personal and political practice. Community building and organizing are important in their own right, but the privileged community of most American feminist thinkers offers a particularly unreal model for others' struggle. Indeed, this culturalist fetish is deepened by the feminist methodological injunction to focus on the personal and local; thus, our women's studies program offers seminars on the authority problems between women faculty and women students and not on more global intellectual and political topics.

Culture, as everything today, is differentially shared and controlled. Our campus boasts a women's reading/discussion group in which most well-connected senior faculty women participate regularly. Of course, there are no men. Moreover, they do not welcome junior women faculty ("they should start their own group"), especially those outside of the humanities-based women's faculty community. In spite of New Left lingo,[10] American feminism reproduces the world's hierarchy virtually on every level. Privileged senior women subordinate junior women; the only difference between them and the rest of the capitalist world is that they run a seminar on it, endlessly wallowing in the self-referencing self-consciousness making themselves their own most engaging analytical topic.

Although economism, the reduction of everything to class, surely is misguided, feminist fixation on the cultural closes off the economy and polity from critical scrutiny. Like the fetish of the textual, culture's fetishism reflects a lot about the social situation of privileged women relatively unburdened of economic difficulties. Women's studies programs these days typically scramble to "find" women faculty and students interested in economics because they know they have neglected it. Women's studies departments tend to be located in or near humanities departments and thus lack a social science orientation fruitfully relating culture and political economy.[11]

This is somewhat less true of the overall American women's movement in which issues of comparable worth and affirmative action are central to the agenda.[12] But feminist theory, my topic here, is academized in exactly the way Marxist thought usually is. Women's studies programs are not responsible for the larger women's movement, but to the extent to which they represent the universal interest of women their avoidance of economics is telling. Where the male left has tended to neglect sexuality, housework, and culture as epiphenomenal, feminists reify culture, virtually in counterposition. This gets us nowhere.

Historically, the fetish of culture emerged from women's experience in the New Left where issues of culture and everyday life were more important than economic concerns. Although, as Marcuse (1969) has argued, this helped mitigate orthodox Marxist economism as well as democratized the New Left, today it continues to mislead. This is not an either/or—economics instead of culture. Critical theory thinks the interrelations between the two by illuminating the analytical possibilities of a thoroughgoing materialism. Feminist thought is idealist by default. By rejecting male economism, feminists abandon the realm of political economy—of structure generally.

Biographically it is easy to see why this happens. Most academic feminists are upper-middle class and so go to movies and concerts, thus valorizing cultural politics. Epistemologically it is also easy to see why this happens where feminist method inherently disqualifies nonexperiential knowledge as male. Culture is accessible to immediate experience, especially where culture is regarded nonmaterially, as non-Marxist-feminists do. Dating from Millett (1970), the topic of much feminist research is literature, film, art, and music. As numerous left aestheticians like Marcuse, Benjamin, and Adorno have shown, cultural topics can readily be treated materialistically, as I have tried to do here.[13] Yet feminist method is nonmaterialist, and thus women's studies survey women's oppressions and achievements in the realm of culture without a theory of the totality within which cultural expression and oppression take on significance.

125

It is not obvious that women's depiction in novel or movie is a political topic. To win the point one needs a theory of the political, of *totality*. This is not to endorse a "Marxist" theory of art; that only begs the question which Marx—Lukacs's, Goldmann's, Adorno's? If words cannot do our work for us, likewise we cannot read novel or film without constructs demonstrating the politics of one's reading. That middle-class feminist professors go to movies does not mean that feminist film criticism is legitimate as political work. The issue has to be argued, and in *terms*, in *concepts*, *theoretically*. And in this world theory will frequently have absolutely nothing to do with people's direct experiences but will think experience as it has been channeled, even rendered unconscious, by huge structuring forces of economy, polity, sexuality, culture—text.

None of this means that we cannot develop appropriate methodologies or approaches to cultural studies. Yet critical theory interrogates the rights of disciplines to exist and of people within disciplines to continue to study what they do, even if their topics have empirical referents in today's world. Feminists exist, but that does not mean there should be feminist methodology. Culture exists, but that does not mean we should study it. For all that, in this book I have tried to exemplify better method in a concrete approach to culture. In what way is it feminist? For that matter, how is it Marxist? To answer these questions requires more than a few slogans or emotional commitment. It requires a theory of the totality within which we comprehend sex and class domination and thus elaborate methods and topics with which to do critical work. My method might be called critique, in its multiple senses, and my topic is fast capitalism—a capitalism in which books are things and things books. As such, sex is a kind of text and text is a kind of sex, a way of reproducing reproduction's own production subordinate to a productivist rule of value.

As it stands, feminism is too frequently just a lifestyle, a mode of cultural self-expression and identification separating outsiders and insiders. This is especially true in the university where senior feminists evaluate other women for cultural, not intellectual, correctness. A friend of mine is in trouble because she blow-dries her hair and wears preppie clothes, even though she does not shave her legs. Cultural commitment replaces intellectual and political criteria with which to evaluate true belief. Dress, use of cosmetics, taste in culture, sexual identity, and expression all signify feminist appropriateness. But these things really connote one's degree of obedience to pregiven standards set by senior feminists with which to control other women. No matter how vigorously these feminists might proclaim women's community, they shatter community with their power-tripping and cultural hyper-evaluativeness—what amounts to the love of self. This is not to say that we do not or should not evaluate other people but that these should be explicitly *political* evaluations comprising a nest of intellectual and political attitudes and actions; and they should reflect a democracy of mood instead of indulging difference only as a slogan. The feminist left does not avoid the male left's corruption by the authoritarianism they both profess to oppose.

American feminism is too cultural, hierarchical, liberal, trivial. American Marxism scarcely exists. American feminists, like almost everyone else, cannot transcend the essentially individualistic grounds of our political history, and thus they formulate their defiance in irrelevant and self-aggrandizing ways. Many academic feminists I know are "in therapy," acknowledging that the problem is themselves. I am not denying that the personal is also political or that we all share the emotional problematics of the time. I insist, though, that American academic feminists inflate the political nature of the personal in projecting and then trying to resolve their own lack of love, authority, identity. Marxists have always been accused of doing this. Yet feminism differs in two ways: it thematizes the personal as a strategic battleground, and it is inappropriate on the left for women to be criticized.

Although the personal is political, it also remains personal.[14] American feminists depoliticize politics and economics by attending too much to themselves. People matter, but they do not willy-nilly constitute the totality. Similarly, there is nothing wrong with interrogating feminist theory and practice even if the critic is either a man or a woman who blow-dries her hair. Individualism reveals illiberalism where it substitutes itself for everyone and everything else. But the self is not a political agenda, even though social change would doubtless allow us to become authentic versions of whatever we were meant to be. Feminists who want everyone to be like them thus work out their own personality and identity problems; political strategy is but an excuse for private psychodrama. And cultural ephemera like dress and hair styles matter so much because feminists recognize that in fast capitalism dress and hair are texts, signifying where traditional signifiers like words and books lose salience.

This characterization is overdrawn. There are political women who understand the dialectical nonidentity of personality and politics and who shelter and thus nurture diversity.[15] Yet they are not the norm. American academic feminism is a sorority rush including some women —not the preppies but those who wear Birkenstocks, perhaps, and celebrate their obesity—and excluding others—quantitative, conventional, just different. This differentiation does not divide around sexual preference these days, for lesbian feminism as a political practice is virtually dead. Liberal academic feminism is relentlessly straight, even familied. *It is tenured. It is bourgeois*—like virtually everything else.

The options are more than two: either tenured feminism with its proscriptive dress and thought codes or an antifeminism denying the relevance of issues of gender. Of course, some take a third (and fourth and fifth) position already. But I am interested in the eclipse of feminist reason as a trend exactly paralleling the overall eclipse of reason. I have tried to understand this in terms of the degradation of significance. Feminist mind goes the way of all mind where we lose the ability to write and read books standing at one remove from the reality they address. There is no reason why Marxists and feminists should not be caught up in fast capitalism, granted exemption from the falling rate of intelligence (Jacoby 1976). But I address the falling rate of Marxist and feminist intelligence because it is chic to grant them exemptions, especially feminism. Ours is an age of fetishes: Derrida, postmodernism, television, post-Marxism, women's studies, economism. All of these are slogans. None of them as slogans can do our thinking for us.

Feminists want to do all the talking where before—for virtually all civilization—they were made to listen. But feminism is historicized by its location in place and time. Thus, American feminism brings with it the liberal individualism and authoritarianism denying it a grasp of the totality, the biggest problem of all. Feminist theory risks being cant where it rejects a structural understanding within which gender is simply a moment *as a project of male mind*. Feminism in rejecting Marxism does more than resist Marxism's territoriality. It eschews the claim of a universal reason extended beyond Hegel by Marx, if imperfectly. At root, feminism is a biologism where it differentiates social being around the axis of sexuality, in this unwittingly converging with the dominant biologism of sexists who would prepare women for their inexorable role as mothers and lovers. Marxism is only a code word for male abstraction, antipathy to a poetizing feminism.

All oppressed tend to take on the roles assigned them by the dominant. Feminism in its individualism and cultural fetishes acts like a woman, avoiding an approach to the public world that would understand its complex circuitries. Feminist epistemology is soft, ethnographic, social-historical—anything but theorizing and totalizing. But that is what women always have done. Patriarchy denies women the capacity to think globally and to write and talk complexly precisely because it wants those powers for itself. Ironically, then, feminism celebrates its own engendered stupidity as a signifier of its femininity, its not-maleness. A graduate student from women's studies told me that quantitative method is immoral; rather, immoral is the refusal to understand issues of morality in terms of a larger structural framework within which the politics of language and knowledge could be addressed.

Marxism has been cant virtually from the beginning because Marx wrote holy books, usurping the intellectual terrain and giving hagiophiles something to do in the meantime. Feminism has become cant centering not on a definitive text or body of knowledge but on cultural and emotional affiliation. Feminism is to be a feminist, whatever that is supposed to mean in the moment. Both lose the ability to mediate, to think, their own relations to things in a way affording insight into what they have become and what they yet need to be. I do not have a version that resolves every irony of the relationship between the personal and political but at least I have a version. My analysis of fast capitalism particularly addresses the way mind and voice themselves are disciplined in losing the capacity to signify and thus oppose a larger world. Feminist critique describes modes of women's cultural disfiguration; yet it offers little structured understanding of this and thus few insights into where to intervene politically.

In reinterpreting feminism as a critique of the subordination of private to public, reproduction to production, I seem to take male liberties with the women's movement and women's issues. But they are my issues where I understand differential dominations to belong to the same complex circuitry of world history. We are all women to the extent to which we participate in the devaluation of our activity; we are all workers, too, to the extent to which we participate in contracts, especially labor contracts, that work against our interests. Saying this is not meant to obliterate differences, for some of us are more "women" than others and some more proletarian. Nonetheless at root there is a commonality of interests and oppressions among the world's billions —precisely the hardest thing to think, and enact, where we are so fragmented.

I dispute that feminism is even *about* sexuality except in a trivial and obvious sense.[16] It is about how valueless activity, accepting its own valuelessness, reproduces its own subordination and enriches those who control the realm of value. Surely sexuality is involved where women have been assigned historical responsibility for the domain of reproduction and where, in turn, they have been sexually subjugated

129

under patriarchy. But just as Marxism is not about the working class per se, so feminism is not limited to the concerns of women, although it includes many of those concerns.

American feminism today is mainstream. As ever the forces of reaction continue to roll back certain legislative and cultural gains of the women's movement, but feminism as lifestyle is here to stay. In itself this does not spell the political irrelevance of feminism. However taken together with feminism's own thoughtlessness, especially its aversion to theory, the institutionalization of feminism in a superficial personal and cultural politics only adds momentum to fast capitalism. Similarly, the proliferation of "Marxist" academic journals and "Marxist" academics only quickens the falling rate of intelligence. At stake is what it means to be feminist and Marxist, how feminism and Marxism think and thus oppose the world. I do not want to be read as anti-Marxist and antifeminist, and yet I risk this precisely because I contest the established names and the work they do (and do not do) in addressing the degradation of Marxism and feminism into identifiable cultural practices—*Capital* study groups, attendance at women's theater.

Marxism and feminism have not comprehended their own degradation into text-objects. That bookstores now have women's studies and Marxist sections[17] does not necessarily mean progress, especially if, as I contend, the texts of feminism and Marxism have degraded simply into *owning those books,* not understanding and then reformulating them. To be a feminist is just another cultural choice, like vegetarianism, marriage, children, vacation, leisure activities. I have taught women's studies courses before, and I was amazed how little the women's studies majors really understand about what they are doing. Although they seem to share classroom power, the political nature of their work is suppressed partly by design of the faculty who are cultural liberals and partly because what it means to learn feminism has been degraded into acquiring certain books, clothes, language.[18] And even feminist process is ultimately belied by the fact that it is the "feminist" professor who calls the shots.

Of course, the mainstream students and courses are no different except in the sense that they never intended to be political. Other students wear their identities on their sleeve—fraternity and sorority membership, sports letter jackets, designer labels. Text has been degraded for them, too, and thus the opportunity to rethink the world given in the immediacy of the things surrounding them. It is largely the fault of feminist and Marxist faculty that the thoughtlessness of their own students is not interrogated in liberating them from simple obedience. *Capital* and *The Second Sex* must be read, but simply reading them does not constitute a Marxist or feminist commitment, especially where they are only labels, slogans, cliches. Left students say "patriarchy" and "class analysis" without having learned the traditions from which these words derive complexly.

A Buffalo campus group of feminists, including women's studies faculty, circulated a questionnaire about faculty research interests, hoping to build a "network" of feminist scholars on campus. We were supposed to say what types of "feminist research" we were doing; but how can one be feminist and split one's research into political and apolitical halves? The subtext is that only work recognizable as "feminist"—like Birkenstocks or Izod labels—counts. But work announcing itself as feminist may not be feminist, and work silent on its explicit intellectual and political affiliation might be the most feminist of all. The problem is that we were expected to know what they meant *and that we accepted that definition of feminist intellectual work.*[19] Again, mind succumbs to the temptation to let dispersed texts do our thinking for us.[20]

Fast capitalism robs thought of significance; thus, we let words think for us. Marxism and feminism are not immune. More than Marxism, feminism seems to need no explication. At least since the 1920s there has been much disputation on the left. Feminism has its own debates, but feminism is claimed in a way appearing to require no further explanation. A feminist is a feminist. Usually this signifies what one is *not,* namely sexist. But there is much more to feminism than its negation, although in a sexist society nonsexism can be an important signifier, especially for women and men typically outside of conventional politics. The feminist left is simply lazy where it takes for granted a common commitment to a certain view of totality encoded in its own name for itself, "feminism."

Let me conclude with a caveat. Marxism and feminism have been swallowed and thoroughly digested by the mainstream disciplines. They have been plundered for research insights and hypotheses. This is not simply a mode of cooptation but also a way of reformulating defiant voices in affirmative terms, disciplining them. Many disciplinary liberals suggest that Marxism and feminism offer valuable insights but should not constitute full-blown intellectual or political identities, given their tendencies to exaggerate. Indeed, this disciplining happens *within* Marxism and feminism where its scholars clamor to professionalize their work in legitimating its place in the university. Although in a limited sense it is probably better to be inside rather than outside the university in the late twentieth century—where else to go?—the self-disciplining of Marxism and feminism only accelerates their degradation into terms of dominant discourse. I am *not* saying feminism is useful only in raising interesting questions for I claim feminism fully. I am only suggesting that feminism like Marxism tends to degenerate into its own objectifications—reading lists, dress, cant —thus silencing the questioning mind within it. I would dediscipline feminism and Marxism. I would scandalize them, making them less mainstream, less academic, and not more.

In any case, Marxism and feminism have become fetishistic like everything else where their texts become things doing our thinking for us. "More" Marxism and feminism will not fix it—more courses, more graduate students, more academic publications. As always, the only way out is through. We must comprehend the totality within which these sorts of things happen to us largely because we are oblivious to them.

CHAPTER 8

Critique's Community

FAST CAPITALISM ROBS words of meaning, assigning those words to something else, calling forth a world they inscribe in their sense. I claim feminism and Marxism, yet I recognize that all claims are suspect where there are no more books—where the relationship between text and world has changed. What can it mean to write theory when writing disperses into the exterior environment compelling conformist readings? Is a book a book when only 35 people read and understand it? *These* are the crucial political questions of the time. Preventing rape and organizing unions have important local significance—*for me, too*. I run with my woman friend so she will not be assaulted by the legions of sick men who yell sexual epithets at her; I work in my faculty labor union so that the state of New York and campus administrators do not achieve even more control over our work and lives. I am trying to get our campus bookstore not to sell magazines objectifying women. I help people fight their tenure cases, as once I needed their help. I encourage students to *be free,* whatever that might mean.[1]

Although these things matter, they are not the central issues of the time. The most crucial agenda of politics is in reversing the order of value subordinating valueless to valued activity, playing itself out in many different domains of local struggle. *But it is difficult to be political where the world swallows mediation,* where we do not know what it means to write books for a public that can read them. Until we figure out how to write books again and ensure that they are not dispersed into the compelling "texts" of money, science, edifice, and figure, all agitational problematics have secondary importance. It is a matter not simply of writing public books but of understanding what the eclipse of textuality *tells us* about fast capitalism in which significance—thought—degrades into hollow things. Given my background and training, I try to do this theoretical work in writing, soliciting correction by readers working along the same lines.

Although there are a number of us, we are not a sect, nor do we want to be. Jacoby (1987) talks of the "last" generation of critical intellectuals now over 45, but he knows that is a regulative notion; people already interrogate the possibility of interrogation in a variety of local and larger domains. For me Marxism and feminism not only do not participate in this rethinking but hinder it by virtue of their canonical investments. Yet I still claim Marxism and feminism because I am not about to give up the words for what they could say if liberated to *say what they mean*. Thus, ironically, a lot of energy must be spent denying others' claims to be feminists and Marxists where they only reproduce the world's hierarchies in their own troubled lives.

Much (e.g., Lasswell 1930) has been written about psychopathology and politics. The argument suggests that some of the most troubled are the most politically involved. The male and female lefts do not betray this. Research is not required to know this: Gary Hart lied about changing his name and age as well as about his sexual dalliances; Joe Biden courageously concealed law school plagiarism while delivering stump speeches littered with unacknowledged phrases from Kennedy and Churchill. This is no iron law, either. One might understand it this way: People who feel their own estrangement and can theorize it by imagining solutions (their candidacy, a revolutionary party) bring with them the deforming problems spurring them on in the first place. To understand deeply the world's inhumanity, Marx surely knew his own inhumanity, as we all must. Indeed, writing is no less a neurotic compulsion than are more overt kinds of politics.

In the case of Marxism, authoritarianism is ratified in the interim solution of a dictatorship of the proletariat. As Soviet practice indicates, this dictatorship, once installed, never seems to go away. Feminism's authoritarianism is less rooted in doctrine, although it is nonetheless present. For feminist leaders other women are like children whose consciousness must be rectified; they need to be mannered in appropriate cultural, emotional, and sexual styles. It is no accident that academic women, especially those in women's studies, hold seminars on authority problems between older and younger women;[2] these seminars address the epochal problems of mothers and daughters in a patriarchal society.

At least Marxism and feminism still proclaim community, if they vitiate it in the difficult period between now and the dawn of a really better society. Marxism offers a glimpse of the totality and then attempts to impose a sweeping world-historical reason on it. It thinks structurally. Feminism addresses the way women oppress themselves unthinkingly by living out roles appearing natural, not historical. They each make consciousness central in changing history, even if the source of true consciousness is different for each of them—for Marxists, from the concerted clash of structurally opposed classes, for feminists from group discussion. Where Marxism is too often obstinately proletarian in slavish imitation of Marx's world, feminism is too often unself-consciously middle- and upper-middle class, projecting the trivial problems of academic and corporate women in utter obliviousness to the desperate lot of almost everyone else.

Critique's discontent with labels and slogans, including those of Marxism and feminism, tempts it to conjure up a whole new language with which to overcome the fateful dualities of western civilization. It must try, even if it trades on past usages in making itself understood. When I say Marxism and feminism, I mean my Marxism and feminism; I call upon pregiven images, and yet by using them in service of seemingly heterodox ideas of the political I make Marxism and feminism do new analytical work. It is also true that Marxism has not been feminist enough, nor feminism Marxist enough. But to splice them solves nothing; in fact, it misleads by implying that the two independent traditions are by themselves basically sound. I do not think they are. And yet saying so risks either fueling reaction—ah ha, Marxism was wrong all along—or irrelevance, private language.

Nonetheless Marxism and feminism are inadequate, too encrusted with unsifted historical sediment to separate what is worth preserving from the original legacies and what needs to be abandoned. This is more a problem for Marxists than feminists simply because Marxism has more literature behind it. For feminism, revisionism revises debates held only a few years ago. Both Marxism and feminism have lost much analytical utility because they are too dualist: the former too economistic, and the latter insufficiently economic. They reproduce the facile either/ors of bourgeois civilization by thinking they oppose them. Again, dualism is not merely a problem of language that can be resolved in neologisms but a political problem as well. As long as public cleaves from private and subordinates it, dualism has truth content.

Critical theory overcomes them both by preserving them. This does not mean that critical theory written by the original Frankfurt School was either without blindspots (e.g., its silence on gender) or can be applied willy-nilly as method today. Critique must pass over Adorno and Habermas while learning from them the rule of antimethodism; substantial criticism neither agrees to ignore its object nor allows its object to overwhelm it with its own mystifying presentation. Critique asks the question of its answer where we thought we knew all along that we were Marxist, feminist, antiracist, friends of nature. We can be again, although I believe these words will be very different from what they are today, notably in how they understand their own textuality in an era when textuality is most at stake.

Critique is not a frustrated author trying to gain purchase by attaching itself to well-read versions. It is directly political action, nothing less. The notion that radicals can be scholars is ludicrous when scholarship methodizes thought in subtracting from it the Dionysian, the passionate rebel driving any version of the world. The university today is not the site of critical transformation. This is not simply because it is another corporation, Nisbet's (1971) academic capitalism having ravaged the autonomy of mind. The alternative is not the so-called life of the mind for that forgets the body in the fashion of every idealism. Instead, rebellion wants to rescue itself from *discipline*, the excuse currently offered not to address a wider universe of concerns.

We cannot just *do this*—write clearer, more popular books or turn away from the university. Where would we go? Instead we must fight to advocate simultaneously the autonomy of thought when thought becomes a thing and the driving passion of thought to change the world. Both can be true, as I think Marx demonstrated. No abstractions have been more concrete than surplus value, alienation, falling rate of profit. Critique would even retain some of his concepts by adding to them. The goal is not just another architectonic system, adding new theories to old, but a reinvigoration of text's intervention in the world that the world threatens to swallow. Writing may be most directly effective where most abstract, given the affirmative nature of concreteness in a pragmatic culture.

Beyond saying that, I cannot be more programmatic. To recommend a certain "kind" of writing, or topic, should already write in that voice. If it does not, then it is empty. One cannot imagine a book on how to write critique; one can only criticize. In particular, writing, in reversing its tendency to become a thing, writes about how it tends to become a thing. Issues of form and content blur to the point of virtual indistinguishability. The best we can do is *reauthor the world as the text—the history—it has become,* thus opening the way for new texts and new histories. If in doing so we run the risk of overvaluing the textual and reproduction generally, we need only look outward to the world to reassure ourselves that productivism holds sway. There is little danger in overvaluing the textual where textuality has virtually no purchase today, even if it seems to have a lot. Anyway, we can only address the world in a text risking the impression that textuality is everything. But text is only a way of gaining autonomy from the things we would make differently.

In my concluding remarks, let me return to the notion of discourse as power, expressing our relationship to the public. Reason's eclipse contingently forces us to reconceptualize conception where otherwise thought and language are dispersed into social nature merely as iterable things—money, science, edifice, and figure. The text gains such significance today because its significance erodes in fast capitalism. One day writing will be only one among many possible modes of creative self-expression; today it is the most credible vehicle of opposition where we no longer enjoy a contemplative relation to the object world and thus cannot appraise it evaluatively or analytically. All mind is sucked into the vortex of the phenomenal present, losing the capacity to reason the world differently. My argument, thus, is about history and the way writing inserts us into it.

The problem with positivism chasing social laws is that the account of those laws conceals the necessity of accounts compelling adjustment and affirmation. A seamless world needs no ideological support, no falsehoods masquerading as the truth. The world needs disguised texts to compel readers' conformity, denying them the capacity to write. This already reveals history's openness. Too frequently we choose not to see it. Nevertheless the present and future are inherently discontinuous; only text connects them today. It could as well rupture them in reformulating the possibility of social being. It all depends on our failure to read "fate" as a narrative.

The notion of text risks becoming a metaphor, as in deconstruction. The world is not *like* a text; it *is* a text where the notion of significance has changed. One day we might create a world in which books are reduced in cosmic significance, losing their desperate tension with the world swallowing them and thus all thought. That is the sense of Marx's image of an all-around person who criticizes after dinner (Marx and Engels 1949); he meant neither that criticism is everything nor that it is nothing. It is a mode of self-expression and creation available to us. Today I would say more than that; critique must do enormous work in reauthorizing a world otherwise enacted thoughtlessly. It frees us to do all of the things we are meant to do in a world without domination, and at the same time it is a paradigmatic mode of our congress with topics and the world. As such, critique both pre-figures and opposes at once.

It is difficult for many strategically inclined people on the left to accept that critique as a text both educates and constitutes a nucleic form of association itself. However trivial it seems today, with thought bureaucratized in the university, our address to topics and readers constitutes a thoroughly political relationship. As such, critique intends to bring about a world it estranges from the present one by authorizing and thus reformulating it. Critique in joining anger and hope acts politically, avoiding its fetish character. Without understanding its own political nature, writing spirals away from history in the centerless word play of the deconstructors. Critique that does not look to the history bringing it forth misrepresents itself as method; yet it opposes method as a ruse of reason—reason circularly reduced to principles of its operation.

Instead critique insists on its own value as a mind unwilling to accept texts' dispersal into things resisting their narration. In this sense it argues for a different order of value by representing it; reproduction is no longer subordinate to or derivative from the originary activity bringing it forth. Critique need not be unable to formulate plans or organize. Although Adorno was famous for not being able to cross the street without assistance as an emblem of his critical distance,[3] we can make our way across streets and otherwise act strategically without sacrificing reason's autonomy. Indeed the one makes way for the other. Without a sense of our connection to a larger public and to history, autonomy is experienced merely as estrangement, even isolation.

Every defiant risks that—going unread, unheard, unloved. Many risk more—imprisonment, poverty, death. For what it is worth I was once fired from a university job and almost was again. At stake were my politics, however much this was mediated by other things. At the first job, the story was that the department needed someone in quantitative methods, and thus I was sacrificed. In the second case, I was almost denied tenure because my outside letters of reference were not from people in mainstream departments, nor was my work published in the discipline's leading journals—no, indeed. To get tenure I had to pass as a safe, academicizing Marxist, not the other kind.

Although these experiences are common in many occupations, they need not be. Critique in being autonomous need not be overwhelmed by the administrative apparatus having little use for dissent. Things can be structured differently, especially where critique loses its isolation and comes to constitute a new mainstream. Yet critique also runs the opposite risk where it is simply swallowed, defanged, domesticated, as so many of us who work in the bourgeois university. The most sophisticated managers today recognize that a little dissidence is good public relations; even more, they recognize that the cantakerous spirit often stimulates new ideas if properly rewarded, mollified. Thus, Marxist and feminist circles have their own stars in the university.

In itself this is not bad, for it helps to legitimize defiance as an intellectual and hence political possibility. Yet most left stars buy too deeply into a world rewarding them handsomely. Some of the most obedient university citizens are the left's big names who stand up for the bourgeois life of the mind. But the price of being sucked in is a certain distance from the world one originally attacked. Again, psychopathology takes political forms where outsiders formulate theory behind their own desire to be insiders. A law of critique seems to be that the most persistent and effective rebels are those born rich or nearly so; they are insiders already—people like Marx, Castro, Mao. For those born poor the temptation of belonging is often so great that their intellectual defiance is organizationally curbed as soon as they hit the big time. Indeed, they are then paraded as examples of "responsible" critics; as a member of my department was overheard to say (not about me), "He is my kind of Marxist"—disciplined, professionalized, tame.

Our fame is usually not our own doing but simply happens, or does not. To the extent to which the culture of letters—now the bureaucratic university—has its own authority ladder, notoriety often polishes the rough edges off thought originally opposed to all authority structures as indefensible. Those who "make it" make it *over* others and are tempted to stay there. Nothing requires notorious thought to forget its passionate origins in opposition. It might even sharpen it. But how often does this happen? More likely is the case where the critic, in Sartre's terms, becomes an institution, agreeing not only to join the mainstream but to say that the mainstream by definition is now more ecumenical. Is this true? It depends on the sort of compromises the person has made to belong. Discipline cannot contain genuine dissent, for that dissent opposes all discipline, even if it joins it better to fight it.

American sociology is not a good test of these intuitions for no one is really famous anymore. Gouldner is dead, and even he was extremely ambivalent about the discipline's legitimacy—that is, he was not sure it was illegitimate. C. Wright Mills is reputable only after the fact, and even now he is largely unread; he is noted because he brashly polemicized in a Texas accent.[4] For their part, critical theorists inhabit a number of disciplines, usually history and philosophy departments. Fredric Jameson is a literary theorist, as such largely unknown in the social sciences. Perhaps only Habermas stands out as a citizen of many disciplines. In his case the cost of legitimizing critical theory in the bourgeois university, where before Horkheimer and Adorno were doomed to nearly total obscurity, has been in his own terms to "professionalize" it.[5] He now reads like a Parsonian; gone is the snap, crackle, and pop of the original Frankfurt School. Habermas's political impact on the established disciplines is an empirical question: where is he cited, read, really used by mainstream scholars? Virtually nowhere. With Derrida and Foucault, he remains largely a name.

I do not imply that Habermas should estrange himself further; at least he compels people to take seriously a variety of difficult oppositional vocabularies. Yet people say "Habermas" without knowing him or, even less, the Marxist and neo-Marxist traditions with which he is in dialogue. And for every Habermas there are scores of thinkers who go unnoticed. Yet within disciplines even mediocre people are known by virtue of attending professional conferences and promoting themselves relentlessly. They construct gossip about themselves in order to have their names repeated in developing a certain professional charisma. So-and-so—certainly not Habermas's equal—just left Virginia for Riverside; big deal. Unless it professionalizes itself in the same way, criticism remains obscure. And if it joins the academic meetmarket, it is banalized.

There are few universal intellectuals who have mastered wide-ranging literatures and yet focus their reading on problems of world-historical importance. Habermas and Foucault stand out as exceptions and, before them, Adorno, Horkheimer, Marcuse, and Sartre. They defied their professionalization, remained public intellectuals, and yet kept their distance. Of course, German and French intellectual culture made way for them. It is hard to imagine Adorno going to conferences and pressing the flesh. Publicity for American academics amounts to being on "Donahue" or the "Today Show." Since the 1920s, when European intellectuals first began to assess the failure of the Russian Revolution without abandoning the whole edifice of historical materialism, times have become worse for critique. It is not entirely up to us how we fare in balancing publicity and disengagement. In the United States, at least, the issue is largely decided for us.

Analytic philosophers would resolve all this by plain language as if we have a reception problem. But the problem of reception has much more to do with the level and content of our concepts than with style pure and simple, if there is any such thing. Literary stylization merely for the sake of obscurity is not a political gesture anymore than is the attempt to expunge complexity and allusion from one's writing. It is difficult to write clearly for a stupid audience, where I follow Sartre in saying that people are born smart but taught to be stupid.[6] Analytic philosophy refuses to think on dubious epistemological grounds. It avoids problems of history in favor of pedantic exercises; it grounds all this in a notion of philosophy's basis in ordinary language. Thus, it assures that nothing of substance or spark will be said.

Critique can manage the tension between distance and immersion where it refuses to methodologize its passion. Much social theory is about other people, not about the world giving rise to numerous articulations. I do not mean that at times we should not address Marx or Marcuse, as I have done, but that these are largely digressions necessary to make sense of the empirical world. Writing's topic is the way writing occludes oppression; sometimes it has to get to its topic through a discussion of the way other voices conceal the topic or, as in my argument here, are themselves concealed. The play of authors cited in authority chains only reproduces the world's hierarchy in the nucleic social units connecting author to wider literature, especially to discipline. Other people are pertinent to one's narration not in support but as exemplifications of other routes, other versions. As a literary production science can forge any illusion out of cited scholarship. Therefore, we should trade on the work of others only where we want to read them against themselves or to show the example of their critique as an alternative to our own. Accumulating experts does nothing but demonstrate one's own investment in a model of scholarship deciding epistemological questions by majority rule, a game we on the left will inevitably lose.

Critique is born of its engagement with a world it hates but also loves. No amount of "scholarship" can make it forget its desire to bring about a certain state of affairs. Versions content only to contemplate aestheticize. There is a place for them but not under the name critique; they belong in art departments, studios, or on stage. Critique shrieks of political passion without losing its distance from things giving it a purchase on independence.[7] I dislike so much of Marxism and feminism because under their own names they would rob minds of independence; ideological faith and apostasy are not adequate grounds on which to write writing or live lives. The left in fearing the mounting forces of regression cleanses itself of dissent in tightening ranks. But this only reproduces the discipline of the larger world.

The choice is not between remorselessly tight organization or anarchist spontaneism; indeed, the bourgeois world would have us make that choice, losing either way. The left needs to prize independence while directing its rage concertedly toward a dominant object, prefiguring a diverse world in the diversity of its versions. This does not mean that Marxist and feminist writing can say anything but that the issue of what it can say ought not be decided outside of history, timelessly. Indeed, Marxism and feminism are rich where they encourage dissent from within in order to focus their dissent from without. But today the left tends to forget this because, like everyone else, they would prefer to let slogans do their thinking for them, especially names differentiating those "for" and those "against."

It is Marxist irony that Marx's indefatigable example of intellectual independence now justifies dogma.[8] Sometimes the left disciplines itself even more harshly than does the bourgeois world, a hollow asceticism preparing for the eventual judgment day. Although only superficially more pluralist, American feminism is equally monolithic, especially its academic version where tenured feminists call the shots. Who needs even more discipline? But this does not mean that we should sit still for all possible uses of the words we use; frequently they are distorted in being coopted. In the university these days we hear a lot about Marxist this, feminist that. We assume that they are. But thought sleeps at the wheel where we fail to interrogate Marxist and feminist namings as the imposters they are. We must struggle to call things by their proper names, even acknowledging that propriety is located in history, not pregiven.

By debating the meanings of the words we use to describe ourselves and the world we do more than establish truth; in fact, we do not, for there is no definitive account of accounts. Instead we build a critical community—organization—in which we nurture and refine our opposition. Critique's community is comprised of the competing versions that correct each other according to a norm of gentle speech, thus prefiguring a future world in which this norm is generalized. Thus, to be a Marxist and feminist requires one to hear different accounts both of theory and the world in a way humbling one's own version and engaging with other versions as its missing sense. This community shelters truth by understanding its literary corrigibility, refusing to chase after the various versions of the absolute bedeviling western civilization since the Greeks.

This community does more than talk amongst itself for it attends to its relation to a broader public unprepared for its postulate of a dominationless order of things. Sometimes, though, to be political requires retreat, rehabilitation, reformulation. In those times, like now, critique's community shelters. This is especially important where we have lost sight of what it means to speak and write publicly in fast capitalism. Community's critique helps us find our voices once again by redrawing the line between its text and the world today engulfing it. Critique also does the important analytic work of authorizing money, science, edifice, and figure that it then turns into literary accounts as a way of proposing a different history. Critique and construction converge in these texts made to say differently what they fail to say today in fast capitalism.

Critique's community substitutes its norm of dialogical reciprocity for the rule of discipline prevailing in the exterior world today. It proposes itself as an alternative mode of social organization where it rejects the rule of discipline only suppressing reason on specious ontological grounds. In dedisciplining, critique offers thought an alternative public context, not defined by hierarchy and fealty to canons. It makes canon a literary accomplishment to which all may add narratively, and then it turns its literary artifice into a constructive political theory where it suggests a mode of intertextuality as the basis of a more rational polity. Where discipline hierarchizes and deauthorizes—the essence of fast capitalism—critique democratizes and authorizes, inherently portraying truth as a corrigible accomplishment of everyday practical reason in a society in which dialogue chances, indeed social intelligence, are more or less equally shared.

Fast capitalism shatters community and then recreates artificial communities—sociology calls them aggregates—around common cultural texts of money, science, edifice, and figure. Real community requires a self-generated site of meaning intersubjectively constituted and reconstituted. We must write the book of books over and over again. This is not to say that "community" should be a new slogan; too soon the word community will lose its power. Indeed, it probably lost it long ago. Critique intends community by hearing its own undecidability, its inherent lack of closure, in the focused way it attacks a world seemingly impervious to other versions. Critique's lack of closure not only makes way for but also requires other voices. Thus, in a decent community language in Habermas's terms would intend understanding as much as a single version of the truth.

It is difficult in an age of science to accept that writing might be done differently, especially science's own text. Once we accept the corrigibility of all versions, we assault versions pretending the absolute while celebrating narrativeness for its own sake as the glue of critique's community. This sounds impossible only because today it is. The Archimedeanism of western civilization defies critique to be absolute in its own right, even where it denounces absolutism as dangerous hubris. That we want text back at a time when it is swallowed in things does not mean that any one text would claim eternity. Language dialectically intends the truth of ambiguity absolutely. We must dwell within the circle of its irony, lest we commit a new sin of pride oppressing people and their versions anew. One anchor of this cosmic humility is community, reminding us that we are alone together and thus reducing the pain of our isolation.

A Marxist who writes like this courts hilarity on the part of hardened politicos. But Marxism has paid too little attention to the narrative problems of its critique, notably how the nucleic social units of writing and response prefigure a whole social order. Where Marxist reason is inured to the ironies of its absolute critique of absolutism, it is no less oppressive than a positivist reason inscribed directly in the world as text. The struggle is not simply over history's meaning but over a way to say it that does not oppress, indeed requiring responses as a medium of the truth. Critique intends community by explaining how it has been bypassed in the past. Yet it recognizes that its order is inherently fragile, depending on a norm of mutuality bringing people together in the common project of writing history together—even if the story can never be complete or told without difficulty.

Marxism must meditate on these things if it is not to neglect the irony of its own narrativeness in certainty that these things need not be said. After all, Marx was no more than a writer; and like all of us he led a damaged life. We must always begin at the beginning, making plain how a different world is possible in terms that do not deny the implacable presence of the past. We must then complexly address the circuitries of power in which we ourselves are involved. Marxist analysis is incomplete without a poetizing vision going beyond mere architecture. We must know how we can tell the story of a new world without feeling that we are merely mouthing somebody else's words. While we all end up dead, there are different ways to die. We die, but in the meantime we can live decent lives as a way of living history differently. Critique thinks the world otherwise in order to show the possibility of different mortal worlds. In showing how, it already changes the world, albeit initially only in small ways.

The most we can say is that critique by hearing its own mortal insufficiency builds community with other self-limiting versions. Traditionally this has been called organization or mobilization. I have tried to understand the problem of left community differently because it seems to me that the meaning of the public is very much at issue today. In the way critique formulates that problem—for me, fast capitalism —it foretells its own answer. Traditional Marxism and feminism give guidance, but not enough. As texts they are integrated too readily at a time of many specialized academic books and bookstores but no general reading public, or writers able to bridge the gap. This is not writers' "fault"; yet they must understand it as a way of illuminating the general nature of the degradation of signification today.

In no way must community be founded on commitment to doctrine, whether it be Marx, Frankfurt, or feminism. In fact, it may not be where doctrine requires minds not to think. Mindlessness cannot be "correct" where it sacrifices the person for larger causes. Instead community relies on the willingness to solicit others' responses as gentle correction, indeed as the sinews of a nonauthoritarian polity. Writing able to hear itself as the corrigible perspective of a single author need not abandon self-confidence or tenacity. The more we overcome hubris, the more compelling our versions will be. Our writing must intend to achieve consensus without canonizing consensus in a way making us only acolytes.

By opposing the dominant center, marginal versions like Marxism and feminism tend to establish their own center as a counterposition of sorts. That is necessary. Without developing highly structured reformulations of positivist culture and its deceptions, critique remains groundless. Yet Marxism and feminism as texts intend more than truth by positivist standards. They want to be community itself, language games allowing all sorts of dissension, indeed encouraging it as the essence of human heterogeneity. Marx's unity of theory and practice is rarely read correctly. Instead of subordinating thought to the rule of political exigency, he understood how text is already a nucleic social relationship acting politically by suggesting a different account of the dominant world.

Marxism and feminism are too positivist in spite of themselves. They enter into discourse with the textless world on grounds of validity already established by a positivist culture. The fit of concept to thing, the positivist criterion of truth, only perpetuates given things. By accepting that standard critique attempts to formulate new representations, allegedly freezing history in the lens of science. But science is only one among many literary possibilities. As a form of practice, science intervenes in the world of which it purports to be an adequate account, *thus changing it*. Marxism and feminism will fail to best positivist versions without reifying the world to which they bear a merely representational relationship. History vitiates absolute understanding; thus, positivism is wrong. In joining positivism on its own terrain, the left loses, even strengthening the positivist version with insights drawn from marginal perspectives.

Nonpositivist versions of science need not relinquish objective knowledge; they understand the narrative contribution of subjectivity and intersubjectivity to the world at hand. That is, critique under-stands its own authoriality as the literary possibility of a different history. That science makes up the world does not deny it objectivity but only suggests that the world can be conjured differently. Phenome-nology educates science about its own historical contribution to what positivism contends is a timeless social nature. This historical contribu-tion is none other than politics, the intention of rhetoric to bring about a certain state of affairs. Marxism and feminism need phenomenology to remind them of their own literary, and hence political, contribution to the world they oppose with nonpositivist accounts of social being.

In a positivist culture everyone is taught to play the game. The left in trying to beat positivism at its own game—better science, computers, grants—only reinforces the culture disciplining defiance. This is not to eschew abstraction and number in themselves for they are necessary to understand and thus oppose the regime of figure and number in fast capitalism. But evidence decides no philosophical dispute, notably about the nature and possibilities of the social world. Critique makes its best case where it models a world it would create by its own galva-nizing example of openness and tenacious humility.[9] It must reject the prevailing standard of value—fidelity to the given. I do not mean that we should refuse to understand the world but instead to understand the way understanding itself reproduces it in a positivist mode. That is the most effective stance. We must refuse the dualities offered by western civilization as inadequate—either subject or object, fiction or science, women or men, labor or capital.

In the meantime, the problem of political struggle is largely rhe-torical. How best to get across when the language, even book itself, is claimed by a positivist culture? This is an empirical problem. Gen-erally, education must acknowledge and then try to unravel the dif-ference between false and true perception. There is no rule under which critical pedagogy can proceed. Liberalism hopes that reason will dispel myth, but its standard of reason is drawn circularly from the prevailing order—reason as technical efficiency, popularity, pro-ductivity. Didactic approaches to pedagogy also fail because they teach slogans but not how to think the slogans in reformulating them. Politi-cal education is a tautology; all education does the difficult work of opening concepts to new formulations of them.

I conclude by noting that I have only so much control over my own reception. This is the problem with which I began. Misreadings pro-liferate in a world in which book culture is all but dead. Worse than misreadings are methodologizations, academizations. This book has not been a "contribution to scholarship" if that means I added to a preexisting body of knowledge structured by a hierarchy of experts. I have tried to decompose Marxist and feminist knowledge about capitalism and sexism by viewing them differently. I have tried to make empirical and political sense of the local problem of distorted communication by reading fast capitalism. In this I have done some political work. Not much, I suspect, but more than nothing. And that is a lot today.

Notes

Introduction. Writing a Book When Books Do Not Exist

1. For example, see my *Western Marxism: An Introduction* (Santa Monica: Goodyear, 1979) for a general discussion of Marxism. Also see Martin Jay's *The Dialectical Imagination* (Boston: Little Brown, 1973) as well as *Marxism and Totality* (Berkeley: University of California Press, 1984). For a good introduction to the corpus of critical theory as a whole, see David Held's *Introduction to Critical Theory* (Berkeley: University of California Press, 1980). For a sampling of original Frankfurt works, see Theodor Adorno, *Negative Dialectics* (New York: Seabury, 1973); Max Horkheimer and Theodor Adorno, *Dialectic of Enlightenment* (New York: Herder and Herder, 1972); Max Horkheimer, *Eclipse of Reason* (New York: Seabury, 1974); Jurgen Habermas, *Knowledge and Human Interests* (Boston: Beacon, 1971) and *The Theory of Communicative Action*, Vol. 1 (Boston: Beacon, 1984) and Vol. 2 (Boston: Beacon, 1987); Herbert Marcuse, *Eros and Civilization* (New York: Vintage, 1955) and *One-Dimensional Man* (Boston: Beacon, 1964). For discussions of feminist theory, see Alison Jaggar, *Feminist Politics and Human Nature* (Totowa, N.J.: Roman and Allanheld, 1983) and Josephine Donovan, *Feminist Theory* (New York: Ungar, 1985). For discussions of deconstruction, see Jonathan Culler, *On Deconstruction* (Ithaca: Cornell University Press, 1982) and Michael Ryan, *Marxism and Deconstruction* (Baltimore: Johns Hopkins University Press, 1982). For readings in deconstruction, see Jacques Derrida, *Of Grammatology* (Baltimore: Johns Hopkins University Press, 1976) and *Writing and Difference* (Chicago: University of Chicago Press, 1978). For works combining feminism and poststructuralism, see Julie Kristeva, *Desire in Language* (New York: Columbia University Press, 1980) and Luce Irigaray, *This Sex Which is Not One* (Ithaca: Cornell University Press, 1985).

2. I have read Adorno and Marcuse together in works such as *Western Marxism*; "A Critical Theory of Dialogue," *Humanities in Society* 4, no. 1 (Winter 1981): 7–30; "The Dialectic of Desire: The Holocaust, Monopoly Capitalism and Radical Anamnesis," *Dialectical Anthropology* 8, nos. 1–2 (1983): 75–86; "On Happiness and the Damaged Life," in John O'Neill, ed., *On Critical Theory* (New York: Seabury, 1976); and "Marcuse's Freudian Marxism," *Dialectical Anthropology* 8, no. 4 (1982): 319–36.

3. An early reflection on the issue of public and private I have found useful is John O'Neill's, "Public and Private Space," in his *Sociology as a Skin Trade* (New York: Harper and Row, 1972).

4. For other discussions of the aesthetics and social theory of "reading," see Harold Bloom, *A Map of Misreading* (New York: Oxford University Press, 1975); Rosalind Coward and John Ellis, *Language and Materialism: Developments in Semiology and the Theory of the Subject* (London: Routledge and Kegan Paul, 1977); and Wolfgang Iser, *The Act of Reading: A Theory of Aesthetic Response* (Baltimore: Johns Hopkins University Press, 1978).

5. For Sartre's discussion of political literature, see *What is Literature?* (New York: Harper and Row, 1965).

6. Theodor Adorno, *Negative Dialectics*, p. 4.

7. For a discussion of Adorno, and particularly of his relation to post-structuralism, see Martin Jay, *Adorno* (Cambridge: Harvard University Press, 1984). Also see his "Habermas and Modernism," *Praxis International* 4, no. 1 (1984): 1–14, where he raises issues of cultural critique I address here, albeit in different ways.

8. Although I am not sure he would agree with the tenor of this book, I draw something about the political nature of narrative from Fredric Jameson's *The Political Unconscious* (Ithaca: Cornell University Press, 1981). I also draw general inspiration about the Marxism/deconstruction problematic from Terry Eagleton's work, particularly *Literary Theory* (Minneapolis: University of Minnesota Press, 1983).

9. The two basic Frankfurt versions of a neo-Marxist critique of ideology are Jurgen Habermas's "Technology and Science as 'Ideology,' " in his *Toward a Rational Society* (Boston: Beacon, 1970) and Marcuse's *One-Dimensional Man* and his *An Essay on Liberation* (Boston: Beacon, 1969). I have addressed these two sources of the Frankfurt theory of ideology in my "Marcuse and Habermas on New Science," *Polity* 14, no. 2 (Winter 1976): 158–81.

10. Marx read money in *Capital*, vol. 1 (Moscow: Progress Publishers, n.d.). Louis Althusser and Etienne Balibar have read Marx reading money in their *Reading Capital* (London: New Left Books, 1970).

11. An example of this reading is my own *Socio(onto)logy: A Disciplinary Reading* (Champaign: University of Illinois Press, 1989).

12. For an example of the reading of edifice, see Michel Foucault's *Discipline and Punish: The Birth of the Prison* (London: Allen Lane, Penguin Press, 1979); also see David Harvey, *Consciousness and the Urban Experience* (Baltimore: Johns Hopkins University Press, 1985).

13. Horkheimer and Adorno make the critique of mathematization central in their *Dialectic of Enlightenment*, especially "The Concept of Enlightenment" chapter. Also see Ludwig Wittgenstein, *Remarks on the Foundations of Mathematics* (Cambridge, Mass.: MIT Press, 1978).

14. For a general discussion of Habermas's work, see Thomas McCarthy, *The Critical Theory of Jurgen Habermas* (Cambridge: MIT Press, 1978).

15. One attempt to "apply" Habermas, collecting a variety of Habermasian readings of contemporary social problems, is John Forester's edited *Critical Theory and Public Life* (Cambridge: MIT Press, 1985).

16. For discussions of the politics of postmodernism and poststructuralism, see Nancy Fraser, "The French Derrideans: Politicizing Deconstruction or Deconstructing the Political?" *New German Critique* 33 (1984): 127–54. Also see Andreas Huyssen, "Mapping the Postmodern," *New German Critique* 33 (1984): 5–52; finally, see Selya Benhabib, "Epistemologies of Postmodernism: A Rejoinder to Jean-Francois Lyotard," *New German Critique* 33 (1984): 103–26. Benhabib responds to one of the central texts of postmodernism, Jean-Francois Lyotard's *The Postmodern Condition: A Report of Knowledge* (Minneapolis: University of Minnesota Press, 1984).

17. Lyotard's *The Postmodern Condition* represents the more conservative valence of post-Marxism. The less anti-Marxist valence is represented by Jean Baudrillard, *The Mirror of Production* (St. Louis: Telos Press, 1975).

18. A typical postmodernist celebration of itself is Arthur Kroker and David Cook's *The Postmodern Scene: Excremental Culture and Hyper-Aesthetics* (New York: St. Martin's, 1986). Although some consume culture as a narcotic, postmodernists sedate themselves with cultural criticism. Under sway of this, the material and political context of textuality disappears. Against that tendency, this book shows what useful work cultural critique can do once harnessed to a larger critical theory. Of course, the original Frankfurt thinkers knew this all along. But it has been forgotten because they go unread, uncomprehended. The fad of Adorno has given way to the fads of Foucault, Derrida, even Habermas.

19. For a sociologizing account of book culture, see Lewis Coser, Charles Kadushin, and Walter Powell, *Books: The Culture and Commerce of Publishing* (New York: Basic Books, 1982).

20. Selya Benhabib examines the implications of Habermas's communicative ethics in this regard in *Critique, Norm and Utopia* (New York: Columbia University Press, 1987).

21. I gave a paper on poststructuralist Marxism at a Marxism conference held at SUNY-Buffalo in 1986. Someone from the audience stood up and said that he wanted more, not less, authoritarianism on the left; its problem is that New Left democracy went too far. Someone else said that I was unfair to Lenin in conflating him with Stalinism. Alright—they are different. Leninism is Stalinism minus the cult of personality.

22. How big is this community? I do not know, although I can count Russell Jacoby's *The Last Intellectuals: American Culture in the Age of Academe* (New York:

Basic, 1987) as a companion volume. I can perhaps also count Joel Kovel's *The Age of Desire: Case Histories of a Radical Psychoanalyst* (New York: Pantheon, 1981). There are others.

Chapter 2. The Domination of Reproduction

1. Guy Debord says some of the same things in his *Society of the Spectacle* (Detroit: Black and Red Press, 1972). The problem with the usual analysis of the quick pace of modernization and meaning is that it ontologizes it as an irrevocable feature of "everyday life" in the late twentieth century. See, for example, Henri Lefebvre, *Everyday Life in the Modern World* (New York: Harper and Row, 1971).

2. My use of the word "text" parallels its use by the group around the journal *Social Text*, including Jameson and Stanley Aronowitz. See Aronowitz's *The Crisis in Historical Materialism* (New York: Praeger, 1981).

3. For another sort of perspective on ideology informed by some of the same sources I cite here, see John B. Thompson, *Studies in the Theory of Ideology* (Berkeley: University of California Press, 1984) and his *Critical Hermeneutics: A Study in the Thought of Paul Ricoeur and Jurgen Habermas* (Cambridge: Cambridge University Press, 1981).

4. I have formulated an early version of my Marxism/feminism in "Marxism, Feminism and Deconstruction," in Christine Gailey and Viana Muller, eds. *Dialectical Anthropology*, forthcoming.

5. See Dieter Misgeld, "Critical Theory and Hermeneutics: The Debate Between Habermas and Gadamer," in John O'Neill, ed., *On Critical Theory*. Also see Misgeld, "Education and Cultural Invasion: Critical Social Theory, Education as Institution and *Pedagogy of the Oppressed*," in John Forester, ed., *Critical Theory and Public Life*.

6. This notion of a literary version of science is developed at much greater length in my *Socio(onto)logy*. Also see Karin D. Knorr, "Producing and Reproducing Knowledge: Descriptive or Constructive? Toward a Model of Research Production," *Social Science Information* 16 (1977): 969–96. As well, see John O'Neill, "The Literary Production of Natural and Social Science Inquiry," *The Canadian Journal of Sociology* 6 (1981): 105–20.

7. For other perspectives on the political possibilities of cultural critique, see John Brenkman, *Culture and Domination* (Ithaca: Cornell University Press, 1987); Frank Lentricchia, *After the New Criticism* (Chicago: University of Chicago Press, 1980); and Mark O'Kane, "Marxism, Deconstruction and Ideology: Notes towards an Articulation," *New German Critique* 33 (1984): 219–47.

8. Paul Piccone has explored this theme in his "Beyond Identity Theory," in John O'Neill, ed., *On Critical Theory*; "The Changing Function of Critical Theory," *New German Critique* 12 (Fall 1977): 29–38; and "The Crisis of One-Dimensionality," *Telos* 35 (Spring 1978): 43–54.

9. For example, see Shoshana Felman, "Rereading Femininity," *Yale French*

Studies 62 (1981): 19–44. Also see Gloria Steinem, "What it Would be Like if Women Win," *Time*, August 21, 1970, 22–23.

10. For a discussion of the left's tendency to undo itself, see Russell Jacoby, *Dialectic of Defeat* (New York: Cambridge University Press, 1982).

11. Jacoby addresses the problem of the academization of Marxism in his *The Last Intellectuals*.

12. The notion of a thin boundary between text and world is suggested differently in Jacques Lacan, *Écrits* (London: Tavistock, 1977) and Roland Barthes, "The Death of the Author," in Stephen Heath, ed., *Image-Music-Text: Roland Barthes* (London: Fontana, 1977) and his *Writing Degree Zero* (New York: Hill and Wang, 1968). Unlike these people, though, I understand the thin boundary in historical terms; poststructuralism asserts that the boundary is always thin—indeed, that there is nothing outside the text.

13. See Peter Rabinowitz, "Truth in Fiction: A Reexamination of Audiences," *Critical Inquiry* 4 (1977): 121–42.

14. Language as a forum of sexual politics is examined in numerous ways. For example, see Leslie Friedman, *Sex Role Stereotyping in the Mass Media: An Annotated Bibliography* (New York: Garland, 1977) and Dale Spender, *Man Made Language* (London: Routledge and Kegan Paul, 1980).

15. See Julia Kristeva, "La femme, ce n'est jamais ca," *Tel Quel* 59 (1974): 19–24. Also see Annette Kolodny, "Dancing through the Minefield: Some Observations on the Theory, Practice and Politics of a Feminist Literary Criticism," *Feminist Studies* 6, no. 1 (Spring 1980): 1–25. Finally, see Elaine Marks and Isabelle de Courtivron, eds., *New French Feminisms: An Anthology* (New York: Schocken, 1981).

16. See Sara Evans, *Personal Politics: The Roots of Women's Liberation in the Civil Rights Movement and the New Left* (New York: Vintage, 1980).

17. Jean Elshtain points to some of these insights in her *Public Man, Private Woman* (Princeton: Princeton University Press, 1981).

18. See his essay "Subject and Object," in Andrew Arato and Eike Gebhardt, eds., *The Essential Frankfurt School Reader* (New York: Urizen, 1978).

19. I have considered this problem in my "The Dialectic of Desire: The Holocaust, Monopoly Capitalism and Radical Anamnesis."

20. For views of the politics of deconstruction, see Andrew Parker, "Of Politics and Limits: Derrida Re-Marx," *SCE Reports* 8 (1980): 83–104.

21. This sociosexual approach to domination emerges most clearly in Marcuse's *Eros and Civilization*. For a reading of Marcuse, see Gad Horowitz, *Repression: Basic and Surplus Repression in Psychoanalytic Theory* (Toronto: University of Toronto Press, 1977). For further discussion, see my "Marcuse's Freudian Marxism."

22. For a discussion of this issue, see Terry Eagleton, "Marxism, Structuralism, and Poststructuralism," *Diacritics* 15, no. 4 (Winter 1985): 2–56. See Alex Callinicos, "Postmodernism, Poststructuralism and PostMarxism?" *Theory, Culture and Society* 2, no. 3 (1985): 85–101. Also see Jacques Derrida, *Positions* (Chicago: University of Chicago Press, 1981).

23. Adorno's most systematic statement of his aesthetic-critical theory is his *Aesthetic Theory* (London: Routledge and Kegan Paul, 1984).

24. I make an early move in this direction of rethinking in my "Dialectical Sensibility I: Critical Theory, Scientism and Empiricism," *Canadian Journal of Political and Social Theory* 1, no. 1 (Winter 1977): 3–34, and in my "Dialectical Sensibility II: Towards a New Intellectuality," *Canadian Journal of Political and Social Theory* 1, no. 2 (Spring-Summer 1977): 47–57.

25. See my essay on Habermas's relevance for latter-day critical theory, "The Dialectic of Deindustrialization: An Essay on Advanced Capitalism," in John Forester, ed., *Critical Theory and Public Life*.

26. I have said this in my "Marxism 'or' the Frankfurt School?" *Philosophy of the Social Sciences* 14 (March 1983): 347–65.

27. For discussions of the epistemological and political implications of fascism, see Max Horkheimer's essay, "The German Jews," in his *Critique of Instrumental Reason* (New York: Seabury, 1974); Herbert Marcuse's essay, "The Struggle Against Liberalism in the Totalitarian View of the State," in his *Negations* (Boston: Beacon, 1968); Franz Neumann's *Behemoth* (London: Gollancz, 1942); and his *The Democratic and the Authoritarian State* (Glencoe, Ill.: Free Press, 1957).

28. For recent examples of the essentially conservative and biologistic implications of feminist epistemology, see Heather Jon Maroney, "Embracing Motherhood: New Feminist Theory," and Mary O'Brien, "Feminism and Revolution," both in Roberta Hamilton and Michele Barrett, eds., *The Politics of Diversity: Feminism, Marxism and Nationalism* (Montreal: Book Center, 1986). For instance, Maroney wrote: "Perhaps the most interesting contribution of the new motherhood problematic is its critical re-examination of the culture/ nature distinction in relation to the prospects for a liberated technology and its location of this intersecting problematic at the point of birth. Here it shares the malestream philosophical perception of the unity of women and nature but interprets this as an evolutionary strength rather than a less-than-human weakness. It argues that birth, nature and female power and creativity are indeed linked and moreover that they each and all conflict with the outcomes of the male reproductive condition: exploitation, mechanistic rationalization and death" (p. 423). And O'Brien commented: "[T]he process of reproduction entails a *separation* of men from nature in the necessary alienation of the male seed in copulation. . . . The profound significance for materialist dialectical science of the fact that man's reproductive consciousness is an alienated consciousness has not been examined with sufficient thoroughness. In Marx's perception of human consciousness, consciousness resists alienation in terms of both thinking and doing. Have men, then, resisted their experienced alienation from biological continuity? The historical record shows quite clearly that they have, in both ideological and practical ways. The most common and most profound mode of resistance which they have employed is the familiar one of appropriation. Men have erected a huge social edifice to facilitate and justify

that appropriation of women's children which we call patriarchy" (p. 429).

29. For a discussion of the implications of Marx's reading of money, see Gayatri Chakravorty Spivak, "Scattered Speculations on the Question of Value," *Diacritics* 15, no. 4 (Winter 1985): 73–93. Also see Marc Shell, *Money, Language and Thought: Literary and Philosophical Economies from the Medieval to the Modern Era* (Berkeley: University of California Press, 1982); and Georg Simmel, *Philosophy of Money* (London: Routledge and Kegan Paul, 1978).

30. I consider this irony in my *Socio(onto)logy*, particularly in Section Five, "Sociology as a Literary Production." Marcuse has considered this in another way in his chapter "The New Sensibility" in *An Essay on Liberation*.

31. Alan Blum has considered the implications of talk for the world in his *Theorizing* (London: Heinemann Educational Books, 1974); John O'Neill considers this differently in his *Making Sense Together: An Introduction to Wild Sociology* (New York: Harper and Row, 1974).

Chapter 3. Books and Things: Texts in a Material World

1. For a general discussion of positivism and of some alternatives to it, see Norman Stockman, *Antipositivist Theories of the Sciences* (Dordrecht: D. Reidel, 1984). Also see Fredric Jameson's "Science Versus Ideology," *Humanities in Society* 6, nos. 2–3 (1983): 283–302.

2. This notion of the degradation of signification is clearly traceable to Horkheimer's notion of "eclipse of reason," a central Frankfurt motif. See his *Eclipse of Reason*.

3. See Fredric Jameson, "Postmodernism, or the Cultural Logic of Late Capitalism," *New Left Review* 146 (July-August 1984): 53–92; also his "Postmodernism and Consumer Society," in Hal Foster, ed., *The Anti-Aesthetic: Essays on Postmodern Culture* (Port Townsend, Wash.: Bay Press, 1983).

4. For my earlier address to discourse theory, see my "A Critical Theory of Dialogue." Discourse is a generic term for what others call ideology, textuality, even culture. Its use is suggested by Terry Eagleton in his *Literary Theory*, especially pp. 206 and 210.

5. The formulation of critical theory as discourse theory is suggested by Antonio Gramsci, *Selections from the Prison Notebooks* (London: Lawrence and Wishart, 1971); Paulo Freire, *Pedagogy of the Oppressed* (New York: Seabury, 1970); Jurgen Habermas, *Communication and the Evolution of Society* (Boston: Beacon, 1979) and *The Theory of Communicative Action*, vols. 1 and 2; and John O'Neill, "Critique and Remembrance," in his edited *On Critical Theory*.

6. This concern about methodologization is the substance of Jacoby's critique of Jameson's "reading" of the L. A. hotel. See Jacoby's *The Last Intellectuals*.

7. For a different sort of critique, see Charles Newman, *The Post-Modern Aura: The Act of Fiction in an Age of Inflation* (Evanston: Northwestern University Press, 1985). He is writing about postmodernism, and here I am writing about

poststructuralism; although I realize they are not identical, there are some important overlaps. One might say that poststructuralism is the theoretical reconstitution of the postmodernist rejection of ideology, politics, history.

8. My prose here seems opaque, even "difficult." Simplification oversimplifies a complex reality. My main point is that language in structuring reality is structured by it, thus becoming a material force. Deconstruction goes part of the way toward this understanding but stops short of understanding the historicity of the text/world relationship, preferring to view it as static, ontologically unalterable. That is why some on the left reject all textual/cultural analysis—unnecessarily, it seems to me. Fredric Jameson's *The Political Unconscious* is one version of a materialist account of the text/world relationship, although one not much less difficult than the one here, particularly given its grounding in literary-theoretic problematics.

9. See Karl Marx and Friedrich Engels, *The German Ideology* (New York: International Publishers, 1949).

10. The politics of authorial commitment are considered in different ways by Sartre and Adorno. See Theodor Adorno, "Commitment," in Andrew Arato and Eike Gebhardt, eds., *The Essential Frankfurt School Reader*; also see Walter Benjamin's "The Author as Producer" in the same volume.

11. Theodor Adorno, *Negative Dialectics*, p. 406.

12. See Bertolt Brecht, *Gesammelte Werke*, vols. 7 and 8 (Frankfurt: Suhrkamp, 1972). Also see Herbert Marcuse's discussion of aesthetic theory in his *Counterrevolution and Revolt* (Boston: Beacon, 1972), especially the chapter entitled "Art and Revolution," and his *The Aesthetic Dimension* (Boston: Beacon, 1978).

13. Habermas criticizes the romantic idealism and "mysticism" of the original Frankfurt School in *Knowledge and Human Interests*, pp. 32–33. I respond in "Marcuse and Habermas on New Science."

14. Paul Connerton has considered the overtotalization of the Frankfurt concept of domination in his *The Tragedy of Enlightenment* (Cambridge: Cambridge University Press, 1980), particularly in the chapter "The Critique of Critical Theory."

15. Habermas comes to terms with the continuity of Marxism and modernism in vol. 1 of *The Theory of Communicative Action*, especially Sect. 4, "From Lukacs to Adorno: Rationalization as Reification." Also see vol. 2, especially sect. 7, part 3 "The Theory of Modernity." See David Rasmussen, "Communicative Action and the Fate of Modernity," *Theory, Culture and Society* 2, no. 3 (1985): 133–44.

16. To offer only one example of the orthodox-Marxist critique of the Frankfurt School pivoting around their alleged lack of practice, see Phil Slater's *Origin and Significance of the Frankfurt School* (London: Routledge and Kegan Paul, 1977); and see my response, "Marxism 'or' the Frankfurt School?" My Ch. 5 here is also an answer of sorts.

17. For reflections on the notion of affirmation, see Herbert Marcuse, "The Affirmative Character of Culture" in his *Negations*.

18. John O'Neill has addressed this in his *For Marx Against Althusser* (Washington, D.C.: University Press of America, 1982).

19. Hannah Arendt also asks this question but answers it differently in *The Human Condition* (Chicago: University of Chicago Press, 1958).

20. The end-of-ideology thesis is offered explicitly in Daniel Bell's *The End of Ideology* (New York: Basic, 1976). For a different perspective, see Axel Honneth, "An Aversion Against the Universal: A Commentary on Lyotard's *Postmodern Condition*," *Theory, Culture and Society* 2, no. 3 (1985): 147–56. Against Bell and his conservative ilk, I maintain that ideology obviously has not "ended." Yet Marxism usually fails to comprehend *where* and *how* ideology is today. It has been displaced into social nature much as Habermas argued that economic crisis tendencies are now displaced into the political sphere in his *Legitimation Crisis* (Boston: Beacon, 1975). In an era beyond books, it is hard, but not impossible, to detect ideologizing claims—that is my thesis here.

21. See James Rule, *Insight and Social Betterment* (New York: Oxford University Press, 1978). Also see Robin Blackburn, ed., *Ideology in Social Science* (London: Fontana, 1972). Finally, see Paul Diesing, *Science and Ideology in the Policy Sciences* (New York: Aldine, 1982).

22. My argument here is a reprise of Marcuse's analysis of one-dimensionality, albeit enriched empirically with insights from literary theory enabling us to understand *what is happening* to suppress critique—notably the absence of a textual culture. See Marcuse's *One-Dimensional Man*. Also in this Weberian age, see Marcuse's critique of Weber, "Industrialization and Capitalism in the Work of Max Weber," in his *Negations*.

23. Maurice Merleau-Ponty helps me think about this. See his *Adventures of the Dialectic* (Evanston: Northwestern University Press, 1973); *Humanism and Terror* (Boston: Beacon, 1972); *Sense and Non-Sense* (Evanston: Northwestern University Press, 1964); and *Signs* (Evanston: Northwestern University Press, 1964). Particularly see his "Concerning Marxism" and "Marxism and Philosophy" in *Sense and Non-Sense*. Also consult John O'Neill's book on Merleau-Ponty, *Perception, Expression and History: The Social Phenomenology of Maurice Merleau-Ponty* (Evanston: Northwestern University Press, 1970).

24. Weber is the culture hero of modern social thought. He appears everywhere: Habermas's two-volume *The Theory of Communicative Action*; Peter Berger, Brigitte Berger, and Hansfried Kellner, *The Homeless Mind* (New York: Random House, 1974); and Anthony Giddens, *Social Theory and Modern Sociology* (London: Polity, 1987). People love Weber because like Nietzsche, yet without his desperate insight, he suffered his age tragically without offering utopian alternatives; thus, he is safe.

25. See Umberto Eco, *The Role of the Reader: Explorations in the Semiotics of Texts* (Bloomington: Indiana University Press, 1979). Also see Elizabeth Flynn and Patrocinio Schweickart, eds., *Gender and Reading: Essays on Readers, Texts and Contexts* (Baltimore: Johns Hopkins University Press, 1986).

Chapter 4. The Degradation of Signification

1. For a discussion of Marx's textuality, see John O'Neill's "On Theory and Criticism in Marx" in his *Sociology as a Skin Trade*.

2. Louis Althusser has tried to conceptualize ideology as a form of practice, not simply inert textuality. See his *For Marx* (London: Allen Lane, 1969). In other respects, too, he is surprisingly close to the Frankfurt School, notably in his notion of what it means to read Marx. "I said that Marx left us no *Dialectics*. . . . I hope to be able to show how we can find in these texts . . . the theoretical answer to our question: what is the specificity of the Marxist dialectic?" (p. 182).

3. For some examples of this emerging Marxist-feminist perspective on value, see Zillah Eisenstein, ed., *Capitalist Patriarchy and the Case for Socialist Feminism* (New York: Monthly Review Press, 1979); also see Leslie Rabine, "Searching for the Connections: Marxist-Feminists and Women's Studies," *Humanities in Society* 6, nos. 2–3 (1983): 195–221.

4. Isaac Balbus has considered the issue of Marxian productivism in his *Marxism and Domination: A Neo-Hegelian, Feminist, Psychoanalytic Theory of Sexual, Political and Technological Liberation* (Princeton: Princeton University Press, 1982). *Fast Capitalism* is my quite different version of the same problem.

5. See Herbert Marcuse, "The Foundation of Historical Materialism" in his *Studies in Critical Philosophy* (Boston: Beacon, 1973); also John O'Neill, "The Concept of Estrangement in the Early and Later Writings of Karl Marx" and "Embodiment and History in Hegel and Marx," both in his *Sociology as a Skin Trade*. Finally, see my discussion of the Hegel-Marx problem in my *Western Marxism*.

6. See Paul Piccone, "Beyond Identity Theory," in John O'Neill, ed., *On Critical Theory*.

7. This issue of the domination of reproduction, raised in Ch. 2, is central for modern feminism. People read the problem differently. See, for example, Nancy Chodorow, *The Reproduction of Mothering* (Berkeley: University of California Press, 1978) and see Adrienne Rich, *Of Woman Born: Motherhood as Experience and Institution* (New York: Norton, 1976).

8. See Walter Benjamin's discussion of aura and artistic fungibility in his "Art in the Age of Mechanical Reproduction," in his *Illuminations* (New York: Schocken, 1969).

9. See Russell Jacoby, "A Falling Rate of Intelligence?" *Telos* 27 (Spring 1976): 141–46. It is interesting to read Jacoby's *The Last Intellectuals* in light of his earlier *Telos* piece. His entire oeuvre develops the falling rate of intelligence in its various formulations—social amnesia, left defeat, repression of psychoanalysis, the academization of intelligence.

10. An early formulation of these themes is found in Bruce Brown, *Marx, Freud and the Critique of Everyday Life* (New York: Monthly Review Press, 1973).

11. Max Horkheimer in 1937 already understood the falseness of this dichotomy for Marxists. See his "Traditional and Critical Theory" in his *Critical Theory* (New York: Herder and Herder, 1972).

12. Habermas in Volume Two of his *The Theory of Communicative Action* discusses what he calls the colonization of the lifeworld. See especially sect. 6, "Intermediate Reflections: System and Lifeworld." Also see John O'Neill's "Decolonization and the Ideal Speech Community: Some Issues in the Theory and Practice of Communicative Competence," in John Forester, ed., *Critical Theory and Public Life.*

13. See Michael Edward Lynch, "Art and Artifact in Laboratory Science: A Study of Shop Work and Shop Talk in a Research Laboratory" (Ph.D. diss. in Social Sciences, University of California, Irvine, 1979). Studies such as this indicate that the "hardest" science is narratively crafted.

14. Fredric Jameson addresses the necessity of this historicization in "Ideology of the Text," *Salmagundi* 31 (1975–76): 204–46.

15. The urge to simplify, to reduce, runs deep, even on the left. C. Wright Mills's synopsis of Parsons in *The Sociological Imagination* (New York: Oxford University Press, 1959) is a well-known example. But to fight a discipline one needs another discipline, or at least a sustained critique refusing to telescope bad text into a few pithy paragraphs. Mills in shortening Parsons does not undo him but merely reinforces a positivist culture in which simplification stands for knowledge.

16. For discussion of this metabolism see William Leiss, *The Limits to Satisfaction: An Essay on Needs and Commodities* (Toronto: University of Toronto Press, 1976) and his "Needs, Exchanges and the Fetishism of Objects," *Canadian Journal of Political and Social Theory* 2, no. 3 (Fall 1978): 27–48.

17. Such as, hermeneutics: Richard Palmer, *Hermeneutics* (Evanston: Northwestern University Press, 1969); E. D. Hirsch, *Validity in Interpretation* (New Haven: Yale University Press, 1967); reception theory: Wolfgang Iser, *The Implied Reader: Patterns of Communication in Prose Fiction from Bunyan to Beckett* (Baltimore: Johns Hopkins University Press, 1974); Stanley Fish, *Is There a Text in the Class?* (Cambridge, Mass.: Harvard University Press, 1980); Umberto Eco, *The Role of the Reader*; Jane Tompkins, ed., *Reader-Response Criticism* (Baltimore: Johns Hopkins University Press, 1980); structuralism and semiotics: Fredric Jameson, *The Prison-House of Language* (Princeton: Princeton University Press, 1972); Michael Riffaterre, *Semiotics of Poetry* (Bloomington: Indiana University Press, 1978); Jonathan Culler, *Structuralist Poetics* (Ithaca: Cornell University Press, 1975); poststructuralism: Jacques Derrida, *Speech and Phenomena* (Evanston: Northwestern University Press, 1973) and *Writing and Difference*; Roland Barthes, *The Pleasure of the Text* (New York: Hill and Wang, 1975) and *Writing Degree Zero*; Michel Foucault, *The Archaeology of Knowledge*, (New York: Harper and Row, 1976) and *The Order of Things*, (New York: Vintage, 1973); Paul de Man, *Allegories of Reading* (New Haven: Yale University Press, 1979); Josue V. Harari, ed., *Textual Strategies* (Ithaca: Cornell University Press, 1979); and feminist criticism: Annette Kolodny, "Dancing Through the Minefield"; Kate Millett, *Sexual Politics* (Garden City: Doubleday, 1970); Josephine Donovan, *Feminist Literary Criticism* (Lexington: Heath, 1975); Elaine Marks and Isabelle de Courtivron, eds., *New French Feminisms: An Anthology.*

18. For a version of this argument, see Terry Eagleton, *Marxism and Literary Criticism*.

19. See Herbert Marcuse, "A Study on Authority" in his *Studies in Critical Philosophy*; also see Max Horkheimer, "Rise and Decline of the Individual," in his *Eclipse of Reason*.

20. Christopher Lasch, *The Culture of Narcissism* (New York: Norton, 1979); *Haven in a Heartless World: The Family Besieged* (New York: Basic, 1977); and *The Minimal Self* (New York: Norton, 1984).

21. Richard Sennett, *The Fall of Public Man*.

22. Russell Jacoby, *The Last Intellectuals*.

23. For a discussion of the administration of the body in late capitalism, see John O'Neill, *Five Bodies* (Ithaca: Cornell University Press, 1985).

24. Adorno was most self-conscious about his relation to his public in his short essays and aphorisms *Minima Moralia: Reflections from Damaged Life* (London: New Left Books, 1974). Also see Gillian Rose (on Adorno), *The Melancholy Science: An Introduction to the Thought of Theodor Adorno* (London: Macmillan, 1978).

25. See Russell Jacoby's essay "The Politics of Subjectivity," in his *Social Amnesia* (Boston: Beacon, 1975). Also see my "On Happiness and the Damaged Life," in John O'Neill, ed., *On Critical Theory*, for a reflection on the objectivity of the subject.

26. Honest conservatism discloses itself politically where deconstruction does not. See Allan Bloom, *The Closing of the American Mind* (New York: Simon and Schuster, 1987).

Chapter 5. Thinking Otherwise:
Radical Hermeneutics as Critical Theory

1. See Dieter Misgeld, "Critical Theory and Hermeneutics," in John O'Neill, ed., *On Critical Theory*. See Jurgen Habermas, *Zur Logik der Sozialwissenschaften* (Frankfurt: Suhrkamp, 1970) for a critique of Gadamer's hermeneutics. See Hans-Georg Gadamer, *Truth and Method* (New York: Seabury, 1975).

2. Jurgen Habermas, "Towards a Theory of Communicative Competence," *Inquiry* 13 (1970): 360–75; also see his *Theory and Practice* (Boston: Beacon, 1973); finally, see his "Wahrheitstheorien," in *Wirklichkeit und Reflexion: Walter Schulz zum 60. Geburtstag* (Pfullingen: Neske, 1973).

3. Marx's "reading" of money is not simply interpretive; it is also political. He wants to see not only what money conceals and thus can be made to reveal, but he also disputes the standard of value encoded and thus reproduced in money. For an example of a politicizing reading of Marx's "reading," see Harry Cleaver, *Reading Capital Politically* (Austin: University of Texas Press, 1979).

4. It seems to me that Marcuse from *One-Dimensional Man* to *An Essay on Liberation* moves toward a version of critique that acknowledges its own

political nature—indeed, its responsibility to attend to the way it remakes the world by its own talk.

5. Michael Ryan's *Marxism and Deconstruction* offers the single best reading of critical theory and deconstruction addressing their common opposition to this notion of a single master narrative, notably that of the Enlightenment and its domination of nature.

6. Marcuse first understood this under the general concept of "repressive tolerance." See Herbert Marcuse et al., *A Critique of Pure Tolerance* (Boston: Beacon, 1965). In these regressive times, we are increasingly surrounded by repressive intolerance—the old-fashioned kind.

7. For another critique of positivist sociology, see Horkheimer and Adorno's collection of essays published under the general editorship of the Institute for Social Research, *Aspects of Sociology* (Boston: Beacon, 1972).

8. John O'Neill in a quite different way addresses the methodical suppression of the grounds of sociological abstraction in the lifeworld in his *Making Sense Together: An Introduction to Wild Sociology*. In general, this is the project of a phenomenological Marxism, which could be another name for what I am doing here. See, for example, Enzo Paci, *The Function of the Sciences and the Meaning of Man* (Evanston: Northwestern University Press, 1972); and see Paul Piccone, "Phenomenological Marxism," *Telos* 9 (Fall 1971): 3–31.

9. For a discussion of the left's right, see Paul Breines, "Redeeming Redemption," *Telos* 65 (Fall 1985): 152–58.

10. Horkheimer and Adorno discuss the degeneration of social science in these terms in their *Aspects of Sociology*, especially the chapter entitled "The Concept of Sociology."

11. Horkheimer and Adorno in *Aspects of Sociology* anticipate my discussion here: "Nothing remains then of ideology but that which exists itself, the models of a behavior which submits to the overwhelming power of the existing conditions. It is hardly an accident that the most influential philosophers today are those who attach themselves to the word "existence," as if the reduplication of mere present existence, by means of the highest abstract determinations which can be derived from this, were equivalent with its meaning. This corresponds to a great degree to the state within men's minds. They accept the ridiculous situation, which every day, in the face of the open possibility of happiness, threatens them with avoidable catastrophe; to be sure, they no longer accept it as the expression of an idea, in the way that they may still feel about the bourgeois system of national states, but make their peace in the name of realism, with that which is given. From the outset the individuals experience themselves as chess pieces, and yet become acquiescent to this. However, since new ideology hardly says more than that things are the way they are, its own falsity also shrinks away to the thin axiom that it could not be otherwise than it is. While human beings bow to this untruth, at the same time they still see through it secretly. The glorification of power and of the irresistible nature of present existence is at the same time the condition for divesting it of its magic. The ideology is no longer a veil, but the threatening face of the world.

161

It is not only due to its involvement with propaganda, but due to its own character, that it goes over into terror. However, because ideology and reality are converging in this manner, because reality, due to the lack of any other convincing ideology, becomes its own ideology, it requires only a small effort of mind to throw off this all-powerful and at the same time empty illusion; but to make this effort seems to be the most difficult thing of all" (pp. 202–3).

12. But existentialism, too, tends to become method, forgetting its original critique of speculative idealism. See Theodor Adorno, *The Jargon of Authenticity* (Evanston: Northwestern University Press, 1970). Also see John O'Neill, "Can Phenomenology Be Critical?" in his *Sociology as a Skin Trade*.

13. For example, see Marx's *Economic and Philosophic Manuscripts* (Moscow: Foreign Languages Publishing House, 1961). See especially the section "The Power of Money in Bourgeois Society," pp. 136–41. Marx makes exactly my point about money as a hidden text in fast capitalism (he did not foresee its extent): "That which is for me through the medium of *money*—that for which I can pay (i.e., which money can buy)—that am *I*, the possessor of the money. The extent of the power of money is the extent of my power. Money's properties are my properties and essential powers—the properties and powers of its possessors. Thus, what I *am* and *am capable* of is by no means determined by my individuality" (p. 138).

14. See Karl Marx, *Capital*, Vol. 1, especially Chapter 3 "Money, or the Circulation of Commodities," pp. 97–144.

15. See, for example, Simone de Beauvoir, *The Second Sex* (New York: Knopf, 1953).

16. See the Second Preface to Herbert Marcuse's *Reason and Revolution* (Boston: Beacon, 1960), "A Note on Dialectic" for discussion of this issue.

17. See Marcuse et al.'s *A Critique of Pure Tolerance* for this discussion.

18. Marcuse argues for a dialectic of transformative process and product in his *An Essay on Liberation*, especially the chapter "The New Sensibility." I have thought about this in my "On Happiness and the Damaged Life," in John O'Neill, ed., *On Critical Theory*.

19. Bruce Ackerman goes part way toward this understanding of dialogue in his *Social Justice in the Liberal State* (New Haven: Yale University Press, 1980).

20. Marcuse evokes this mortal notion of radicalism in his *Eros and Civilization*, especially in the chapter "Eros and Thanatos."

21. The search for new language, if not a whole new social order encoded in that language, was Wittgenstein's project. See his *Philosophical Investigations* (Oxford: Basil Blackwell, 1953).

22. In a largely sympathetic account, H. Stuart Hughes discusses these translation problems in his *The Sea Change: The Migration of Social Thought, 1930–1965* (New York: Harper and Row, 1975). "Not until he was gone did the wider public outside Germany begin to appreciate the loss that Western intellectual life had sustained. And this was in part Adorno's own fault in insisting on a mode of expression which was 'mannered, hermetic and remote from ordinary discourse.' It was not merely that the Gallicisms of his early

work and the Americanisms of his postexile writings raised special linguistic hurdles. It was that he consciously chose 'a style refined and formalized to the point of complete artificiality'" (p. 169).

23. From Hughes's *The Sea Change*: "[I]n their application of the dialectical method the Frankfurt philosophers had tried to cast off what was stiff and schematic in the way it was conventionally understood. Scarcely less conscientiously than Wittgenstein, they had striven to think in terms of a universe of fluid relationships. Yet once more only up to a point. Despite all that they had renounced in the Hegelian or Marxist tradition—despite the intricate many-sidedness of their perceptions—one aspect of their philosophical inheritance they steadfastly refused to give up: 'the conviction that an all-embracing or fundamental structure of being could be discovered'" (p. 170).

24. Originally I sought this standard of otherness elsewhere. See my "Marcuse's Freudian Marxism" and my "On Happiness and the Damaged Life," in John O'Neill, ed., *On Critical Theory*. In other words, I did not have a total theory. Perhaps I still do not, but at least it is more totalizing. All writing is an exercise in intellectual autobiography. We so fear this because the trace of authoriality signals open political possibility. Thus, we discipline it.

25. Althusser calls this "theoretical practice." See his *For Marx*, especially the chapter "On the Materialist Dialectic." "The only Theory able to raise, if not to pose, the essential question of the status of these disciplines, to criticize ideology in all its guises, including the disguises of technical practice as sciences, is the Theory of theoretical practice (as distinct from ideological practice): the materialist dialectic or dialectical materialism, the conception of the Marxist dialectic in its *specificity*" (pp. 171–72). "Theoretical practice produces knowledges which can then figure as *means* that will serve the ends of a technical practice. Any technical practice is defined by its ends: such and such effects to be produced in such and such an object in such and such a situation. The means depend on the ends. Any theoretical practice uses among other means knowledges which intervene as procedures: either knowledges borrowed from outside, from existing sciences, or 'knowledges' produced by the technical practice itself in pursuance of its ends. In every case, the relation between technique and knowledge is an *external,* unreflected relation, radically different from the internal, reflected relation between a science and its knowledges. It is this exteriority which justifies Lenin's thesis of the necessity to *import* Marxist theory into the spontaneous political practice of the working class. Left to itself, a spontaneous (technical) practice produces only the 'theory' it needs as a means to produce the ends assigned to it: this 'theory' is never more than the reflection of this end, uncriticized, unknown, in its means of realization, that is, it is a *by-product* of the reflection of the technical practice's end on its means. A 'theory' which does not question the end whose *by-product* it is remains a prisoner of this end and of the 'realities' which have imposed it as an end. Examples of this are many of the branches of psychology and sociology, and of Economics, of Politics, of Art, etc. . . . This point is crucial if we are to identify the most dangerous ideological

menace: the creation and success of so-called theories which have nothing to do with real theory but are mere *by-products* of technical activity. A belief in the 'spontaneous' theoretical virtue of technique lies at the root of this ideology, the ideology constituting the essence of Technocratic Thought" (p. 171).

26. Having said this, it is difficult to avoid being subordinated to the great names with which we litter our writing. A prepublication reviewer of my *Socio(onto)logy: A Disciplinary Reading* suggested that I was combining Marcuse and Derrida in my disciplinary critique. On reflection I found this observation interesting and correct. In fact, it helped me see the logic of my argument more clearly when doing revisions. Yet, although the reviewer did not intend this, had I more self-consciously called my book a Marcusean-Derridean version of sociology I would surely be read as a subordinate to these established traditions and thus lose the distinctiveness of my voice, an especially troubling problem where I view my argument as 95 percent Marcusean and 5 percent Derridean, deconstruction useful only in its occasionally political moments. The reviewer was trying to suggest the import of my project to an editor and thus s/he used these names as code words. Yet the names can get out of control and make me only a Marcusean or Derridean.

27. See Howard Becker, *Writing for Social Scientists* (Chicago: University of Chicago Press, 1986).

Chapter 6. Avoiding the Fetish of the Textual

1. For a discussion of the so-called linguistic turn in critical theory, see Albrecht Wellmer, "Communications and Emancipation: Reflections on the Linguistic Turn in Critical Theory," in John O'Neill, ed., *On Critical Theory*.

2. Isaac Balbus discusses some of the implications of this territoriality on the part of Marxists in his *Marxism and Domination*.

3. For one version of a Marxist-feminist synthesis, see Eli Zaretsky, *Capitalism, The Family and Personal Life* (New York: Harper and Row, 1976).

4. Although this is perhaps not her intent, Mary O'Brien reflects what one might call the radical-feminist perspective in her trenchant critique of Marxism. See her *The Politics of Reproduction* (London: Routledge and Kegan Paul, 1981).

5. Christopher Lasch is controversial among feminists because in repeating the Frankfurt School's theory of the necessity of patriarchal authority he seems politically to challenge the women's movement. See his *Haven in a Heartless World*. Also see Max Horkheimer's "Authority and the Family," a chapter in his *Critical Theory*. I recently heard Lasch give a talk in which he criticized homosexuals, abortion advocates, the divorced, and the childless for refusing to sacrifice themselves for future generations. Lasch's haven in a heartless world is no haven after all; the "left" here converges with the right.

6. Feminism redefines the political, as does much of critical theory. See Jean Elshtain, *Public Man, Private Woman*. Why do feminists and critical theorists usually not talk? The Frankfurt School idealizes the patriarchal family

in an unfortunate way, and many American feminists are averse to theoretical abstraction as a moment of male mind.

7. For example, see Roland Barthes, *The Pleasure of the Text*. Also see Marcuse's version of new science and technology in his *An Essay on Liberation*.

8. Yet neither do structures endure ontologically, the source of poststructuralist dissatisfaction with so-called structuralism. However, this debate fails to proceed historically, thus politically. Structures sometime structure. For some reflections along these lines, see Alvin Gouldner's *The Two Marxisms: Contradictions and Anomalies in the Development of Theory* (New York: Seabury, 1980). And see Stanley Diamond's *In Search of the Primitive* (New Brunswick, N. J.: Transaction, 1974). Finally, see Jean-Paul Sartre's unread classic, *Critique of Dialectical Reason* (London: New Left Books, 1976).

9. See Claude Lévi-Strauss, *The Savage Mind* (Chicago: University of Chicago Press, 1966) and his *Totemism* (Boston: Beacon, 1963).

10. See Michel Foucault, *The Order of Things*.

11. See Nancy Fraser, "The French Derrideans: Politicizing Deconstruction or Deconstructing the Political?"

12. As far as I am concerned, the Frankfurt thesis of total administration is raised early on in Horkheimer's "The Authoritarian State," *Telos* 15 (Spring 1973): 3–20. Also see Horkheimer's *Dawn and Decline* (New York: Seabury, 1978).

13. See his "Wahrheitstheorien," in *Wirklichkeit und Reflexion*. Also see Habermas's *Theory and Practice*.

14. For good examples of critiques addressing nondiscursive "texts," see Theodor Adorno's "A Social Critique of Radio Music," *Kenyon Review* 8, no.2 (Spring, 1945): 208–17, and his "The Stars Down to Earth: The Los Angeles Times Astrology Column: A Study in Secondary Superstition," *Telos* 19 (Spring 1974): 13–90.

15. Maurice Merleau-Ponty anticipates much of this discussion. He remains a highly pertinent philosopher. See his *Signs*. See also his *Sense and Non-Sense*: "But there is more to be said. Marxism not only tolerates freedom and the individual but, as 'materialism,' even gives man a dizzying responsibility, as it were. Insofar as he reduced history to the history of the spirit, Hegel found the final synthesis heralded and guaranteed in his own consciousness, in his certainty at having understood history completely, and in the very realization of his philosophy. How could he help being optimistic, when history was consciousness's return to itself and the internal logic of the idea as he lived it in himself testified to the necessity of this return and to man's possibility of attaining totality and freedom from anxiety? That is the textbook Hegel, but there are other ways to interpret him: he could be, and we think he must be, made much more Marxist; one could base his logic on his phenomenology and not his phenomenology on his logic. But whether it bears the name of Hegel or Marx, a philosophy which renounces absolute Spirit as history's motive force, which makes history walk on its own feet and which admits no other reason in things than that revealed by their meeting and interaction, could not affirm

a priori man's possibility for wholeness, postulate a final synthesis resolving all contradictions or affirm its inevitable realization. Such a philosophy continues to see the revolutionary event as contingent and finds the date of the revolution written on no wall nor in any metaphysical heaven. The breakdown of capitalism may lead the world to chaos instead of to the revolution if men do not understand the situation and do not want to intervene, just as childbirth may result in the death of both mother and baby if no one is there to assist nature. Although synthesis exists *de jure* in Hegel, it can never be more than *de facto* in Marxism. If there is a Hegelian quietism, there is necessarily a Marxist unrest. Although Hegel's solid and enduring foundation in theology makes it possible for him blindly to leave everything to the natural course of events, Marxist praxis—which can rely on nothing but coexistence among men—does not have the same resource. It cannot assign history a particular end in advance; it cannot even affirm the dogma of "total man" before he actually comes into being. If all our contradictions are someday to be resolved, then that day will be the first we know of it. Engels' learned talk about the way necessity reabsorbs historical accidents is much admired, but how does he know that history is and will continue to be rational if he is no longer a theist or an idealist? Marxism is unique in that it invites us to make the logic of history triumph over its contingency without offering any metaphysical guarantees" (pp. 81–82).

16. See Jurgen Habermas, *Zur Rekonstruktion des Historischen Materialismus* (Frankfurt: Suhrkamp, 1976). Four of these essays have been translated in his *Communication and the Evolution of Society*. Also see "Towards a Reconstruction of Historical Materialism," *Theory and Society* 2 (1975): 287–300.

17. See Jurgen Habermas, "A Postscript to *Knowledge and Human Interests*," *Philosophy of the Social Sciences* 3 (1975): 157–89.

18. See Theodor Adorno, "Why Philosophy?" in Walter Leifer, ed., *Man and Philosophy* (Munich: Max Hueber, 1964).

19. See Theodor Adorno, "Is Marx Obsolete?" *Diogenes* 64 (Winter 1968): 1–16.

20. See Theodor Adorno, "Scientific Experiences of a European Scholar in America," in Donald Fleming and Bernard Bailyn, eds., *The Intellectual Migration* (Cambridge: Harvard University Press, 1969).

21. For example, see Michael Harrington, *The Other America* (New York: Macmillan, 1963); also see his *The Twilight of Capitalism* (New York: Simon and Schuster, 1976).

22. After all, Adorno wrote about *television*. Someone completely resigned would not have bothered. This is not to say he thought we could simply "change" television—better programs, for example. We could learn from it about the world it reflects and thus reproduces. See his "How to Look at Television," *Quarterly of Film, Radio and Television* 8 (Spring 1954): 213–35.

23. Phil Slater says this, among other things, in his *Origin and Significance of the Frankfurt School*.

Chapter 7. Avoiding the Fetish of the Sexual

1. Radical or cultural feminism dismisses the male/Marxist left because it believes that gender domination is more important than class domination, reproducing the either/or of bourgeois society. See, for example, Shulamith Firestone, *The Dialectic of Sex* (New York: Morrow, 1970). Although so-called radical feminism is now conveniently compartmentalized (see Jaggar, *Feminist Politics and Human Nature*, or Donovan, *Feminist Theory*) I would submit that virtually every species of feminism today in resisting Marxist economism subordinates class domination to that of gender. So-called Marxist-feminism is an effort to reintroduce concepts of class through the backdoor, having recognized the mistake. See, for example, Zillah Eistenstein, ed., *Capitalist Patriarchy and the Case for Socialist Feminism*. In any case, Marxists and feminists continue to defend themselves against each other. After division, conquest is sure to follow.

2. See my "Marxism, Feminism, Deconstruction," in Christine Gailey and Viana Muller, eds., *Dialectical Anthropology: The Critical Ethnology of Stanley Diamond*.

3. See Nancy Chodorow, *The Reproduction of Mothering*.

4. I realize that "just" is a big word. But feminist biologism is no solution either analytically or politically. See Mary Daly, *Beyond God the Father: Toward a Philosophy of Women's Liberation* (Boston: Beacon, 1973). Daly exemplifies the worst elements of much feminism—mysticism, antieconomism, biologism. It is difficult to take her seriously in a political sense yet, again, I would suggest that Daly's version of feminism is prevalent in an increasingly reactionary women's movement.

5. For examples of this persuasion, see Sandra Harding and Jean O'Barr, eds., *Sex and Scientific Inquiry* (Chicago: University of Chicago Press, 1987); also see Sandra Harding, *Feminism and Methodology* (Bloomington: Indiana University Press, 1988).

6. See, for example, Peter Berger and Thomas Luckmann, *The Social Construction of Reality* (Garden City, N.Y.: Doubleday, 1967); also see Hugh Mehan and Houston Wood, *The Reality of Ethnomethodology* (New York: Wiley, 1975).

7. See Adrienne Rich, *Of Woman Born*; also see her *On Lies, Secrets and Silence* (New York: Norton, 1979).

8. While not methodologically canonical here, Ann Oakley's *Subject Women* (New York: Pantheon, 1981), is an example of the self-referential nature of a lot of women's studies.

9. For some examples of this methodological humanism from within feminism, see Shulamit Reinharz, "Feminist Distrust: Problems of Context and Content in Sociological Work," in David Berg and Ken Smiths, eds., *Exploring Clinical Methods for Social Research* (Beverly Hills: Sage, 1985); "Feminist Research Methodology Groups: Origins, Forms, Functions," in Vivian Patraka and Louise A. Tilly, eds., *Feminist Re-visions: What Has Been and Might Be* (Ann Arbor: Women's Studies Program, 1983); "Experiential Analysis: A Contribution to Feminist Research Methodology," in Gloria Bowles and Renata Duelli-

Klein, eds., *Theories of Women's Studies* (Boston: Routledge and Kegan Paul, 1983). See Toby Jayaratne, "The Quantitative/qualitative Dilemma" (paper delivered at the Fifth Annual Women's Studies Association Meetings, Columbus, Ohio, 1983).

10. See Sara Evans, *Personal Politics*.

11. A friend of mine who does quantitative work on gender inequality submitted a paper to *Signs*. It was rejected. The editor, Jean O'Barr, said that the paper was not rejected because it was too quantitative but because the journals' editors did not accept the assumption underlying the paper about the nature of the relationship between housework and paid labor. In essence, my friend argues that women's household time detracts from the time they can spend in paid labor. O'Barr avers that this assumes that women are somehow to be regarded naturally as responsible for domestic labor. Instead, she implies, *Signs* would rather view domestic labor as a choice. This is interesting on two levels: first, the paper was rejected without a reading, the hallmark of "refereed" scholarship. Although *Signs* does not claim to be a refereed journal, as the flagship of feminist scholarship in the United States it clearly has a powerful gatekeeping role. Second, O'Barr gives voice to a thoroughgoing liberal feminism, deemphasizing the sexual division of labor. After all, many women are still almost entirely responsible for housework. This is not their choice; patriarchal capitalism denies them options. Analyzing the way this detracts from their paid labor time need not be conservative. Indeed, denying it —as if everyone could hire a maid—is deeply ideological. Tenured feminism holds sway.

12. See Linda Blum, "Reevaluating Women's Work: The Significance of the Comparable Worth Movement" (Ph.D. diss., Department of Sociology, University of California, Berkeley, 1987). Also see her "Possibilities and Limits of the Comparable Worth Movement," *Gender and Society* 1, no. 4 (1987): 380–99. Finally, see Paula England, *Comparable Worth: Theories and Evidence* (New York: Aldine, 1989).

13. See Herbert Marcuse's *The Aesthetic Dimension* for a discussion of Marxist theories of aesthetics.

14. See Russell Jacoby, "The Politics of Subjectivity," in his *Social Amnesia*.

15. For example, see Jane Flax, "Tragedy or Emancipation?: On the 'Decline' of Contemporary American Families," in Mark E. Kann, ed., *The Future of American Democracy* (Philadelphia: Temple University Press, 1983).

16. Although I am not sure she would agree, Barbara Ehrenreich seems to be saying much the same thing in her *The Hearts of Men* (New York: Doubleday, 1983). She reverses the usual feminist tendency to ignore men in studying women. Ehrenreich sees that masculine and feminine are different words, different practices, for the same thing.

17. And, in Ithaca, New York, also gay studies and men's studies shelves.

18. I gave a talk of some of these themes in two women's studies classes at Buffalo and the instructor, a tenured feminist, told me I was "too pessimistic."

168

We just cannot get it right—too male, too left, too gloomy, too this, too that.

19. See Ellen DuBois, et al., *Feminist Scholarship: Kindling in the Groves of Academe* (Champaign: University of Illinois Press, 1985) for a version of feminist scholarship.

20. Ann Oakley, *Subject Women*: "Feminism can be defined in many ways and just how to define it is one task of the women's movement at the moment. . . . Ultimately any feminism is about putting women first; it is about judging women's interests (however defined) to be important and to be insufficiently represented and accommodated within mainstream politics/academia" (p. 335). The subtext here screams to be read. Oakley says that women should have priority, and then she says only that they should be judged "important." Feminism is *not* about addressing suppressed issues of gender inequality but about "putting women first," the liberal authoritarianism of the women's movement clearly revealed.

Chapter 8. Critique's Community

1. For example, see Theodore Mills Norton and Bertell Ollman, eds., *Studies in Socialist Pedagogy* (New York: Monthly Review Press, 1978). Also see the special issue of *Humanities in Society* on "Marxists and the University," 6, nos. 2–3 (Spring and Summer 1983). In particular, see Carl Boggs, "The Intellectuals and Social Movements: Some Reflections on Academic Marxism," 223–39.

2. The Sociologists for Women in Society publish a periodical newsletter containing a Ms. Manners-like column offering advice to women academics. Many of the mock letters inquire about appropriate modes of conduct among academic women. Although useful in some respects, this clearly suggests that feminism ought to be largely a mannered practice.

3. See H. Stuart Hughes, *The Sea Change*, especially pp. 142–43 and 168–70.

4. For example, few read C. Wright Mills's *The Marxists* (New York: Dell, 1962).

5. Even Habermas succumbs. He has an avowedly political perspective in his redevelopment of critical theory, yet he can write a paragraph like this: "To be sure, these remarks touch upon only the motivational background to this work and not its actual theme. I have written this book for those who have a professional interest in the foundations of social theory." *The Theory of Communicative Action*, vol. 1, *xlii*.

6. Simone de Beauvoir, *Adieux: A Farewell to Sartre* (New York: Pantheon, 1984).

7. Maurice Merleau-Ponty, *Signs*. "A concrete philosophy is not a happy one. It must stick close to experience, and yet not limit itself to the empirical which marks it internally. As difficult as it is under these conditions to imagine the future of philosophy, two things seem certain: it will never regain the

conviction of holding the keys to nature or history in its concepts, and it will not renounce its radicalism, that search for presuppositions and foundations which has produced the great philosophies" (p. 157).

8. Merleau-Ponty, *Signs*: "It is this family of interrogations concerning Marxist ontology which is cleverly eliminated if Marxism is from the start declared valid as a truth for some later date. These questions have always constituted the pathos and profound life of Marxism, which was the trial or test of the creative negation, the realization-destruction, In forgetting them, we repudiate Marxism as revolution. In any case, if we grant without debate both Marxism's claim to be not a philosophy but the expression of a single great historical fact and its criticism of all philosophy as an alibi and sin against history, and if we confirm in another connection the present lack of any proletarian movement on a worldwide scale, we retire Marxism to inactive status and define ourselves as honorary Marxists. If philosophy alone is decreed at fault in the divorce between philosophy and politics, the divorce will be a failure. For divorces as well as marriages can fail" (p. 9).

9. See John O'Neill, *Perception, Expression and History*: "It is the nature of human consciousness to realize itself in the world and among men and its embodiment is the essential mode of its opening toward the world and to others. The problem of community and coexistence only arises for an embodied consciousness driven by its basic needs into a social division of labor and engaged by its deepest need in a life and death struggle for intersubjective recognition. Embodied consciousness never experiences an original innocence to which any violence would be an irreparable harm; it knows only different kinds of violence. For consciousness finds itself already engaged in the world, in definite situations in which its resources are never merely its own but derive from the exploitation of its position as the husband of this woman, the child of these parents, the master of these slaves. As such the intentions of embodied consciousness already presuppose a common matrix of justice and injustice, truth and deception, out of which they emerge as acts of love, hate, honesty, and deceit. This is the ground presupposed by political discussion and political choice. We never act upon isolated individuals, as the liberal imagines, but always within a community which possesses a common measure of the good and evil it knows. As soon as we have lived we already know what it means for subjects to treat one another as objects, placing into jeopardy the community of subjectivity which is the originary goal of embodied consciousness. None of us reaches manhood outside of this history of the violence we hold for one another. None of us can bear it apart from the attempt within this violence to establish love and communion" (pp. 81–82).

Bibliography

Ackerman, Bruce. *Social Justice in the Liberal State*. New Haven: Yale University Press, 1980.

Adorno, Theodor. *Aesthetic Theory*. London: Routledge and Kegan Paul, 1984.

———. "Commitment." In Andrew Arato and Eike Gebhardt, eds. *The Essential Frankfurt School Reader*. New York: Urizen, 1978.

———. "How to Look at Television." *Quarterly of Film, Radio and Television* 8 (Spring 1954): 213–35.

———. *The Jargon of Authenticity*. Evanston: Northwestern University Press, 1970.

———. "Is Marx Obsolete?" *Diogenes* 64 (Winter 1968): 1–16.

———. *Minima Moralia: Reflections from Damaged Life*. London: New Left Books, 1974.

———. *Negative Dialectics*. New York: Seabury, 1973a.

———. *Philosophy of Modern Music*. New York: Seabury, 1973b.

———. "Scientific Experiences of a European Scholar in America." In Donald Fleming and Bernard Bailyn, eds. *The Intellectual Migration*. Cambridge: Harvard University Press, 1969.

———. "A Social Critique of Radio Music." *Kenyon Review* 8, no. 2 (Spring 1945): 208–17.

———. "The Stars Down to Earth: The Los Angeles Times Astrology Column: A Study in Secondary Superstition." *Telos* 19 (Spring 1974): 13–90.

———. "Subject and Object." In Andrew Arato and Eike Gebhardt, eds., *The Essential Frankfurt School Reader*. New York: Urizen, 1978.

———. "Why Philosophy?" In Walter Leifer, ed. *Man and Philosophy*. Munich: Max Hueber, 1964.

Agger, Ben. "A Critical Theory of Dialogue." *Humanities in Society* 4, no. 1 (Winter 1981): 7–30.

――. "The Dialectic of Deindustrialization: An Essay on Advanced Capitalism." In John Forester, ed., *Critical Theory and Public Life*. Cambridge: MIT Press, 1985.

――. "The Dialectic of Desire: The Holocaust, Monopoly Capitalism and Radical Anamnesis." *Dialectical Anthropology* 8, nos. 1–2 (1983a): 75–86.

――. "Dialectical Sensibility I: Critical Theory, Scientism and Empiricism." *Canadian Journal of Political and Social Theory* 1, no. 1 (Winter 1977a): 3–34.

――. "Dialectical Sensibility II: Towards a New Intellectuality." *Canadian Journal of Political and Social Theory* 1, no. 2 (Spring-Summer 1977b): 47–57.

――. "Marcuse's Aesthetic Politics: Ideology-Critique and Socialist Ontology." *Dialectical Anthropology*, forthcoming.

――. "Marcuse's Freudian Marxism." *Dialectical Anthropology* 8, no. 4 (1982): 319–36.

――. "Marcuse and Habermas on New Science." *Polity* 14, no. 2 (Winter 1976): 158–81.

――. "Marxism, Feminism, Deconstruction." In Christine Gailey and Viana Muller, eds., *Dialectical Anthropology: The Critical Ethnology of Stanley Diamond*. forthcoming.

――. "Marxism 'or' the Frankfurt School?" *Philosophy of the Social Sciences* 14 (March 1983b): 347–65.

――. "On Science as Domination." In Alkis Kontos, ed., *Domination*. Toronto: University of Toronto Press, 1975.

――. *Socio(onto)logy: A Disciplinary Reading*. Champaign: University of Illinois Press, 1989.

――. *Western Marxism: An Introduction*. Santa Monica: Goodyear, 1979.

――. "Work and Authority in Marcuse and Habermas." *Human Studies* 2 (1979): 191–208.

Agger, Ben, and Allan Rachlin. "Left-Wing Scholarship: Current Contradictions of Academic Production." *Humanities in Society* 6, nos. 2–3 (1983): 241–56.

Althusser, Louis. *For Marx*. London: Allen Lane, 1969.

Althusser, Louis, and Etienne Balibar. *Reading Capital*. London: New Left Books, 1970.

Arato, Andrew, and Eike Gebhardt eds. *The Essential Frankfurt School Reader*. New York: Urizen, 1978.

Arendt, Hannah. *The Human Condition*. Chicago: University of Chicago Press, 1958.

Aronowitz, Stanley. *The Crisis in Historical Materialism*. New York: Praeger, 1981.

Balbus, Isaac. *Marxism and Domination: A Neo-Hegelian, Feminist, Psychoanalytic Theory of Sexual, Political and Technological Liberation*. Princeton: Princeton University Press, 1982.

Baran, Paul, and Paul Sweezy. *Monopoly Capital*. New York: Monthly Review Press, 1966.

Barthes, Roland. "The Death of the Author." In Stephen Heath, ed., *Image-Music-Text: Roland Barthes*. London: Fontana, 1977.

———. *The Pleasure of the Text*. New York: Hill and Wang, 1975.

———. *Writing Degree Zero*. New York: Hill and Wang, 1968.

Baudrillard, Jean. *The Mirror of Production*. St. Louis: Telos Press, 1975.

Becker, Howard. *Writing for Social Scientists*. Chicago: University of Chicago Press, 1986.

Bell, Daniel. *The End of Ideology*. New York: Basic, 1976.

Benhabib, Selya. *Critique, Norm and Utopia*. New York: Columbia, 1987.

———. "Epistemologies of Postmodernism: A Rejoinder to Jean-Francois Lyotard." *New German Critique* 33 (1984): 103–26.

Benjamin, Walter. "Art in the Age of Mechanical Reproduction." In his *Illuminations*. New York: Schocken, 1969.

———. "The Author as Producer." In Andrew Arato and Eike Gebhardt, eds., *The Essential Frankfurt School Reader*. New York: Urizen, 1978.

Berger, Peter, Brigitte Berger, and Hansfried Kellner. *The Homeless Mind*. New York: Random House, 1974.

Berger, Peter, and Thomas Luckmann. *The Social Construction of Reality*. Garden City: Doubleday, 1967.

Berman, Marshall. *All That is Solid Melts into Air*. New York: Simon and Schuster, 1982.

Blackburn, Robin, ed. *Ideology in Social Science*. London: Fontana, 1972.

Bloom, Allan. *The Closing of the American Mind*. New York: Simon and Schuster, 1987.

Bloom, Harold. *A Map of Misreading*. New York: Oxford University Press, 1975.

Blum, Alan. *Theorizing*. London: Heinemann, 1974.

Blum, Linda. "Possibilities and Limits of the Comparable Worth Movement." *Gender and Society* 1, no. 4 (1987): 380–99.

———. "Reevaluating Women's Work: The Significance of the Comparable Worth Movement." Ph.D. diss., Department of Sociology, University of California, Berkeley, 1987.

Boggs, Carl. "The Intellectuals and Social Movements: Some Reflections on Academic Marxism." *Humanities in Society* 6, nos. 2–3 (Spring and Summer 1983): 223–39.

Brecht, Bertolt. *Gesammelte Werke*. Vols. 7 and 8. Frankfurt: Suhrkamp, 1972.

Breines, Paul. "Redeeming Redemption." *Telos* 65 (Fall 1985): 152–58.

Brenkman, John. *Culture and Domination*. Ithaca: Cornell University Press, 1987.

Brown, Bruce. *Marx, Freud and the Critique of Everyday Life*. New York: Monthly Review Press, 1973.

Callinicos, Alex. "Postmodernism, Post-structuralism, Post-Marxism?" *Theory, Culture and Society* 2, no. 3 (1985): 85–101.

Chodorow, Nancy. *The Reproduction of Mothering*. Berkeley: University of California Press, 1978.

Cleaver, Harry. *Reading* Capital *Politically*. Austin: University of Texas Press, 1979.

Connerton, Paul. *The Tragedy of Enlightenment*. Cambridge: Cambridge University Press, 1980.

Coser, Lewis, Charles Kadushin, and Walter Powell. *Books: The Culture and Commerce of Publishing*. New York: Basic, 1982.

Coward, Rosalind, and John Ellis. *Language and Materialism: Developments in Semiology and the Theory of the Subject*. London: Routledge and Kegan Paul, 1977.

Culler, Jonathan. *On Deconstruction*. Ithaca: Cornell University Press, 1982.

———. *Structuralist Poetics: Structuralism, Linguistics and the Study of Literature*. Ithaca: Cornell University Press, 1975.

Daly, Mary. *Beyond God the Father: Toward a Philosophy of Women's Liberation*. Boston: Beacon, 1973.

de Beauvoir, Simone. *Adieux: A Farewell to Sartre*. New York: Pantheon, 1984.

———. *The Second Sex*. New York: Knopf, 1953.

Debord, Guy. *Society of the Spectacle*. Detroit: Black and Red Press, 1972.

de Man, Paul. *Allegories of Reading*. New Haven: Yale University Press, 1979.

Derrida, Jacques. *Glas*. Lincoln: University of Nebraska Press, 1987.

———. *Of Grammatology*. Baltimore: Johns Hopkins University Press, 1976.

———. *Positions*. Chicago: University of Chicago Press, 1981.

———. *Speech and Phenomena*. Evanston: Northwestern University Press, 1973.

———. *Writing and Difference*. Chicago: University of Chicago Press, 1978.

Diamond, Stanley. *In Search of the Primitive*. New Brunswick, N.J.: Transaction, 1974.

Diesing, Paul. *Science and Ideology in the Policy Sciences*. New York: Aldine, 1982.

Donovan, Josephine, ed. *Feminist Literary Criticism*. Lexington: Heath, 1975.

———. *Feminist Theory*. New York: Ungar, 1985.

DuBois, Ellen et al. *Feminist Scholarship: Kindling in the Groves of Academe*. Champaign: University of Illinois Press, 1985.

Eagleton, Terry. *Literary Theory*. Minneapolis: University of Minnesota Press, 1983.

———. *Marxism and Literary Criticism*. London: Methuen, 1976.

———. "Marxism, Structuralism and Poststructuralism." *Diacritics* 15, no. 4 (Winter 1985): 2–56.

Eco, Umberto. *The Role of the Reader: Explorations in the Semiotics of Texts*. Bloomington: Indiana University Press, 1979.

Ehrenreich, Barbara. *The Hearts of Men*. New York: Doubleday, 1983.

Eisenstein, Zillah, ed. *Capitalist Patriarchy and the Case for Socialist Feminism*. New York: Monthly Review Press, 1979.

Elshtain, Jean. *Public Man, Private Woman*. Princeton: Princeton University Press, 1981.

Engels, Friedrich. *The Origin of the Family, Private Property and the State.* Moscow: Progress Publishers, 1948.

England, Paula. *Comparable Worth: Theories and Evidence.* New York: Aldine, 1989.

Evans, Sarah. *Personal Politics: The Roots of Women's Liberation in the Civil Rights Movement and the New Left.* New York: Vintage, 1980.

Felman, Shoshana. "Rereading Femininity." *Yale French Studies* 62 (1981): 19–44.

Firestone, Shulamith. *The Dialectic of Sex.* New York: Morrow, 1970.

Fish, Stanley. *Is There a Text in the Class?* Cambridge, Mass.: Harvard University Press, 1980.

Flax, Jane. "Tragedy or Emancipation?: On the 'Decline' of Contemporary American Families." In Mark Kann, ed., *The Future of American Democracy.* Philadelphia: Temple University Press, 1983.

Flynn, Elizabeth, and Patrocinio Schweickart, eds. *Gender and Reading: Essays on Readers, Texts and Contexts.* Baltimore: Johns Hopkins University Press, 1986.

Forester, John, ed. *Critical Theory and Public Life.* Cambridge: MIT Press, 1985.

Foucault, Michel. *The Archaelogy of Knowledge.* New York: Harper and Row, 1976.

———. *Discipline and Punish: The Birth of the Prison.* London: Allen Lane, Penguin, 1979.

———. *The Order of Things.* New York: Vintage, 1973.

Fraser, Nancy. "The French Derrideans: Politicizing Deconstruction or Deconstructing the Political?" *New German Critique* 33 (1984): 127–54.

Freire, Paulo. *Pedagogy of the Oppressed.* New York: Seabury, 1970.

Friedman, Leslie. *Sex Role Stereotyping in the Mass Media: An Annotated Bibliography.* New York: Garland, 1977.

Gadamer, Hans-Georg. *Truth and Method.* New York: Seabury, 1975.

Giddens, Anthony. *Social Theory and Modern Sociology.* London: Polity, 1987.

Gouldner, Alvin. *The Two Marxisms: Contradictions and Anomalies in the Development of Theory.* New York: Seabury, 1980.

Gramsci, Antonio. *Selections from the Prison Notebooks.* London: Lawrence and Wishart, 1971.

Habermas, Jurgen. *Communication and the Evolution of Society.* Boston: Beacon, 1979.

———. *Knowledge and Human Interests.* Boston: Beacon, 1971.

———. *Legitimation Crisis.* Boston: Beacon, 1975.

———. *Zur Logik der Sozialwissenschaften.* Frankfurt: Suhrkamp, 1970a.

———. "Modernity versus Postmodernity." *New German Critique* 22 (1981): 3–14.

———. "A Postscript to *Knowledge and Human Interests.*" *Philosophy of the Social Sciences* 3 (1975): 157–89.

———. *Zur Rekonstruktion des Historischen Materialismus.* Frankfurt: Suhrkamp, 1976.

———. "Technology and Science as 'Ideology.'" In his *Toward a Rational Society*. Boston: Beacon, 1970b.

———. *The Theory of Communicative Action*. Vol. 1. Boston: Beacon, 1984.

———. *The Theory of Communicative Action*. Vol. 2. Boston: Beacon, 1987.

———. *Theory and Practice*. Boston: Beacon, 1973.

———. *Toward a Rational Society*. Boston: Beacon, 1970c.

———. "Towards a Reconstruction of Historical Materialism." *Theory and Society* 2 (1975): 287–300.

———. "Towards a Theory of Communicative Competence." *Inquiry* 13 (1970d): 360–375.

———. "Wahrheitstheorien." In *Wirklichkeit und Reflexion: Walter Schulz zum 60. Geburtstag*. Pfullingen: Neske, 1973.

Harari, Josue V., ed. *Textual Strategies*. Ithaca: Cornell University Press, 1979.

Harding, Sandra. *Feminism and Methodology*. Bloomington: Indiana University Press, 1988.

———. *The Science Question in Feminism*. Ithaca: Cornell University Press, 1986.

Harding, Sandra, and Jean O'Barr, eds. *Sex and Scientific Inquiry*. Chicago: University of Chicago Press, 1987.

Harrington, Michael. *The Other America*. New York: Macmillan, 1963.

———. *The Twilight of Capitalism*. New York: Simon and Schuster, 1976.

Harvey, David. *Consciousness and the Urban Experience*. Baltimore: Johns Hopkins University Press, 1985.

Held, David. *An Introduction to Critical Theory*. Berkeley: University of California Press, 1980.

Hirsch, E. D. *Validity in Interpretation.* New Haven: Yale University Press, 1967.

Honneth, Axel. "An Aversion Against the Universal: A Commentary on Lyotard's *Postmodern Condition*." *Theory, Culture and Society* 2, no. 3 (1985): 147–56.

Honneth, Axel, Eberhard Knodler-Bunte, and Arno Widmann. "The Dialectics of Rationalization: An Interview with Jurgen Habermas." *Telos* 49 (1981): 5–31.

Horkheimer, Max. "The Authoritarian State." *Telos* 15 (Spring 1973): 3–20.

———. *Critical Theory*. New York: Herder and Herder, 1972a.

———. *Critique of Instrumental Reason*. New York: Seabury, 1974a.

———. *Dawn and Decline*. New York: Seabury, 1978.

———. *Eclipse of Reason*. New York: Seabury, 1974b.

———. "The German Jews." In his *Critique of Instrumental Reason*. New York: Seabury, 1974.

———. "Rise and Decline of the Individual." In his *Eclipse of Reason*. New York: Seabury, 1974.

———. "Traditional and Critical Theory." (first published in 1937). In his *Critical Theory*. New York: Herder and Herder, 1972b.

Horkheimer, Max, and Theodor Adorno. *Dialectic of Enlightenment*. New York: Herder and Herder, 1972.

Horowitz, Gad. *Repression: Basic and Surplus Repression in Psychoanalytic Theory.* Toronto: University of Toronto Press, 1977.

Hughes, H. Stuart. *The Sea Change: The Migration of Social Thought, 1930–1965.* New York: Harper and Row, 1975.

Huyssen, Andreas. "Mapping the Postmodern." *New German Critique* 33 (1984): 5–52.

Institute for Social Research. *Aspects of Sociology.* Boston: Beacon, 1972.

Irigaray, Luce. *This Sex Which is Not One.* Ithaca: Cornell University Press, 1985.

Iser, Wolfgang. *The Act of Reading: A Theory of Aesthetic Response.* Baltimore: Johns Hopkins University Press, 1978.

———. *The Implied Reader: Patterns of Communication in Prose Fiction from Bunyan to Beckett.* Baltimore: Johns Hopkins University Press, 1974.

Jacoby, Russell. *Dialectic of Defeat.* New York: Cambridge University Press, 1982.

———. "A Falling Rate of Intelligence?" *Telos* 27 (Spring 1976): 141–46.

———. *The Last Intellectuals: American Culture in the Age of Academe.* New York: Basic, 1987.

———. "The Politics of Subjectivity." In his *Social Amnesia.* Boston: Beacon, 1975a.

———. *The Repression of Psychoanalysis.* New York: Basic, 1983.

———. *Social Amnesia.* Boston: Beacon, 1975b.

Jaggar, Alison. *Feminist Politics and Human Nature.* Totowa, N.J.: Roman and Allanheld, 1983.

Jameson, Fredric. "Ideology of the Text." *Salmagundi* 31 (1975–76): 204–46.

———. *The Political Unconscious.* Ithaca: Cornell University Press, 1981.

———. "Postmodernism and Consumer Society." In Hal Foster, ed., *The Anti-Aesthetic: Essays on Postmodern Culture.* Port Townsend, Wash.: Bay Press, 1983.

———. "Postmodernism, or the Cultural Logic of Late Capitalism." *New Left Review,* 146 (July-August 1984): 53–92.

———. *The Prison-House of Language.* Princeton: Princeton University Press, 1972.

———. "Science Versus Ideology." *Humanities in Society* 6, nos. 2–3 (1983): 283–302.

Jay, Martin. *Adorno.* Cambridge: Harvard University Press, 1984a.

———. *The Dialectical Imagination.* Boston: Little Brown, 1973.

———. "Habermas and Modernism." *Praxis International* 4, no. 1 (1984): 1–14.

———. *Marxism and Totality.* Berkeley: University of California Press, 1984b.

Jayaratne, Toby. "The Quantitative/qualitative Dilemma." Paper delivered at the Fifth Annual Women's Studies Association meeting, Columbus, Ohio, 1983.

Knorr, Karin D. "Producing and Reproducing Knowledge: Descriptive or Constructive? Toward a Model of Research Production." *Social Science Information* 16 (1977): 969–96.

Kolodny, Annette. "Dancing through the Minefield: Some Observations on the Theory, Practice and Politics of a Feminist Literary Criticism." *Feminist Studies* 6, no. 1 (Spring 1980): 1–25.

Korsch, Karl. *Marxism and Philosophy*. New York: Monthly Review Press, 1970.

Kovel, Joel. *The Age of Desire: Case Histories of a Radical Psychoanalyst*. New York: Pantheon, 1981.

Kristeva, Julia. *Desire in Language*. New York: Columbia University Press, 1980.

———. "La Femme, ce n'est jamais ca." *Tel Quel* 59 (1974): 19–24.

Kroker, Arthur, and David Cook. *The Postmodern Scene: Excremental Culture and Hyper-aesthetics*. New York: St. Martin's, 1986.

Lacan, Jacques. *Écrits*. London: Tavistock, 1977.

Lasch, Christopher. *The Culture of Narcissism*. New York: Norton, 1979.

———. *Haven in a Heartless World: The Family Besieged*. New York: Basic, 1977.

———. *The Minimal Self*. New York: Norton, 1984.

Lasswell, Harold. *Psychopathology and Politics*. Chicago: University of Chicago Press, 1930.

Lefebvre, Henri. *Everyday Life in the Modern World*. New York: Harper and Row, 1971.

Leiss, William. *The Limits to Satisfaction: An Essay on Needs and Commodities*. Toronto: University of Toronto Press, 1976.

———. "Needs, Exchanges and the Fetishism of Objects." *Canadian Journal of Political and Social Theory* 2, no. 3 (Fall 1978): 27–48.

Lentricchia, Frank. *After the New Criticism*. Chicago: University of Chicago Press, 1980.

Lévi-Strauss, Claude. *The Savage Mind*. Chicago: University of Chicago Press, 1966.

———. *Totemism*. Boston: Beacon, 1963.

Lynch, Michael Edward. "Art and Artifact in Laboratory Science: A Study of Shop Work and Shop Talk in a Research Laboratory." Ph.D. diss. in Social Sciences, University of California, Irvine, 1979.

Lyotard, Jean-Francois. *The Postmodern Condition: A Report of Knowledge*. Minneapolis: University of Minnesota Press, 1984.

Marcuse, Herbert. *The Aesthetic Dimension*. Boston: Beacon, 1978.

———. *Counterrevolution and Revolt*. Boston: Beacon, 1972.

———. *Eros and Civilization*. New York: Vintage, 1955.

———. *An Essay on Liberation*. Boston: Beacon, 1969.

———. *Five Lectures*. Boston: Beacon, 1970.

———. "The Foundation of Historical Materialism." In his *Studies in Critical Philosophy*. Boston: Beacon, 1973.

———. "A Note on Dialectic." Second Preface to *Reason and Revolution*. Boston: Beacon, 1960a.

———. *One-Dimensional Man*. Boston: Beacon, 1964.

————. *Reason and Revolution*. Boston: Beacon, 1960b.

————. "The Struggle Against Liberalism in the Totalitarian View of the State." In his *Negations*. Boston: Beacon, 1968.

————. "A Study on Authority." In his *Studies in Critical Philosophy*. Boston: Beacon, 1973.

Marcuse, Herbert, et al. *A Critique of Pure Tolerance*. Boston: Beacon, 1965.

Marks, Elaine, and Isabelle de Courtivron, eds. *New French Feminisms: An Anthology*. New York: Schocken, 1981.

Maroney, Heather Jon. "Embracing Motherhood: New Feminist Theory." In Roberta Hamilton and Michele Barrett, eds., *The Politics of Diversity: Feminism, Marxism and Nationalism*. Montreal: Book Center, 1986.

Marx, Karl. *Capital*. Vol. 1. Moscow: Progress Publishers, n. d.

————. *Economic and Philosophic Manuscripts*. Moscow: Foreign Languages Publishing House, 1961.

Marx, Karl, and Friedrich Engels. *The Communist Manifesto*. New York: Washington Square Press, 1964.

————. *The German Ideology*. New York: International Publishers, 1949.

McCarthy, Thomas. *The Critical Theory of Jurgen Habermas*. Cambridge: MIT Press, 1978.

Mehan, Hugh, and Houston Wood. *The Reality of Ethnomethodology*. New York: Wiley, 1975.

Merleau-Ponty, Maurice. *Adventures of the Dialectic*. Evanston: Northwestern University Press, 1973.

————. *Humanism and Terror*. Boston: Beacon, 1972.

————. *Sense and Non-Sense*. Evanston: Northwestern University Press, 1964.

————. *Signs*. Evanston: Northwestern University Press, 1964.

Millett, Kate. *Sexual Politics*. Garden City: Doubleday, 1970.

Mills, C. Wright. *The Marxists*. New York: Dell, 1962.

————. *The Power Elite*. New York: Oxford University Press, 1956.

————. *The Sociological Imagination*. New York: Oxford University Press, 1959.

Misgeld, Dieter. "Critical Theory and Hermeneutics: The Debate Between Habermas and Gadamer." In John O'Neill, ed., *On Critical Theory*. New York: Seabury, 1976.

————. "Education and Cultural Invasion: Critical Social Theory, Education as Institution and 'Pedagogy of the Oppressed.'" In John Forester, ed., *Critical Theory and Public Life*. Cambridge: MIT Press, 1985.

Mueller, Claus. *The Politics of Communication*. New York: Oxford University Press, 1973.

Neumann, Franz. *Behemoth*. London: Gollancz, 1942.

————. *The Democratic and the Authoritarian State*. Glencoe, Ill.: Free Press, 1957.

Newman, Charles. *The Post-Modern Aura: The Act of Fiction in an Age of Inflation*. Evanston: Northwestern University Press, 1985.

Nisbet, Robert *The Degradation of the Academic Dogma*. New York: Basic, 1971.

Norton, Theodore Mills, and Bertell Ollman, eds. *Studies in Socialist Pedagogy*. New York: Monthly Review Press, 1978.

Oakley, Ann. *Subject Women*. New York: Pantheon, 1981.

O'Brien, Mary. "Feminism and Revolution." In Roberta Hamilton and Michele Barrett, eds., *The Politics of Diversity: Feminism, Marxism and Nationalism*. Montreal: Book Center, 1986.

———. *The Politics of Reproduction*. London: Routledge and Kegan Paul, 1981.

O'Kane, John. "Marxism, Deconstruction and Ideology: A Note Towards an Articulation." *New German Critique* 33 (1984): 219–47.

O'Neill, John. "The Concept of Estrangement in the Early and Later Writings of Karl Marx." In his *Sociology as a Skin Trade*. New York: Harper and Row, 1972.

———. "Decolonization and the Ideal Speech Community: Some Issues in the Theory and Practice of Communicative Competence." In John Forester, ed., *Critical Theory and Public Life*. Cambridge: MIT Press, 1985.

———. ed., *On Critical Theory*. New York: Seabury, 1976.

———. "Critique and Remembrance." In his edited *On Critical Theory*. New York: Seabury, 1976.

———. "Embodiment and History in Hegel and Marx." In his *Sociology as a Skin Trade*. New York: Harper and Row, 1972.

———. *Five Bodies*. Ithaca: Cornell University Press, 1985.

———. *For Marx Against Althusser*. Washington, D.C.: University Press of America, 1982.

———. "The Literary Production of Natural and Social Science Inquiry." *The Canadian Journal of Sociology* 6 (1981): 105–20.

———. *Making Sense Together: An Introduction to Wild Sociology*. New York: Harper and Row, 1974.

———. "Marxism and Mythology: Psychologizing *Capital*." In his *For Marx Against Althusser*. Washington, D.C.: University Press of America, 1982.

———. "Marxism and the Two Sciences." *Philosophy of the Social Sciences* 11 (1981): 281–302.

———. "Merleau-Ponty's Critique of Marxist Scientism." *Canadian Journal of Political and Social Theory* 2, no. 1 (Winter 1978): 33–62.

———. ed., *Modes of Individualism and Collectivism*. London: Heinemann, 1973.

———. *Perception, Expression and History: The Social Phenomenology of Maurice Merleau-Ponty*. Evanston: Northwestern University Press, 1970.

———. "Public and Private Space." In his *Sociology as a Skin Trade*. New York: Harper and Row, 1972.

———. *Sociology as a Skin Trade*. New York: Harper and Row, 1972.

Paci, Enzo. *The Function of the Sciences and the Meaning of Man*. Evanston: Northwestern University Press, 1972.

Palmer, Richard E. *Hermeneutics*. Evanston: Northwestern University Press, 1969.

Parker, Andrew. "Of Politics and Limits: Derrida Re-Marx." *SCE Reports* 8 (1980): 83–104.

Parsons, Talcott, Robert Bales et al. *Family, Socialization and Interaction Process.* Glencoe, Ill.: Free Press, 1955.

Piccone, Paul. "Beyond Identity Theory." In John O'Neill, ed., *On Critical Theory.* New York: Seabury, 1976.

———. "The Changing Function of Critical Theory." *New German Critique* 12 (Fall 1977): 29–38.

———. "The Crisis of One-Dimensionality." *Telos* 35 (Spring 1978): 43–54.

———. "Phenomenological Marxism." *Telos* 9 (Fall 1971): 3–31.

Rabine, Leslie. "Searching for the Connections: Marxist-Feminists and Women's Studies." *Humanities in Society* 6, nos. 2–3 (1983): 195–221.

Rabinowitz, Peter. "Truth in Fiction: A Reexamination of Audiences." *Critical Inquiry* 4 (1977): 121–42.

Rasmussen, David. "Communicative Action and the Fate of Modernity." *Theory, Culture and Society* 2, no. 3 (1985): 133–44.

Reinharz, Shulamit. "Experiential Analysis: A Contribution to Feminist Research Methodology." In Gloria Bowles and Renata Duelli-Klein, eds., *Theories of Women's Studies.* Boston: Routledge and Kegan Paul, 1983.

———. "Feminist Distrust: Problems of Context and Content in Sociological Work." In David Berg and Ken Smith, eds., *Exploring Clinical Methods for Social Research.* Beverly Hills: Sage, 1985.

———. "Feminist Research Methodology Groups: Origins, Forms, Functions." In Vivian Patraka and Louise A. Tilly, eds., *Feminist Re-Visions: What Has Been and Might Be.* Ann Arbor: Women's Studies Program, 1983.

Rich, Adrienne. *Of Woman Born: Motherhood as Experience and Institution.* New York: Norton, 1976.

———. *On Lies, Secrets and Silence.* New York: Norton, 1979.

Riffaterre, Michael. *Semiotics of Poetry.* Bloomington: Indiana University Press, 1978.

Rose, Gillian. *The Melancholy Science: An Introduction to the Thought of Theodor Adorno.* London: Macmillan, 1978.

Rule, James. *Insight and Social Betterment.* New York: Oxford University Press, 1978.

Ryan, Michael. *Marxism and Deconstruction.* Baltimore: Johns Hopkins University Press, 1982.

Sartre, Jean-Paul. *Critique of Dialectical Reason.* London: New Left Books, 1976.

———. *What is Literature?* New York: Harper and Row, 1965.

Sennett, Richard. *The Fall of Public Man.* New York: Vintage, 1978.

Shell, Marc. *Money, Language and Thought: Literary and Philosophical Economies from the Medieval to the Modern Era.* Berkeley: University of California Press, 1982.

Simmel, Georg. *Philosophy of Money.* London: Routledge and Kegan Paul, 1978.

Slater, Phil. *Origin and Significance of the Frankfurt School*. London: Routledge and Kegan Paul, 1977.

Spender, Dale. *Man Made Language*. London: Routledge and Kegan Paul, 1980.

Spivak, Gayatri Chakravorty. "Scattered Speculations on the Question of Value." *Diacritics* 15, no. 4 (Winter 1985): 73–93.

Steinem, Gloria. "What it Would be Like if Women Win." *Time*, August 21, 1970, 22–23.

Stockman, Norman. *Antipositivist Theories of the Sciences*. Dordrecht: D. Reidel, 1984.

Thompson, John B. *Critical Hermeneutics: A Study in the Thought of Paul Ricoeur and Jurgen Habermas*. Cambridge: Cambridge University Press, 1981.

———. *Studies in the Theory of Ideology*. Berkeley: University of California Press, 1984.

Tompkins, Jane, ed. *Reader-Response Criticism*. Baltimore: Johns Hopkins University Press, 1980.

Wellmer, Albrecht. "Communications and Emancipation: Reflections on the Linguistic Turn in Critical Theory." In John O'Neill, ed., *On Critical Theory*. New York: Seabury, 1976.

Wittgenstein, Ludwig. *Philosophical Investigations*. Oxford: Basil Blackwell, 1953.

———. *Remarks on the Foundations of Mathematics*. Cambridge: MIT Press, 1978.

Zaretsky, Eli. *Capitalism, The Family and Personal Life*. New York: Harper and Row, 1976.

Index

A Note on the Author

Ben Agger, associate professor of sociology at SUNY-Buffalo, is the author of many articles on critical theory, Marxism, feminism, and discourse theory. He has published several related books, including *Western Marxism: An Introduction*, *Social Problems through Conflict and Order* (with S. A. McDaniel), *Socio(onto)logy: A Disciplinary Reading*, and *Reading Science: A Literary and Political Analysis*. He is working on *The Decline of Discourse*, a book about what writers write in advanced capitalism.